P9-DZZ-413

"A TRUE EMOTIONAL PHENOMENON ... ENTERTAINING ... Of particular interest to fans will be the evolution of Johnson's relationship with Bird, his great karmic partner in the game."
—*New York Newsday*

His first challenge came as a boy is Lansing, Michigan, when he was forced to bus across town to an all-white high school. There, he proved himself to be a big player with a big heart, always in the big games. Now, as the former Los Angeles Laker superstar point guard who has battled to five NBA crowns, Magic Johnson faces the biggest challenge of all.

In this dramatic, exciting, and inspirational autobiography, Magic Johnson allows us into his life, into his triumphs and tragedies on and off the court. In his own exuberant style, he tells us of the friends and family who've been constant supporters; the basketball greats he's worked with, including Kareem Abdul-Jabbar, Pat Riley, Larry Bird, Michael Jordan, and Isiah Thomas; his experience as a member of the 1992 Olympic "Dream Team;" and his own brave battle with the HIV virus. It's all here, the glory and the pain, the character, charisma, and courage of the hero called Magic.

"MY LIFE leaves one with a greater understanding of why Mr. Johnson's enforced retirement was so agonizing. . . . The beauty and legacy of Magic Johnson will be as an inspirational athlete and a living symbol of an H.I.V.-infected person attempting to get on with his life."
—*The New York Times Book Review*

MY LIFE

EARVIN "MAGIC" JOHNSON
with WILLIAM NOVAK

FAWCETT CREST • NEW YORK

A Fawcett Crest Book
Published by Ballantine Books
Copyright © 1992 by June Bug Enterprises

All rights reserved under International and Pan-American Copyright Conventions. Published in the United States by Ballantine Books, a division of Random House, Inc., New York, and simultaneously in Canada by Random House of Canada Limited, Toronto.

Library of Congress Catalog Card Number: 92-53637

ISBN 0-449-22254-3

This edition published by arrangement with Random House, Inc.

Printed in Canada

First Ballantine Books Edition: October 1993

Cover photos of Magic Johnson by Neil Leifer

For Cookie

You were right.
I should have married you sooner.

ACKNOWLEDGMENTS

I played center on this one. Bill Novak was the point guard, feeding me the ball at every opportunity. Peter Osnos of Random House was our coach, keeping us on the winning track. And Lon Rosen, our general manager, did just about everything.

—EARVIN JOHNSON

A number of people helped us out, and I'm grateful to all of them. For talking with me and answering my questions, I want to thank Kareem Abdul-Jabbar, Peter Berger, Larry Bird, Vince Bryson, Jerry Buss, Michael Cooper, Wanda Cooper, Greta and Jim Dart, Elizabeth Glaser, Russ Granik, Jud Heathcote, Jim Hill, Christine Johnson, Cookie Johnson, Earvin Johnson, Sr., Pearl Johnson, Mitch Kupchak, Bob McAdoo, Stu Nahan, Linda Rambis, Pat Riley, Dr. David Rogers, Josh Rosenfeld, Bob Ryan, Fred Stabley, Jr., David Stern, and Jerry West.

Over at the Forum, John Black, Stacy Brown, Matt Fleer, Renee Hawkins, Mary Lou Leibich, and Bob Steiner kindly opened their files and answered my questions.

At Random House, Ken Gellman and Betsy Rapoport made many fruitful suggestions. Amy Edelman, our copy editor, offered dozens of improvements. And most of all, thanks to Peter Osnos. A lot of editors identify problems. Peter comes up with solutions.

For their advice and generosity, I'm especially grateful to a few individuals who made a big difference: Steve Axelrod, Michael Cooper, Greta Dart, Jim Dart, Cookie Johnson, Roy S. Johnson, Taren Metson, Michael Ovitz, Stephen Rivers, and Laurie Rosen. Colleen Mohyde helped with the research.

For guiding me toward the right questions, I'm grateful to the authors of several books: *Winnin' Times* by Scott Ostler and Steve Springer; *Show Time* by Pat Riley; *Kareem* by Kareem Abdul-Jabbar and Mignon McCarthy; *Magic* by Earvin Johnson and Richard Lèvin; *Magic's Touch* by Earvin Johnson and Roy S. Johnson; and of course *The Breaks of the Game* by David Halberstam.

Lon Rosen deserves his own paragraph, but where do I start? Perhaps with his superb memory, his good judgment, his fine sense of humor, and his general thoughtfulness. Several of these qualities came together one spring day as I was about to leave my hotel to interview Kareem Abdul-Jabbar. Out of the blue, Lon called to make sure I was wearing clean socks. Sure, Lon, but why? Lon had suddenly remembered that visitors to Kareem's house were asked to remove their shoes, and he didn't want me to be embarrassed. Lon was such a pleasure to work with that I almost forgot we were trying to complete this book in record time.

—William Novak

CONTENTS

PART THREE: NOW

PROLOGUE

Orlando, Florida. It's Sunday, February 9, and I'm playing in the 1992 All-Star Game. I can't believe I'm here.

Just three months ago, I was shocked to learn I had HIV, the virus that causes AIDS. As soon as I heard the news, I stopped playing basketball. Doctor's orders.

When I announced my decision on November 7, I never imagined that I'd be playing today. But the All-Star ballots had already been printed, and despite everything, the fans voted me in. Even so, some people were convinced I couldn't play. Or that I shouldn't.

But I had something to prove. From the moment I discovered that I had this terrible virus, I knew I wanted to keep on playing. That's part of what this All-Star Game is about for me. I want to show myself, and everybody else, that I can still play basketball like I used to.

Here in Orlando, the fans are with me, cheering me on. And my teammates are making me feel welcome. I haven't played in a real game all year, so I'm relieved when I see that I haven't lost a step. And I'm loving it, every minute, every play. My heart is pounding. I don't want this to end. Ever.

It's late in the fourth quarter, and the game is almost over. I've just hit a pair of three-pointers, and I'm feeling terrific. Now Isiah Thomas is bringing the ball up the court for the

East. Isiah is my friend, and I can see what he's thinking: Man, I shouldn't have let you make that last one.

He wants to score on me, I just know it. I've got to shut him down. One of his teammates is in the way. I wave him aside. I want it to be just Isiah and me, one more time.

Suddenly the other eight guys on the court start to melt away. Now it's just the two of us, Isiah and me, back on the playground. Nobody else around. Before you get the reputation of being really good, you've got to go through everybody, one-on-one. Show them your best stuff.

The crowd is going crazy, loving it. These two warriors, old friends and tough rivals, are going at it again.

Now Isiah starts dribbling, the way he always does, getting fancy now, between the legs, behind the back. I wave him toward me. Come on, I'm telling him. Quit stalling. You gonna make your move, or what?

Isiah takes a jump shot. Misses everything. The defense is too tight. Loud cheers from the crowd.

A minute later, here comes Michael Jordan, bringing up the ball. He's grinning. I want him, too. Again I clear everybody out of the way. The crowd is screaming! They love this. I love it, too.

I'm expecting Michael to drive to the basket, to fly up with one of his incredible super-dunks. I'm playing him tight, but he surprises me. Pulls up short for the jumper. *Clang!* Off the rim. The crowd roars.

People have asked if these little one-on-one battles were rehearsed. Sorry, but I'm not that smart. Who could have thought this up?

Thirty seconds left in the game. I get the ball one last time. I'm about to drive for the lay-up, but Isiah is all over me. He's giving me nothing. I toy with him a little, paying him back. Now I step behind the three-point line and throw up a long rainbow. I'm falling back, so I have to shoot it a little higher and a little harder than usual.

Feels good to me and—yes—*swish*. Another one! The fans are screaming. Everybody is stunned. Three three-point shots in a row, and this last one was from the next county. Who says I can't still play this game?

Fourteen seconds left, but nobody picks up the ball. Suddenly I'm surrounded, mobbed by the All-Stars on both teams. They're giving me their affection, their support. And I'm fighting back the tears. I don't think I've ever felt more exhilarated than I am right now. Or more loved.

Those three-pointers were great, but this incredible ending is the best moment of all. Game called on account of hugs.

For as long as I can remember, my life has been about basketball. About being part of a team. About winning, and about championships. About never being satisfied with my play. About working constantly to make myself better. As soon as I realized that I had God-given talent to play this game, I was determined to take it as far as I could.

And I did. Until late on a Friday afternoon in the fall of 1991, when I found myself sitting across the desk from the team doctor in Los Angeles. Wham! When he told me the news, I knew that everything I had accomplished in my life was nothing compared to the battle I was about to begin.

When Dr. Michael Mellman first explained that I had contracted HIV, I had only a vague idea of what he was talking about. In the shock and haze of the week that followed, I still didn't understand exactly what was wrong with me. As I walked down the corridor to the big press conference at the Forum on November 7 to announce my retirement, Lon Rosen, my manager and close friend, pulled me aside. "Tell them you have HIV," he said. "Remember, you don't have AIDS."

I still don't have AIDS. I'm very strong, and I'm definitely in shape. I worked hard to prepare for the Olympics. I had no trouble keeping up with my teammates. And I'm just as committed to taking on this challenge for my life as I ever was to making a mark on the basketball court. That's why I decided to play again: because I still can.

From the moment of that announcement, I was no longer Magic Johnson, basketball star and master of ceremonies for

Showtime. Suddenly I had a new identity. Now I was Earvin "Magic" Johnson, a living symbol of AIDS—a disease that can strike anybody unlucky enough to get in its way.

Almost overnight, I had to start dealing with things that had never been an issue for me before—at least not in public. Like promiscuous sex. Or how I felt about gays. Or the rumors that I was either gay or bisexual. And my relationships with women, and how that part of my life fit into basketball and being a celebrity.

I understood from the start that I would have to answer these questions, as difficult and personal as they are. I would also step out in a completely new direction as a spokesperson, and at times almost a politician, as I tried to get the world to pay more attention to the problem of AIDS. On top of that, I wanted to do everything I could to help educate the millions of kids who were running the risk of getting this disease, but still weren't paying much attention to it.

I was shocked at the enormous reaction to my announcement that I had HIV. I knew I had a following, but the intensity of the public's interest in this story was hard to believe. Some people have said they'll always remember exactly where they were when they heard the news, almost like when President Kennedy was shot. I'd had a lot of success as a basketball player, but I never imagined that anything about me or my life could have that kind of impact.

But that's fine, because now I had an important message to deliver. That anyone can get HIV. That our government must pay far more attention to it. That we need to allocate more money for research and education if we're going to avoid an epidemic like you wouldn't believe.

The year since my November 7 announcement has been a time of incredible emotion for myself and the people around me. My wife, Cookie, and my family have had to cope with a lot of turmoil, including nasty rumors and ridiculous gossip. At the same time, this period has also provided some of the biggest highs of my life: my closeness to Cookie and the birth of our son; the All-Star Game in Orlando and the "retirement" ceremony at the Forum; visits to high schools around the country; my meetings with younger kids, including some with HIV and AIDS; and of course the Olympics, where my teammates and I represented the United States and won the gold medal. It's been an amazing roller coaster, and of course it's far from over. It's still Showtime.

If the doctors are right, the real struggles for me still lie ahead. There's nothing I can do about the past. Of course I regret what happened. I could have prevented this, and I was stupid not to have taken precautions.

But I can still make a difference by doing everything I can to help other people learn from my mistake. And I pray that God, the love of my family, the strength of my own will, and the advances of medical science will allow me to go on trying to make a difference for a very long time.

I would have written this book anyway. But not yet. I had been planning to work on it two or three years down the road, when my basketball career came to a natural close. Instead, it comes now, as I try to prove that HIV is not the end of an athlete's life.

I feel enormously grateful for the life I have enjoyed so far. I really have been blessed. I come from a big, loving family, with parents who have given me not only values, but also the drive to succeed. For too many black Americans race and racism have been a terrible handicap. That didn't happen to me. Because of my skills as an athlete, every conceivable opportunity has been there.

I've had more fun, more good times, more satisfaction, and enjoyed more success and material prosperity than any one person could possibly expect. Until recently, I hadn't really stopped to think about what all that meant. And that's what makes this a different book from the one I always expected to write.

Most of this story is about things that have happened to me and the people I've met along the way. My childhood and my family. My years at Michigan State and the NCAA championship. My years with the Lakers, and my encounters with some of the great ballplayers on our team and around the league. My longtime relationship with Cookie, who will also speak for herself in these pages. And the events that led up to and then followed my announcement about HIV.

So welcome to my life. I hope that what you'll read here will have some meaning. I want it to, as much as I've ever wanted anything. There are some lessons here, and a few morals. There's a lot of good news, and a few things that might be disturbing.

This is Earvin Johnson, Jr., talking to you, son of Earvin and Christine Johnson, husband of Cookie, father of Andre and little Earvin. Magic is who I am on the basketball court. Earvin is who I am.

PART ONE

GROWING UP

CHAPTER 1

LOVE AND DISCIPLINE

I grew up in the kind of black family that people today worry is disappearing. Even though there were nine of us, we had what we needed—two great parents, food on the table, and time for the whole family to be together. To provide for us, my parents worked terribly hard. My father had two full-time jobs, and Mom worked just as hard to keep the household going. Seven kids kept her busy, but she also had jobs outside the home.

This was in Lansing, Michigan, an hour and a half from Detroit. Our family lived in a modest yellow frame house at 814 Middle Street, on the west side of town. It was a stable neighborhood of working people. It wasn't the suburbs, but it wasn't the ghetto, either.

Besides being the state capital, Lansing is also a big factory town. General Motors was really cooking during the 1950s, so there were plenty of jobs. Wages were good, which is why so many blacks, including my parents, moved up to Lansing from the rural South. Most of the fathers I knew, including mine, worked for GM or one of its subsidiaries.

Lansing was a great place to grow up. There was a real small-town atmosphere; people waved to one another and said hello on the street. We knew the whole neighborhood, and the families I grew up with did almost everything together—church, school, Boys' Club, ice skating, and going to basketball games at Sexton, the local high school. Whatever I did, or whatever small trouble I got into, my parents always knew about it—sometimes even before I got home.

You can't get away with much in a community like that. The men would get to the shop and say, "Hey, I saw your boy today." You knew that if you acted up, you would catch hell from whatever adult was around. But that didn't stop your parents from disciplining you again when you got home.

I was born on August 14, 1959, the middle of seven children. Quincy, Larry, and Pearl were older, and Kim and the twins—Evelyn and Yvonne—came along afterward. My mother says I was a jolly baby who smiled a lot, and that I let just about anybody pick me up and play with me. That sounds about right.

Our family was squeezed into three small bedrooms on the second floor: one room for our parents, one for my four sisters, and one for the three boys. The place turned into a real madhouse before school every morning, when we all lined up to use the one bathroom. You learned to be quick.

In addition to the seven of us, my parents had three other kids from before they were married. Michael, Lois, and Mary lived in the South, but they often came to stay with us. And we always considered them part of our family.

I was chubby before I grew tall, and when I was young people called me June Bug. Grown-ups in the neighborhood would be going off to work, and when they passed me with my basketball, I'd hear them say, "There goes that crazy June Bug, hoopin' all day." My parents called me Junior, but to my friends I was E.J., or sometimes just E. People from Lansing still call me that.

My original nickname disappeared a long time ago, which is fine with me. Man, I'm glad I didn't have to go through my professional career with *that* name: "And now, ladies and gentlemen, playing guard for the world-champion Los Angeles Lakers, June Bug Johnson!"

We were a close-knit family, and we had fun together. Just about every Saturday night we had a pizza party. Mom would cook up a batch of homemade pies with onions, peppers, mushrooms, and hamburger. After supper, we'd all move into the living room with big bowls of popcorn to watch TV.

We watched a lot of television when I was a kid, shows like *Barnaby Jones*, *Mannix*, *Columbo*, and *The Man from U.N.C.L.E.* There weren't many black shows on in those days, but we did watch *Sanford and Son*, *The Flip Wilson Show*, and *Julia*, with Diahann Carroll. On Sunday nights Ed Sullivan was our man, partly because he featured so many black entertainers.

But when I think back on how television influenced me, what comes to mind isn't a program, but a commercial for Camay soap. It showed a tall, elegant lady who seemed to live in a castle. She was about to step into a huge, sunken bathtub. For some reason, that tub just called out to me. That's it, I decided. When I grow up, I'm going to live in a big mansion with a gigantic bathtub just like that one.

The next time that commercial came on, I turned to my sister Pearl, who's a year ahead of me. "See that bathtub?" I said. "Someday I'm gonna have one just like that in my house."

"Yeah, right," said Pearl, and I never mentioned it again. But today I have a big house with a huge bathtub that reminds me of the one in that commercial. And Pearl has even been in it.

My other notion of what it meant to be rich came from one of my part-time jobs. There were two successful black businessmen in Lansing, Joel Ferguson and Gregory Eaton, who owned nice homes and drove nice cars, and everybody admired them. I used to clean their offices. Whenever I went over there, I'd sit in those big leather chairs and put my feet up on those wide desks. I'd pretend I owned the place, and I'd start giving orders to my staff: "Do this. Take care of that." I'd imagine that everybody in the whole building worked for me, and that I had the respect of the entire town.

Unlike Detroit, Lansing was mostly white. Just about every black family in town lived on either the west side or the east side. But these two men owned large, beautiful homes, and they could afford to live anywhere they wanted.

In those days, I never dreamed that someday I would play basketball for a living. My goal was to be a rich businessman, just like Mr. Ferguson and Mr. Eaton.

With so many kids to take care of, my parents didn't have much money left over for luxuries. We always had enough to eat, but there were plenty of things I wanted and just couldn't have, like a ten-speed bike or blue jeans. Clothes were a special problem for me because I grew into a new size every two weeks. (My brothers and sisters were all taller than average, but nothing like me.) The fanciest thing I owned was a suit with a reversible jacket that I wore to church. One week it was black, and the next Sunday I turned it around and it was checkered.

My parents believed in work—not only for themselves, but for their children, too. They expected all of us to help out around the house. Like my brothers and sisters, I washed the dishes, took out the trash, vacuumed, cooked, and took care of the twins—although I was only two years older than they were.

Dad didn't believe in handouts. So as a kid, the only way I could get my hands on any spending money was to go out and earn it. By the time I was ten I had my own little neighborhood business. I raked leaves, cleaned yards, and shoveled snow. With the money I earned, I could go to the movies and buy an occasional record.

Dad was my idol, so I paid close attention to the way he handled his money. As a way of forcing himself to save, he always kept two or three uncashed checks in his wallet. There were times when I thought he was a little *too* careful, especially when he wouldn't buy me something I thought I needed. But then I'd hear, "You want five dollars, Junior? Here, take the lawn mower. There's a lot of grass in this town, and I bet you could earn that money real quick."

He hated to borrow, and he often warned us about the dangers of going into debt. One of the happiest days of his life was when he made the final mortgage payment on our house. But he was generous, too. When his friends needed a few bucks, he was always willing to help.

Through basketball and my business interests, I've been blessed with a great income, far more than my father ever dreamed of. A couple of years before Cookie and I got married, I bought a big new house in Beverly Hills that cost me $7.2 million. But I'm still my father's son, and some things just don't change.

When I bought the house, my accountant advised me not to make too large a down payment. For tax purposes, he explained, it was better to pay off the mortgage over many years. I knew he was right, but I just couldn't do it that way. Instead, I put down $6.2 million, which was more than 85 percent of the total price. But I *still* didn't feel right, and a few months later, I wrote out a check for that last million. I just hated the idea of that mortgage—or any debt—hanging over my head.

I rarely saw my father with a drink in his hand, and nobody was allowed to smoke in our house. But my parents had lots of friends, and Dad enjoyed dressing up for parties. I used to look forward to the day I could dress like him. When *GQ* put me on their cover a few years ago, I was so proud that I sent it to him right away.

He loved the old blues singers like B. B. King and Muddy Waters. He had their 45's—the albums were too expensive—and every three minutes, when the record was over, it was my job to go over to the record player and start it again. We'd sit together on the living-room couch on weekend afternoons, and I'd wait for him to doze off. As soon as he was sleeping, I'd take off his record and put on one of mine—the Jackson Five, the Commodores, or the Temptations.

But Dad could hear music in his sleep. Or maybe it was just *my* music he could hear, because he didn't like it much. "Boy," he'd call out, "put that song *back.*"

As I get older, my music tastes are leaning more toward his. A few years ago I, too, became a blues fan. And recently I've been buying some of the same records he used to like.

Whenever I put them on, Cookie teases me and calls me an old man.

If my work ethic and some of my habits come from my father, a lot of my personality comes from my mom. People talk about my smile, but my smile is her smile. Most people can make you happy by doing certain things, but Christine Johnson can make you happy by doing almost anything. She just lights up every place she goes.

Mom gets along with everybody, and she was every kid's mother in our neighborhood. Even today, she's always hosting people or preparing a meal for some large group. During my years with the Lakers, whenever we played in Detroit, she and Dad would drive down from Lansing with a big homemade dinner for the entire team.

She was always working. As soon as the twins were old enough to walk, she took a job as a school custodian. Later, she worked in a cafeteria. After standing all day, she would come home to look after the seven of us, with all our complaints and squabbles. She was usually exhausted, and you could see the tiredness in her face.

Mom is very religious, and when I was young we all went to the Union Missionary Baptist Church. But when I was about ten, a woman started going from house to house, with religious books and Bibles. She was a Seventh-Day Adventist, and when Mom was receptive, she came back again and again. The Adventists are Christians who observe the Old Testament Sabbath and the same biblical dietary laws as Orthodox Jews.

When Mom became an Adventist, things got pretty tense for a while. Dad was deep in the Baptist church, active on all the committees. He and I both sang in the choir. Mom wanted the whole family to become Seventh-Day Adventists, and for a few weeks we all did—except Dad.

I hated it. My peewee-league basketball games were on Saturday, and suddenly I couldn't play anymore. There was no TV from sundown Friday until Saturday night, you couldn't go anywhere in a car on Saturday, except to church, and the only music we could listen to was Christian music.

I was mad that I had to make all these changes. I went to Dad about it, and he was upset, too. Mom had stopped cooking on Saturdays, and she also stopped serving ham, pork, and bacon. That was hard, because Dad was a big ham-and-sausage guy.

For a few weeks, there was war. But my parents loved each other, and they fixed things up. Dad saw that Mom was serious about her new church, and Mom understood that Dad wasn't going to join her. My sisters became Adventists, while Dad and I and my brothers remained Baptists. Mom and Dad still live that way, and they go to church together on Saturday *and* Sunday.

Now just because Mom had a great smile didn't mean she was a pushover. Dad was always working, so Mom handled most of the discipline. She was tough, too. If you didn't do your chores, or there was a problem at school, you were grounded. If something really bad happened, which wasn't very often, she'd wait for Dad to get home.

And Dad was *really* strict. If he came home from work in the middle of the night, and you hadn't shoveled the driveway like he told you to, he'd wake you up and make you do it on the spot—even if it was three in the morning.

Once, when I was nine, my friends and I stole some candy from a neighborhood store. That was bad enough, but I made it worse by lying about it to my father. He was so mad that he made me go outside and get a switch from a tree. I knew what that meant—a whupping. Whuppings were rare, but the worst part was that Dad made you get your own switch. When he picked me up for a whupping, my little legs would be running in the air like a cartoon character who had just stepped over a cliff.

Dad worked the night shift at Fisher Body, which was part of GM. Year after year, I don't believe he was ever out sick or even late for work. Whatever they asked him to do, he did, whether it was in the body shop, in the trim shop, or painting. He worked there for thirty years, and he was proud of his excellent record.

His shift began at 4:48 each afternoon, and he worked

until 3:18 the next morning. The assembly line was exhausting, and dangerous, too. He often came home with burn marks on his clothing and occasionally on his skin. Then he'd take a bath, and he was so wiped out that he'd fall asleep right there in the tub.

As long as I can remember, he always had a second job. At first he pumped gas all day and fixed cars at a Shell station near our house. Later on, he bought a truck and started his own trash-collection business. After he got off work at Fisher, he'd drive over to a truck dealership and clean up their garage. In the morning, he'd drive to all the stores on his route and haul away their rubbish. On Saturdays he would bring along one of us to help out.

He has always loved cars—building them, tinkering with them, talking about them, driving them, buying them. He worked on Oldsmobiles at the plant, but his favorite car was the Buick Electra 225. He always had at least one Buick, and every two years he'd trade it in for a new model. He took great care of these cars, always changing the oil, waxing them, and keeping them clean. Even today, his hobby is buying old cars and fixing them up.

People who write articles about me sometimes describe how I spent my childhood shooting hoops in the driveway. But they don't know my dad. We had a driveway, but Dad would never let us put up a basket. The man loved basketball, no question about that. But he loved cars more.

Both of my parents grew up in the South, and every summer, we all piled into the Buick and drove down to North Carolina and Mississippi to visit our extended family. Along the way, our parents would tell us stories from when they were young. Mom grew up on a farm in Tarboro, North Carolina, one of ten kids. She worked in the fields early in the morning before school, and then again after school.

Dad comes from Wesson, a little Mississippi farm town, where his parents were sharecroppers. His father left when Dad was a boy, and Dad and his brother spent most of their days picking cotton and tobacco and taking care of the animals. Dad used to say that the only time they went to school was when it rained.

Late at night, as we drove through the Mississippi Delta and the rest of the family was asleep, I'd sit up front and talk with Dad. Sometimes we discussed basketball, but mostly he told me stories about growing up on the farm, and all the hard work they had to do.

He talked about segregation, too. When he was a boy, there were separate facilities in restaurants and bus stations, and blacks had to go around to the back. A lot had changed since then, but traces of the old South were still there. Even in the early seventies we used to bring our own food on these trips, and we ate our meals in rest areas along the way. It was a lot cheaper that way, but this wasn't the only reason. When you were down South, you never knew when a restaurant would flat out refuse to serve you.

Dad would remind us that Mississippi was a different world than the one we knew back in Michigan. We had to remember to say "Yes sir" and "No sir" to white folks. As recently as 1990, I was in a restaurant in the Deep South when a white man around my father's age came up to me. He stared at me for a minute, seeming to know my face. "Boy," he said, "you play basketball, don't you?" Here we were in the *nineties,* and this guy was still calling me "boy"! But I held my temper as I recalled what my father always said—that we shouldn't forget these people had come a long, long way.

My dad and I had a special bond that continues to this day, and there's no question that basketball made us especially close. He didn't have much free time when I was a kid, but on Sunday afternoons we would sit together in the living room and watch NBA games on television. This was long before cable came along; there was only one game a week on TV, and that's what you watched.

My father's favorite player was Wilt Chamberlain, but we used to watch all the greats: Kareem Abdul-Jabbar and Oscar Robertson from Milwaukee, Bill Russell and John Havlicek from the Celtics, Elgin Baylor and Jerry West from the Lakers. During the games, my father would point out the subtleties of the pick-and-roll play, and explain the various defensive strategies.

When the game was over, Dad usually fell asleep on the couch. I'd run over to the Main Street courts at the schoolyard to practice some of the moves we had just seen. Sometimes Dad came with me, especially when a retooling at the plant gave him a few days off.

We'd play one-on-one, and he always beat me. He was really good, but he also played tough. Sometimes he'd hold me with one hand while he shot with the other. He poked me in the ribs and pushed me and grabbed me all over the court. I'd get mad, but he'd say, "No, that's not a foul!"— which only made me more frustrated, and pushed me to play harder, despite everything he was doing to harass me.

But that was the point. Dad was teaching me that I wouldn't always get the calls, that I had to play above the contact. He showed me different shots, like the two-handed set shot, which wasn't used anymore, and a running hook shot, which he had pretty well mastered. But above all he taught me how to be aggressive on the court: how to drive to the basket and take the charge; how to put up a shot as I was being hit. If they called the foul, great. And if they didn't, no problem.

He taught me to win against the odds, and never to quit. It was years before I was finally able to beat him one-on-one. But when I did, I knew I had really earned it.

Physically, I'm not the most gifted basketball player in the world. I've never been the fastest runner or the highest jumper. But thanks to my father, nobody will ever outsmart me on the court.

Dad comes from the old school, believing that anyone who plays basketball should work his tail off to become a complete player. He encouraged me to work on my shooting, both inside and out. But I also had to learn how to block out and rebound, how to play defense, how to pass, and how to dribble without looking at the ball.

I wanted to be good, so I practiced and played constantly. As hard as my father worked on his jobs, I worked on the basketball court. But I always found a way to make it fun. When I was alone, I'd play fantasy full-court games between Philadelphia and Detroit. These always boiled down to a one-on-one confrontation between my two favorites, Wilt Chamberlain and Dave Bing. I'd be Chamberlain going one way and Bing going the other.

I was also the announcer, telling the imaginary crowd exactly what was happening on the court: "Here's Wali Jones coming down on the right side. He throws it in to Wilt. There are eleven seconds left, and Detroit is leading by one point. Wilt fakes left, goes right, there's the finger roll—and it's in! Here come the Pistons, with just six seconds remaining in the game. Philadelphia's ahead by one. Quickly now, it's Dave Bing off the pick and roll, a twenty-foot jump shot, at the buzzer, *yes!* And the Detroit Pistons have just won the world championship!"

There I was, all alone on the court at seven in the morning, as happy as I've ever been, yelling, "Dave Bing, ladies and gentlemen. What an exciting player he is to watch!"

I was only seven when Dave Bing was drafted out of Syracuse, but I watched him average 20 points a game in his rookie year. Because of him, the next year the Pistons reached the playoffs for the first time. Soon every kid on the playground was shooting the Dave Bing jumper. They'd come running down the court, pull up, leap into the air, yell, "Bing," and let it fly.

Occasionally I got to see Dave Bing in person at Cobo Arena in Detroit. Going to a basketball game in those days was not as difficult as it is today. Tickets were a whole lot cheaper, and you could usually get one, too.

These games were *fun*—especially in Detroit. The Pistons were not a good team, but that didn't matter because the games were great social events anyway. The crowd, which was mostly black, was really dressed up: the women in their nice coats and fur collars, the men in big hats, and eye-catching hip suits like you would never see back in Lansing.

I miss places like Cobo. When I got to the pros, it bothered me that although black players were dominating the game, there seemed to be fewer and fewer black fans. Most of the teams had moved out to the suburbs, and ticket prices were so high that many of the older fans could no longer afford to come.

But Cobo—that place was special. It was a small, intimate arena where the fans could actually talk to the players: "Whip it on him! Talk to him, Mr. Bing. He can't carry your tennis shoes!" They let you know if you could play, and if you couldn't they let you know that, too.

When I was eleven, a group of us from the Boys' Club took a bus to Cobo to see the Pistons play Milwaukee. Somebody brought me into the Milwaukee locker room so I could ask the great one himself, Kareem Abdul-Jabbar, for an autograph. Suddenly, there he was, standing right in front of me. But I was so nervous that I couldn't even open my mouth. Another kid had to ask him for me.

Kareem signed quickly and dashed right out. He wasn't very friendly about it, and it left me with a bad feeling. Despite that first meeting, Kareem turned out to be the most important teammate I ever had; I'll have a lot more to say about him later on.

Earl Monroe of the Knicks was another of our heroes. His moves on the court were so amazing that people said even Jesus Christ couldn't go one-on-one against him. Guarding him was like trying to keep up with the Invisible Man, because you never knew where he'd turn up next. We all knew him as Earl the Pearl, but one of my father's friends told me that his original nickname was Black Magic.

If Earl hit for 30 points, then everybody on the playground wanted to be Earl. If Dave Bing got off that Sunday, everybody wanted to be Dave. These guys were larger than life, and I worshipped them. I never dreamed that someday I, too, would play in the NBA, and that kids would be talking about me that way. The first time I heard it happen was back in Lansing during the off-season three or four years after I turned pro. I was walking by a playground just as a kid sank a three-pointer. "All *right*!" he yelled. "Just like Magic Johnson." Did he really say that? It gave me chills.

Watching those NBA games with my father, I studied the great players and tried to learn from them all. Bill Russell was always a big favorite of the grown-ups, because they appreciated his brilliant defensive moves. Well, Russell was a great player, all right, but what I admired most about him had nothing to do with his moves. It was all those championships he had won with the Celtics. That's all I ever wanted—to be a winner.

There was one more player I idolized, although he never played in the NBA. Marques Haynes, known as the "World's Greatest Dribbler," started out with the Harlem Globetrotters and then left them in 1953 to form his own team, the Harlem Magicians. Whenever Marques Haynes came to town, my dad would take me to see him.

He was the best ball handler I've ever seen. That man could dribble! Through his legs or his defender's legs and even lying on his back, his ball control was unbelievable. He used to dribble very low, just an inch or two off the ground, which knocked me out. I had tried to do that, so I knew how hard it was. I also practiced dribbling on the outside wall of our house, because somebody told me that was a good way to develop fingertip control.

No matter what else I was doing, I always had a basketball in my hand. If I was running an errand for my mother, I'd dribble on the way to the store. Just to make it interesting, I'd alternate right hand and left, block by block.

I remember waking up when it was still dark outside and wanting to play ball so badly that I'd just lie there, looking out the window, waiting for daybreak. If it was too early to go to the schoolyard, I'd dribble on the street. I'd run around the parked cars and pretend they were players on the other team. All up and down Middle Street people used to open their windows and yell at me for waking them up. But I couldn't help it. The game was just in me.

Mom had strict rules about playing ball in the house, and I knew she meant business. So on rainy days I would make a special indoor basketball by rolling up some of my father's socks. For the basket, I'd take a pencil and draw a little box high up on the wall. Sometimes I played with my sisters, or my brother Larry. But usually I played alone, shooting into the box on the wall or a trash can or making foul shots into a laundry basket at the top of the stairs. One way or another, I had to play.

The weather had to be pretty bad to keep me off the Main Street courts, however. By fourth grade I was even going on winter mornings. Snow wouldn't stop me—I brought a shovel. Sometimes Larry came with me, and we'd play a full-court game, just the two of us. He was always Walt Frazier, and I was Chamberlain. One reason I learned to dribble so well was that every time Wilt had the ball, Frazier would pressure him the whole length of the court.

When the weather turned nice, the schoolyard was always crowded. Those courts were Lansing's proving ground. We barely noticed that the pavement was slanted, or that there were no nets on the baskets. Sometimes we'd bring over a net from some other court, but pretty soon it would be in shreds from all the hooping.

Even the courts took a beating. But every year or two the city would redo the surface, outlining the paint lines, which you couldn't see anymore, and putting in new rims. These renovations always gave me a tremendous lift. What a joy it was to play on those clean, bright lines, and to shoot into those bright orange rims for the two or three days when they were actually parallel to the ground.

If you didn't have a pair of Chucks—Chuck Taylor All Star basketball shoes—you weren't considered a player. Mine were red, with red-and-white laces. We played to 15, shirts against skins, one point per basket, and you had to win by two. If your team won, you stayed on the court. Main Street was crowded with kids waiting their turn, so the only way to keep playing was to keep winning.

And I did. But I didn't always choose the most talented players for my team. I noticed early on that some of these guys just wanted to show off. I preferred the hard workers, the kids who really *wanted* to win. That way we could keep the court all day long.

These were standard five-man pickup games. But within each game there were always one-on-one competitions. These were more about style than scoring. The object was to top the other guy and make him look bad. If he came down and made a move on you, everybody on the sidelines would say, "Oooh." Then they'd wait for you to respond by putting a move on him. The first few points of the game might come from outside shots, but when it got to be winning time you'd take it right to the basket.

The best ball came on late summer afternoons. Sometimes we'd be going so well that our older brothers would drive up and flick on the headlights. Then we would play into the night. The great thing about Main Street was that our parents never had to worry about us. They always knew where we were, and who we were with.

Even so, my mother always made me tell her where I was going. "Come on, Mom," I said. "You *know* that if I'm not home, I'm at the courts." But that wasn't good enough. Even if it was early on a Sunday morning, and everybody was sleeping, I still had to wake her up before I left. She'd open one eye, say, "Uh-huh," and fall back to sleep. I used to think it was because I was young, but now I know better. It's because she's a mother. Even today, whenever I'm back in Lansing, she still waits up for me at night.

I don't know exactly when I understood that basketball was more than just a game for me, or when the outside world started to matter. But I was probably around ten. My fifth-grade teacher, Greta Dart, and her husband, Jim, played a role in my growing up that was second only to my parents. Outside of my family, they were the most important adults in my life. And for all that's happened since, we're still close.

Aside from everything else they taught me in the classroom, on the court, and in their home, they were also my first (and closest) white friends. Getting to know the Darts allowed me to start feeling comfortable with white people. For many black kids in America, that just doesn't happen.

I was in the first class Mrs. Dart ever taught, although she was far too smart to let us know that. She was small, only about five feet tall, and probably didn't weigh more than a hundred pounds. She was also a blue-eyed blonde in a school where 95 percent of the kids were black.

We all liked her, and she and I hit it off right away. I was the tallest kid in the class, a good athlete, and a decent student. I didn't act up much, because my parents would have killed me if I did. The other kids looked up to me, and I enjoyed being a leader. Sometimes, when the class got too noisy, I helped Mrs. Dart settle things down.

I got to know her husband when the sixth graders at our school formed their own basketball team. The fifth-grade boys were jealous, so a few of us met with the principal to ask if we, too, could have a team. "I don't see why not," he said. "But I can't let you use the gym without an adult to supervise. If you can find yourselves a coach, go ahead."

We went straight to Mrs. Dart. "Please?" we said. "You don't actually have to *do* anything. You just have to be there."

"I'm sorry, guys," she said. "I can't do it."

"What about your husband?" somebody asked. All we knew about Mrs. Dart's husband was that he existed. We didn't know that he had played basketball in high school and in the Lansing City League. We just needed an adult. If this guy was available, we were glad to have him. As it turned out, he was more than available; he was *good*.

Mrs. Dart was pretty athletic herself. She was one of the few teachers who actually played kickball with us at recess. Sometimes she and I and one other kid would take on the whole class. I had a big crush on her, although I didn't even know it at the time. But why else did I volunteer to stay after school to help her clean the blackboards and close the windows?

More than any other teacher at Main Street School, Mrs. Dart had a way of inspiring and motivating the class. When she told us about the Presidential Fitness awards, five of us, three boys and two girls, decided to sign up. The program was a real challenge, and involved a lot of running, and plenty of sit-ups, push-ups, and pull-ups. (The pull-ups were *really* hard.) This was the first time I had ever worked toward an athletic goal, and it took weeks of effort and dedication. But I don't think any of us would have signed up if Mrs. Dart hadn't encouraged us. When the medals were awarded, we wore them proudly around the school.

My friendship with Mrs. Dart almost ended when she and I got into an argument that was one of the real tests of my childhood. I was playing in a Saturday-morning basketball league, and our championship game was scheduled for the weekend. A few days earlier I had come to school without my homework. Mrs. Dart told me to stay after class so I could do it.

"I can't," I said. "We've got a practice."

"I'm sorry, Earvin, but you've got to do this assignment."

"But we've got our big game on Saturday."

"I know. But if you don't finish the assignment, you won't be able to play."

"You can't make me miss that game!" I said. Technically, I might have been right. But I never should have said that. Now the two of us were in a contest of wills. When I continued to refuse to do the assignment, Mrs. Dart told the coach that I couldn't play. She also called my parents to tell them what had happened, so now I was in double trouble.

I did everything I could to smooth things over. I called Mrs. Dart at home. I begged her to change her mind. I went to see her after school. "You don't understand," I said. "This is the league championship. The team needs me. I can do the assignment next week."

"No," she said again. "Unless you finish it before the game, you can't play."

I was pretty sure she was bluffing, and I showed up at the game anyway. When the coach told me I couldn't play, I was furious. I was even more angry as I sat on the bench and watched our team lose for the first time all season. We lost that game by one point.

I cried that day, and I vowed that I'd never speak to Mrs. Dart again. I stayed angry at her for weeks. I still don't fully understand why, but after my anger wore off, Mrs. Dart and

I became even closer. Maybe I respected her for following through on her threat. Or maybe I was secretly proud that she saw me as more than just an athlete, that she expected me to be a good student, too.

Jim Dart drove a truck for Vernor's, a well-known Michigan soft-drink company that made only one product—ginger ale. He would drive from one grocery store to the next, delivering cases of Vernor's and stacking them on the shelves. On weekends when my father didn't need me, I'd drive around with Jim and help him on his route.

He also owned several houses, which he rented out to families on the west side of Lansing. My friends and I did a lot of part-time work for the Darts at these houses, cutting grass, painting, and cleaning. In addition to paying us, Jim and Greta were always inviting us over for lunch and doing us other favors.

Jim took good care of me. He's a basketball nut, and he used to take me with him to games at Sexton High, which was right in our neighborhood, and at Michigan State University, just a few miles away. One summer, when he played in a fast-pitch softball league, he got me a job as the batboy. After I finished seventh grade, he sent me to a basketball camp at the university. The program was run by Gus Ganakas, the assistant coach, and he and I became friends. From then on there was always a pass waiting for me at the Michigan State games.

By the time I got to junior high, several families from our neighborhood had moved to a housing project on the other side of town. My friends and I used to go to parties over there. Because it was too far to walk, especially in the winter, we often asked the Darts to drive us. And they did. But we were embarrassed to be seen getting a ride from white people, so we'd always ask to be dropped off and picked up a block or two from where we were actually going. We thought we were getting away with something, but Jim and Greta knew all along. They understood what we were going through, and they were nice enough not to let on.

By then I was playing basketball just about all the time. I

played in every possible league and in every pickup game I could find. I played with kids my age and with older kids who were in high school. Sometimes I walked all the way over to the south side just to play ball. Wherever the game was, that's where you'd find me.

I wasn't the only kid in Lansing who was really good. Over on the east side, I had a rival named Jay Vincent. Jay and I were the same age, and we played against each other so often that we ended up becoming friends. Later, we played on the same team at Michigan State, where we were also room-mates.

I tried football one season, but I guess my heart wasn't in it, because I'd always get to the park an hour or two before practice so I could play basketball. There I was in my football uniform, but because I had walked over in my cleats, I ended up playing basketball in my socks. That's how much I loved the game.

Shortly after I started seventh grade at Dwight Rich Junior High, the coach announced tryouts for the basketball team. A lot of kids wanted to play; there must have been a hundred of us in that gym. I knew I'd make the team, but I figured it would take the coach at least a week to narrow it down to twelve kids.

But he had a better idea. "Okay," he said. "I want all the right-handed kids to line up over here. Lefties, you go to the other side. We'll start with the righties. I want each of you guys to dribble to the basket with your left hand and shoot a left-handed lay-up. Lefties, you'll be doing it with your right hand."

Most kids just couldn't do it, and the coach cut them on the spot. In about twenty minutes, that gym cleared out and Coach Louis Brockhaus had his team.

I made the team because Jim Dart had worked with us on our weak-hand shooting, and also because I had practiced so much. All that dribbling on the street and all those hours of playing by myself had finally paid off. But Coach Brockhaus worked with me on becoming a more physical player, taking the charge, and going after rebounds. On the playground I used to get rebounds easily because of my height. Now, for the first time, I learned to work for them.

In eighth and ninth grades, another coach, Paul Rose-krans, helped me improve my shooting. I was pretty good from the outside, so he worked with me on my inside moves. He had me doing shooting drills, where I practiced each shot twenty-five times in a row. This was a new experience for me, learning the value of repetition.

By ninth grade our team was unstoppable. There was one game against Otto Junior High in which I scored 48 points. I don't know how I did that, because we played six-minute quarters and I sat out for the entire fourth quarter.

It was during junior high that I really shot up. I hit the six-foot mark in seventh grade, and by the end of ninth grade I was up to six-five. Shopping was hard—and expensive, too, because I kept outgrowing my clothes and my shoes. Here, too, Jim and Greta Dart helped me out.

Unlike some big kids, I didn't mind being tall. But there were times when it was a problem—like when I couldn't find a pair of shoes that fit. At dancing parties in people's base-ments, my head would hit the ceiling. Even the tallest girls were so much shorter that during the slow dances I had to bend way over.

Like all tall people, I got my share of "How's the weather up there?" You'd be amazed how often people say that. And they actually think they're being clever! Years later, some-body told me that Wilt Chamberlain used to answer that question by spitting. "I hear it's raining," he'd say.

People expect more from you when you're tall, especially in sports. That's why I've always felt bad for tall guys who don't happen to be athletic. And if you're tall and *black*, forget it—everyone just assumes you're a ballplayer. I have an old friend who's around my height—I stopped growing at six feet, eight and a half inches—and people are always com-ing up to him and saying, "What? You don't play basketball? Man, if I had your height . . ." That's the favorite line on the playground, and I must have heard it a thousand times: "If I had your height, I'd be in the NBA."

But I've noticed over the years that some of the tallest players in the NBA are also the least talented. You get the feeling that somebody decided that height was enough in their case, and the talent would somehow appear on its own. When you see a little guy come into the league, you can almost bet he's good.

My father never saw me play serious basketball until I was in junior high. Our games were on weekday afternoons, but because of his work schedule he couldn't be there. "Dad," I'd tell him the next morning, "I had thirty last night." I'd describe some of the shots I made, but I knew he felt bad that he wasn't there.

Finally, after some of the other fathers started telling him about my success, he asked for permission to leave work to see me. When he was turned down by his supervisor, he went right to the foreman.

"I know all about your boy," the foreman said. "And you've got to be there." After the game against Otto when I scored 48 points, the whole community was talking about Earvin Johnson's son. From then on, Dad didn't miss a game.

My family always supported me, but they never let me get a swelled head. Maybe I was the hero of the game, but when I got home I still had to take out the trash. And no matter how many points I scored on Friday night, Dad would still come in at six-thirty the next morning. "Wake up, son, and jump in the truck. We've got work to do."

Even though people made a big fuss about me in junior high, I didn't believe I was as good as they said. I had heard about dozens of great young players who had come out of big cities like Detroit, New York, Chicago, and Philadelphia. Some of them went on to become college stars, and a few even made it to the NBA. But nobody I had ever heard of had come out of Lansing, Michigan.

I always had doubts about myself, but that turned out to be a big advantage. It kept my expectations low, and it made me work like crazy to keep getting better. It wasn't until eighth grade that I began to realize that I might have a future in basketball. If I kept improving, and kept practicing, maybe I could be a star at Sexton High. That would *really* be something.

CHAPTER 2

BLACK AND WHITE

Sexton High. It was the pride of the west side, and was known throughout the state of Michigan as a basketball powerhouse. The school, which was all black, was only five blocks from our house. Everybody in the neighborhood supported the Big Reds, and we all went to the Sexton games. This was Showtime, Lansing style. The gym was packed, the crowd was yelling, the band was playing, the drums were beating, and the whole place was rocking. The popcorn was popped right there in the gym. When you walked in and smelled that great aroma, you just knew it was basketball time.

All through junior high, I played, and we won, and I waited. Someday my turn would come. I, too, would play for Sexton, where I'd be part of that great tradition. All I could see was Sexton High, and I couldn't wait to get there.

But I hadn't counted on busing.

Some people have the impression that only whites were against forced busing, and that most blacks supported it. Not in Lansing! We hated busing, and nobody hated it more than I did. Our family lived just outside the cutoff line. Suddenly we weren't allowed to go to Sexton with all our friends. All of us except Quincy, who had already started high school, had to take the early bus to Everett, a white school on the south side of town.

I was furious. No black kid wanted to attend an all-white school. But for me, being sent to Everett was an especially cruel punishment. Maybe if Everett had had a great basket-ball team I could have lived with it. Or even a half-decent team. But the Vikings were terrible. They couldn't run, couldn't jump, and worst of all, they couldn't *win*. The idea of playing for Everett was humiliating.

So I did everything in my power to avoid going there. I tried to say that our family had moved. When that didn't work, I claimed that *I* had moved. I said I was living with friends in another part of the neighborhood. I even appealed to the school board. But nothing made any difference.

The previous year, Larry and Pearl had been bused to Everett. Pearl hated it, and Larry had been involved in sev-eral fights. He was a good basketball player, but he was cut from the team after an argument with the coach. He was still mad about it, and he begged me not to play for the Vikings. I loved my brother, but I couldn't go along with what he was asking. The idea of playing for Everett sounded horrible to me, no question about it, but not playing sounded even worse.

As I look back on it today, I see the whole picture very differently. It's true that I hated missing out on Sexton. And for the first few months, I was miserable at Everett. But being bused to Everett turned out to be one of the best things that ever happened to me. It got me out of my own little world and taught me how to understand white people, how to com-municate and deal with them.

And Everett was still a big step up from junior high. In Michigan, high school basketball is almost as important as it is in Indiana, and everybody knows what *that's* like. The fans are passionate. The teams are covered in the media. And the best players become known all over the state.

When school began in September, the atmosphere at Ev-erett was tense. Busing was still relatively new; we were only the second group of black kids to attend the school. The previous year, a few whites had thrown rocks at the buses. Some white parents had even kept their kids out of school rather than let them attend classes with blacks. Things had improved a little, but it was a long time before we stopped feeling like outsiders. Two busloads of kids can get swallowed up pretty fast in a big high school.

At first there was almost no mixing between the two groups. The teachers and administrators were used to a certain kind of school, and a lot of them felt threatened by this sudden influx of blacks. There were about a hundred of us at Everett, and at basketball games, the black kids all sat together under the basket, like a big black dot on a white page.

Because so many of the black kids knew me, I quickly emerged as their leader. But where Larry had been angry and confrontational with the school authorities, I was friendly and diplomatic. When the black students felt alienated by the white rock music that was piped into the lunchroom, I went to see the principal. In a polite and nonthreatening way, I explained the situation. Soon we had black music, too. The black kids started feeling more comfortable, and the white kids liked those Motown songs almost as much as we did.

Then we asked the principal if we could use an empty room for lunch-hour dances. He didn't exactly say no, but he wasn't comfortable about it, either. He told me he was worried that it could make kids late to their early-afternoon classes. I promised him that this wouldn't happen. We got the dance room, and I always made sure that the music was turned off ten minutes before the end of lunch hour.

But not every problem was solved that easily. Shortly before the basketball season began, there were tryouts for cheerleaders. Two or three black girls had gone out, and we all knew they were good. When the cheerleading coach announced the results, and no black girls had been accepted, that didn't seem right.

This time, diplomacy failed. When the administration didn't respond to the problem, I kept the black basketball players out of practice until the matter was resolved. It didn't take long.

Would the racial tensions at Everett influence the basketball team, too? I kept hoping they wouldn't, and I had good reason to be optimistic. I had played for Everett in a few summer-league games, and although I had been the only black starter, things had gone well. I was really hot, and the team played better than I expected. The seniors didn't play in the summer, and that made our success look even more impressive.

But when the seniors returned in the fall, everything changed. On the first day of practice, my teammates froze me out. Time after time I was wide open, but nobody threw me the ball. At first I thought they just didn't see me. But I woke up after a kid named Danny Parks looked right at me and then took a long jumper. Which he missed.

I was furious, but I didn't say a word. Shortly after that, I grabbed a defensive rebound and took the ball all the way down for a basket. I did it again, and a third time, too.

Finally Parks got angry and said, "Hey, pass the goddamn ball."

That did it. I slammed down the ball and glared at him. Then I exploded. "I *knew* this would happen!" I said. "That's why I didn't want to come to this fucking school in the first place!"

"Oh yeah? Well, you people are all the same," he said. "You think you're gonna come in here and do whatever you want? Look, hotshot, your job is to get the rebound. Let *us* do the shooting."

All this time we were moving toward each other. I was really mad, and I was getting ready to punch this guy in the face. But just then some of the other players grabbed me and held me back.

As I was struggling to get loose, George Fox, our coach, ran onto the floor. He sent Parks to the locker room and pulled me over to the side.

"What the hell's going on here?" he said. "What are you so upset about?"

"Can't you see?" I said. "They're freezing me out! I hate these assholes."

"Let me talk to them, Earvin. Everything will be all right."

"No it won't! My brother told me this would happen.

What am I doing here anyway? There must be some other school I can play for."

"Listen, you just have to be more tolerant of these kids. Sometimes they miss a pass."

What the hell was he talking about? Why should *I* have to be tolerant?

"We'll work it out," said Fox, but I didn't believe him.

At first I hoped that the incident would be enough to get me transferred to another school—maybe even Sexton. But I was dreaming. Either I'd find a way to work with these guys, or I wouldn't play basketball.

The coach must have talked to the seniors, because the second practice was better. But they still expected to run the show. They hadn't counted on a black player coming in—especially a freshman who was a lot better than they were.

It was another white senior on the team who helped me out. Some of his friends were giving me the silent treatment, but Randy Shumway made a point of talking to me. The situation improved, so I guess Randy got Parks and the others to settle down.

George Fox was a good coach and an excellent teacher. He worked us hard and stressed the fundamentals, like how to rebound, or what the proper footwork was for different plays. He would make us do these things again and again until they became habit. Everett wasn't exactly loaded with talent, but we practiced intensely and started winning. Although talent is important, the fundamentals will usually win out. And nothing in the world beats hard work.

It was Fox who first understood that I played best as a guard. Normally the biggest kids played forward or center, and the smaller guys handled the ball. But I've always functioned best as the quarterback, reading the defense, making the decisions, and getting the ball to the open man. There was an unwritten rule that you didn't let your big man bring up the ball, that you kept him in the low post, near the basket. But when he saw what I could do, Coach Fox was willing to be flexible.

We got along well. I was a good practice player, and every

coach I've ever played for has appreciated that. I was willing to work for hours on rebounding, shooting, or defense. When practice was boring, I found a way to make it fun. But I always played my heart out.

Some players take it easy during practice. They coast and don't go into high gear until the actual game. I've never understood that mentality. To me, when you're turning that switch on and off, there's always the danger that it can get stuck in "off." From high school through the Lakers, I've always played as intensely in practice as I did in the games.

To Coach Fox, being in the gym and playing for the Vikings were privileges that had to be earned. There were no free rides, not even for the star player. In my second year, I started slacking off a little in practice. Right away, Coach Fox pulled me aside and laid down the law: "Earvin, I don't care how good you are. If you keep this up you won't be starting for us."

That was all the warning I needed. I don't always do the right thing—but when I screw up, you don't have to tell me twice.

The year I came to Everett we were picked to finish last. But we got off to a great start and won our first six games. Then came a game against Jackson Parkside, which I'll never forget. They were picked to finish first, and they were very good. But we were better, and we just destroyed them. I had one of the best games of my entire life, and finished with 36 points, 18 rebounds, and 16 assists. A triple-double, although back then nobody used that phrase.

After the game, Fred Stabley, Jr., a sportswriter for the *Lansing State Journal*, came into our locker room as usual.

"Great game, Earvin," he said.

"Thanks."

"Listen, Earvin, I think you should have a nickname. I was thinking of calling you Dr. J., but that's taken. And so is Big E—Elvin Hayes. How about if I call you Magic?"

I was fifteen years old. My teammates were standing around listening to all of this. I was embarrassed by the question and didn't take it seriously. "Fine," I said. "Whatever you like."

I didn't expect to hear that name again, and for a few weeks I didn't. Fred told me later that when he got back to the office, his colleagues at the paper talked him out of it. "Don't call him Magic," his editor said. "The kid is off to a great start, but it'll never last." A little later, when I had another great game against the same team, Fred started writing about me as Earvin "Magic" Johnson. Within about two months, that name was known all across Michigan.

Magic Johnson. Most people in Lansing liked the name, but my parents sure didn't. Dad felt it was a guaranteed way for people to be disappointed in me, because the name was too much for any player to live up to. He also figured that just about every opponent I would ever run into would now have an extra incentive to stop me. He was right about that, but the additional pressure actually helped me get better.

My mother's objection was a little different. As a religious woman, she didn't want me to forget that my talents came from God. To her, all this talk of "magic" sounded like blasphemy. She worried that the name would put bad ideas into my head. To this day, when somebody refers to me as "Magic" in her presence, she'll correct them by saying, "Earvin," or "Junior," which is how I'm known at home.

With my new name, everything changed. We'd come into the gym at a rival school, and the first thing we'd see would be signs reading NO MAGIC TODAY or WE'LL MAKE THE MAGIC DISAPPEAR. Once, in a game against East Lansing, the whole crowd was hollering in rhythm, "No magic, no magic, no magic tonight." When I was introduced in that game, everybody in the place stood up and turned their backs. Wherever I played I became a target for opposing fans. That was fine with me, because I took it as a compliment. The only part that bothered me was that some of these people probably figured that the new name was my own idea.

The name became a challenge, and I love challenges. The signs and the slogans only served to fire me up. They didn't seem to hurt my teammates, either. For the first time in years,

Everett had a winning season—a great season. The Vikings lost only one game all season, and we made it all the way to the state quarterfinals. We might have won that game, too, if I hadn't called a time-out with ten seconds left. I didn't realize that our last time-out had already been used, so the other team got possession of the ball. Still, for Everett to get that far was a small miracle.

Although the name has been great for me, I have never thought of myself as Magic. And neither have my teammates or my coaches. Pat Riley, the Lakers' coach during most of my NBA career, absolutely hated the name. He thought it conveyed precisely the wrong message. To him, "Magic" sounded like a player who didn't practice hard or work on the fundamentals. But I did both. Constantly.

To me, being known as Magic Johnson has always been an honor and a great motivator. I've spent the rest of my career trying to live up to it.

My second year at Everett was a lot more fun. The seniors had all graduated, so there was far less tension on the team. And there's nothing like winning to help people get along. We even beat Sexton—twice, in fact. And nobody could remember the last time *that* had happened. I was so nervous before those games. I wasn't sure how our guys would hold up under the pressure of Sexton's reputation, and the way they talked trash to our team. And I was jealous of the Sexton players, who included several of my friends.

In our first game against them, I was so pumped up that I missed a lot of my shots. The following week, when they came to our gym, I was ready. Maybe I couldn't play for Sexton, but I could still show them my stuff. I scored 54 points in that game, which turned out to be the most points scored by a high school player in Lansing's history.

Just before that season had begun we had taken a bus to Detroit for an exhibition game against Detroit Northwestern. Like Sexton, they were an all-black team. But these guys played in Detroit, which made us all a little nervous.

When we got into their gym and started warming up, the

home team was already there. And one after another, *they were all dunking the ball.* This was fairly common in black city schools, where teams used to dunk before the game to intimidate their opponents. They also did it to psych up the crowd. Every time a guy dunked during the warm-ups, the fans would all yell in unison, *"Boom!"*

Jaimie Huffman, a white guard on our team, ran up to me, a worried expression on his face. "Come on, Earvin," he said. "*You* guys start dunking." Like that was going to make a difference.

"No," I said. "Let's just wait for the game."

It was only an exhibition game, but everybody in that gym was watching me. I had received a lot of press, and the Detroit media wanted to see what this small-town boy known as Magic was made of. Okay, kid, we've heard a lot about you. Now show us how good you really are.

I thrive on pressure, and I ended up with 40 points, 35 rebounds, and 20 assists. The rest of our team played well, too, and even our second team outscored those guys. If this was any indication, our second season was going to be even better than our first.

I guess it's not surprising that I was paying a high price for my success in basketball. During my first year at Everett, the guidance counselor had a little talk with me. "You may be a great athlete," she said, "but academically, you're barely getting by. I don't know if you're planning to go to college, but unless your grades start improving, you haven't got a chance."

It was true. I was getting C's and D's because I was thinking about nothing but basketball.

"Well, I'm definitely going to college," I said.

"If you're really serious about that, I think you should be going to summer school."

Summer school? That was about the last thing I wanted to do. To be stuck in class when it was hot outside and everybody else was playing? Forget it. Another teacher told me that I was reading at only an eighth-grade level, and that I

ought to do some extra work to catch up. For a while I re-
sisted. But when I took the time to be honest with myself and
really listened to what these teachers were telling me, I knew
they were right.

When summer came along, I took classes at Everett for
three hours every morning. I really applied myself, and I
worked hard. Sure enough, my reading scores improved.
When I continued to work on my reading the following year,
all my grades went up. The improvement was so dramatic
and so satisfying that I decided to go back to summer school
the following year.

But not everybody at Everett High was as supportive as
my teachers. The school's security officer was a guy we called
John the Narc, who used to patrol the hallways, checking for
hall passes and looking out for any evidence of drugs.

John didn't like me. Maybe he resented all the attention I
was getting. Or maybe it was good old-fashioned prejudice.
Whatever the reason, he loved to tell me that I would never
amount to anything. "You think you're really something because you can play ball," he'd say. "But you'll see. You
won't even graduate from here. No black kid ever comes out
of here and is successful. You're just like the rest of them."

I hated him, but I never said a word. I figured that he was
dying for me to talk back so he could get me in trouble.
Instead of responding, I just let it wash over me. I'll show
this asshole, I thought. John the Narc would be shocked to
hear it, but I turned him from my enemy into my biggest
motivator. Starting in eleventh grade, I worked harder at
school than at basketball.

After I graduated, I returned to Everett twice just to see
John. The first time was a few months later, when I brought
along the grades from my first semester at Michigan State. I
had a 3.4 average, and I wanted him to see it.

The second time was two years later, when I signed with
the Los Angeles Lakers. Now, for the first time in my life, I
could afford almost anything I wanted. And what I wanted
most of all was a car—a beautiful blue Mercedes. (Both of
those businessmen whose offices I used to clean as a kid had

driven Mercedeses.) I treated that car like a treasure. Even Dad, Mr. Goodwrench himself, thought I might be overdoing it. "Junior," he said, "if you keep on cleaning that thing, you're gonna wash the paint right off it." But I loved my new car and all it represented. I wanted everybody who saw it to be as happy for me as I was for myself.

I bought the car in Illinois. Although I was about to turn pro, I was on my way back to Michigan State to finish up the semester. But first I had a stop to make. Early in the morning, I shined up the car and waxed it yet again. Then I drove it to Everett High School, right onto the front lawn. I asked one of the students to find John the Narc, and to tell him that some guy had parked his car up on the grass. Sure enough, out came John to deal with the problem. I just sat there behind the wheel with my arms folded. When he came up to the car, I rolled down the window. "Oh, hi, John, is that you? Well, I guess I didn't amount to anything, did I?"

His face turned red—the nicest shade of red I've ever seen.

Starting in eleventh grade, I began taking college-prep courses. There weren't too many blacks in these classes, which gave me an extra push to get to know some of the white kids. Of course it helped that I was the star of the basketball team.

One Friday, in the locker room, one of my white teammates, a guy named Brian, said, "I'm having a kegger tonight."

"What's a kegger?" I asked.

"You're putting me on," he said.

"No really, what's a kegger? I've never heard of it."

"It's a party," he said. "You buy a keg of beer, and your parents aren't home. Don't you guys do that?"

No, I told him, the black kids I knew didn't drink beer. Mostly they drank wine, although I didn't drink at all. One night, my brother Quincy had come home drunk. It was very late, but Mom woke us all up because she wanted us to see what he looked like. The poor guy was stinking and throwing up, and Mom gave him coffee and threw him into the tub.

That was enough of a warning for me, but Dad woke Quincy up at six and made him get on the truck. That made a big impression on me. To this day, I might have one drink at a party, but that's my limit.

In the locker room now, Brian and a couple of other guys were talking about different brands of beer and wine. After a few minutes, Brian said to me, "Why don't you come over tonight?"

"Thanks," I told him, "but I can't make it. We're having our own party."

"What time?"

"Ten, ten-thirty. I'll show up around eleven."

"That late?" he said. "We start at eight o'clock."

"Eight o'clock? We're not even *dressed* yet."

"You know," said Brian, "you could probably go to both."

"Maybe I will," I said. "I'll check with Reggie."

Reggie Chastine was my best friend. He was a feisty little guy, no more than five feet three, but he had the heart of a giant. Despite his size, he joined our team as a starter when I was in eleventh grade. He was a terrific player. The two of us were inseparable. We looked so funny together that people called us Mutt and Jeff.

I was curious about the white kids' party, but I didn't want to show up alone. Besides, Reggie had a car.

It wasn't hard to find Brian's house that night because the music was so loud we could hear it from the car. When Reggie and I walked in, it was like a scene out of an old Western when the bad guy strolls into the saloon. Everything stopped. Most of these kids knew who we were, but they were almost catatonic to see us at their party. Meanwhile, I was desperately searching the room for the guy who had invited me. "Um, is Brian around?"

Brian came out and introduced us around. The first thing I noticed, after my ears got used to the music, was that this was the biggest house I had ever been in. And there were people everywhere: in the kitchen, the living room, the basement. Some were dancing. But most of them were just standing around drinking beer and talking. At our parties, everybody stayed in one room and danced.

Although I never drank a single beer, Reggie and I went to a number of keggers that year. We'd always leave in time to get to our own parties with our friends who went to Sexton. There are always a few blacks who resent it if you have white friends, but I didn't let that deter me. I still had my black friends, including Toni, my girlfriend, who went to Sexton. But now I had some white friends, too.

As black and white kids at Everett started to feel a little more comfortable with one another, each group started to pick up on the way the other talked. The white guys used to say "fucking A," which I had never heard before, or "golly gee," which sounded like something out of a TV sitcom. And we loved it when they tried to talk black: "Yo, what's up, bro?" That always cracked us up because most of them said it without any soul. Naturally, we helped them with their elocution.

In the summer I was back in the neighborhood. I worked at the Boys' Club during the afternoon and shot hoops all evening. At night I sang with four other guys on the corner of Middle and Williams. Jimmy Howell sang lead, and he could get up really high. The rest of us sang backup on songs like "My Girl," "Heard It Through the Grapevine," "Ain't Too Proud to Beg," and other Motown hits. We worked hard on these routines, and we even practiced the dance steps.

It was a great time for pop music, although we all complained that Lansing didn't have a single black radio station. Late at night, if you were in the right spot, you could pick up Detroit. Mostly we listened to top forty, and waited for black songs to come along. I loved that music—the Jackson Five, the Commodores, the Temptations, Stevie Wonder, the Supremes. This was before cassette tapes became popular. It wasn't all that long ago, but we lugged around those big bulky eight-tracks that look so ridiculous and old-fashioned today.

We went to a lot of movies in the summer, especially horror movies. We also hung out at the roller-skating rink.

That was one sport I was never good at. Normally, I'd rather not do something at all than do it badly. But I made an exception for roller skating, because if you were *really* bad, the girls would hold your hand and help you out.

CHAPTER 3

THREE FRIENDS

A lot of who I am today has to do with the people I was close to when I was growing up. There were my parents, of course, and my family, and Jim and Greta Dart. But in my teenage years it was my friends who seemed to matter most.

What my pal Reggie Chastine lacked in height, he more than made up in self-confidence. He had so much faith in his own abilities that it was almost as if he could peel off some of his extra self-assurance and hand it over to me.

I definitely needed it. This might sound strange, given everything that happened to me later, but when I started high school I was full of doubts about just how good I really was. Would I be able to keep up with guys on other teams who could run right past me and jump right over me? Sure, I was a big deal in Lansing, but Lansing was nothing. What would happen when we played some of those really strong teams from Detroit?

"Are you kidding?" Reggie would say. "You're going all the way, man. I don't care *where* you're from. I just know where you're going, and that's the NBA."

He was a year ahead of me at Everett, but we did everything together. He would pick me up every morning so we could drive to school together. After class, we'd practice together with the team. During the final minutes of a game, when we were blowing out the other team and the subs had come in, the two of us would sit together on the bench. We'd pretend to watch the game, but we were actually scanning the crowd, looking for pretty girls. Sometimes Reggie would pick out a couple of girls who were sitting together. He'd write them a note and the team manager would bring it over, asking them to wait for us after the game. Sometimes they did. Once, after a game in Jackson, Reggie met a girl he really liked. Before long, he was driving to Jackson to see her on weekends.

When Reggie graduated, he won a basketball scholarship to Eastern Michigan University. That summer I often drove with him to Jackson, where I had a girlfriend, too. I forget why, but just before one of these trips I had to cancel out at the last minute. Reggie promised to call when he got there. When I didn't hear from him, I figured something had come up.

Early the next morning I got a call from Reggie's younger brother. He told me that the night before, Reggie's car had been hit by a drunk driver who had run a stop sign. Reggie, my best friend, had been killed instantly.

No! No! No! As soon as I hung up the phone, I left my house and started running. I ran for hours, it seemed, the tears streaming down my face. I didn't know where I was headed, but I just kept going. I couldn't stop, didn't *want* to stop. If I stopped running, that would make it true.

I couldn't believe that Reggie's life was over just like that. He had plans. He had a *future*! I was going to watch him play in college. And Reggie was going to come back to see us at Everett.

In his senior year we had reached the semifinals. And this season, which was starting in just a few weeks, we had a good chance to go all the way, to win the state championship. "I know you guys can take it," Reggie had told us when he graduated. "And I'll be back to cheer you on."

This was my first experience with death, and it was devastating. When you're young, and you lose somebody your own age, it's a shock you never forget. The whole community was stunned. Everybody loved Reggie, this scrappy little fighter who not only made the team, but became a starter.

He had so much heart. He feared nobody. And he taught me about courage when I really needed to learn it.

I don't know how I ever made it through his funeral. His teammates were the pallbearers, and in Reggie's honor we wore our warm-ups and basketball shoes. But for me the pain was only beginning. We'd had so many good times together, and now a huge chunk of my life had been ripped away. That I was supposed to have been with him in the car only made it worse. For months after the accident I wanted to call his house, but I couldn't bring myself to do it. All over town I kept running into girls we had dated, or other people who reminded me of him. And every time that happened, the pain started up all over again.

I miss him even today. I thought about Reggie over the past year, wishing he could have been there for me. I thought about him especially during the 1992 All-Star Game. And Reggie had been on my mind when I played my first NBA game, and every time the Lakers won a world championship. He believed in me before I believed in myself, and I know how much joy and pride he would have taken in my success. I also know that Reggie Chastine would have been a great source of strength in what I'm dealing with today.

When school started again that September we dedicated our season to his memory. Everett had another great year, our best ever. One of our games, against Eastern High, was even on television—the first time that had ever happened in Michigan. Eastern had a very strong team that was led by Jay Vincent, my longtime friend and rival. We played them in Jenison Field House at Michigan State University, the same arena where the Michigan State Spartans played in the Big Ten Conference. But unlike the Spartans during those years, we filled every seat in the house.

We beat Eastern, and we blew through everybody that year, too. But along the way I had to make a big adjustment in my playing style. I started the season at an incredible pace—maybe Reggie's death had something to do with it, but during the first couple of weeks it seemed like nobody could stop me, I was averaging around 45 points a game. Coach

Fox was smart enough to see that my performance, as great as it was, was actually hurting the team. "Earvin," he said, "you're scoring too much. If we're going to win the championship this year, it'll take a team effort. The other guys have to get used to taking some of the important shots. You've got the whole crowd watching you, and that's fine. The other team is watching you, and that's fine, too. But you've also got your four teammates watching you, and that's a problem. Half the time they're just standing around waiting for you to do something. You need to distribute the ball. Get these other guys more involved."

I listened, and I changed my game. Instead of 45 points a night, I started scoring 25 or 30. I did a lot more passing, and I took over a game only when it was absolutely necessary.

This was the same lesson Michael Jordan had to learn in the NBA during the late 1980s. His individual performances were amazing, but during his first few years, the Bulls just weren't winning. Michael realized that, and when he started sharing the wealth, Chicago became the best team in all of basketball.

That year, for the first time ever, Everett made it all the way to the state championships. Our opponent in the final game was Birmingham Brother Rice, a Catholic high school with a very strong team. The game was played at the University of Michigan. Brother Rice got off to a fast start, but we caught them in the second half, and played them tough. With time running out, we were ahead by two. Then one of their guys hit an amazing desperation shot from beyond half-court. Hello, overtime.

Now it was our turn to run. I scored the first eight points of the overtime. Then, with three minutes left, I fouled out. But our guys hung tough, and they knew how to win without me. We beat Brother Rice, 62–56. Finally!

It was an incredible feeling to go all the way. But for me, something was missing. While my teammates were whooping it up in the locker room, I stepped into a dark hallway to be alone. There would be plenty of time to celebrate when

we got back to Lansing, but right now I couldn't stop thinking about Reggie. It wasn't right. He should have been there
with us, or at least watching us. At that moment, with the
shouts of my teammates echoing in the background, I missed
him terribly.

"We did it, man," I said through my tears. "You said we
could, and we did. We did it for you."

Terry Furlow was a different kind of friend than Reggie.
Reggie and I were tight. Terry was more like an older brother.

Terry played for the Spartans, and went on to become one
of the all-time top scorers in the Big Ten. I met him back in
the tenth grade, when I started hanging around the Michigan
State gym and he invited me to join a pickup game. The first
time I got into a game I was so nervous that I didn't take a
single shot the whole time. And although I was fouled a few
times, I didn't say a word—I was too scared. It was a new
experience for me to play in a game where I wasn't the best,
or even close. These guys were a few years older than I was,
and most of them were better. As the new guy, and the youngest, I kept my mouth shut so that nobody would get mad at
me.

But somebody did. Terry didn't like the way his team was
losing because this young kid wasn't calling any fouls. After
we straightened that out, Terry asked me to play on his team
every time I showed up. I was shaky at first, but within a
month or two I was starting to hold my own. I didn't dominate like I did on the playground. But at least I wasn't a
liability. When I played with older, bigger guys, I concen-
trated on my passing. No matter where I've played, this has
always made my teammates happy.

During my high school years Terry took me under his wing
and more or less adopted me as his little brother. "Young
fella," he said, "you're gonna hang out with me." After the
pickup games, the two of us would play one-on-one. I thought
I was pretty good, but Terry was a terrific shooter. For weeks
on end he destroyed me every single time we played. It was
always 15–0. It was a couple of months before I finally scored

my first point against him. Gradually I scored three, five, and as many as eight points against him. A few months after that I even started to challenge him. Finally, after about two years of these games, I actually beat him. He was so proud that he took me out for a soda.

Terry Furlow was a genuine sports hero at the university. He was a big deal on campus, the kind of guy people wanted to be around. One night, when I was in the tenth or eleventh grade, he invited me to go with him and his friends to a party at Michigan State. I checked with my parents. They said I could go as long as I didn't stay out too late.

When we got there, he was surprised to see that somebody was collecting money at the door. "Never mind that," he said. "I'm Terry Furlow, and I don't pay for no parties. I got all my people with me, and this young fella is with me, too." They let us in for free. When the people at the party saw Terry, everybody came up and slapped him five.

As soon as Terry got inside he made his presence known. "Man, I can't *see* in here. The Fur-Low is in the house, so turn up the lights." People put up with him because he was such a great character.

When Terry started showing up at my games, I was thrilled. He always came in style—dressed in a fancy suit with three or four guys in tow and a beautiful girl on each arm. It was heady stuff to be in high school and to have a whole little section of glamorous college students cheering me on.

The first time Terry showed up at Everett, I went out of my way to put on a show for him. I hit my first 12 shots, and finished with something like 40 points, 20 rebounds, and 17 assists.

When I saw him the next day at Michigan State, I waited for him to congratulate me on my great performance. "You played all right, young fella," he said. "But when you went in for that left-handed lay-up, you took it with your right hand!" Given all the things I had done *right* in that game, I couldn't believe that he'd picked up on something like that. But I was still glad he had been there to see me in action.

In 1976, Terry was a first-round draft choice of the Philadelphia 76ers. As soon as he turned pro, he bought himself a blue Mercedes. He used to drive it back to Michigan, where his mother lived. The first time I saw that car, I fell in love with it. And that's when I promised myself that if I ever made it to the NBA, that was the car I would drive, too.

After Terry turned pro, people said he was taking drugs. Maybe that's why Philadelphia was so quick to trade him to Cleveland. He went from there to Atlanta, and from Atlanta to Utah. He never talked about drugs with me, and never tried to influence me in that direction. A couple of times I asked him if the rumors were true, but he always changed the subject.

In 1980, at the end of my rookie year in the NBA, Terry Furlow was killed in a car accident. He was going a hundred miles an hour when he smashed into a bridge abutment. Evidence of cocaine was found in his car.

Reggie gave me his friendship and his support. Terry taught me about basketball and about style. I couldn't save either one of them from dying young. I wish I could have, because they had both given me so much.

Another person who made a difference in those high school years was George Gervin, who was then playing in the old ABA. One summer afternoon I went to see a game at St. Cecilia's, a small cracker-box gym in Detroit where some of the pros used to play in the off-season. One team was led by Campy "Mr. Moves" Russell, who played for Cleveland, and the other by George Gervin. Gervin, who was known as "Ice" because he never seemed to sweat, played most of his career with the San Antonio Spurs. He was one of the all-time greats. In the late 1970s and early 1980s, he led the NBA in scoring four times during a five-year period. Only Wilt Chamberlain and Michael Jordan have been more successful in that department.

The Iceman was born in Detroit and played for Eastern Michigan University. He was a local favorite in Detroit, and that hot little gym was packed to the rafters. But Campy

Russell was on fire that day. He must have had 40 points at the half. Campy was really getting off on Gervin, and the crowd was mad. "Come on, Ice," they yelled. "Put on a show. Don't let him give you that shit."

As the second half began, the whole crowd stood up together. "Ice! Ice! Ice!" they hollered in unison. The effect on Gervin was just amazing. He turned into a different player in the third quarter, hitting about fifteen shots in a row. Then he missed one or two to show he was human. But in the fourth quarter he hit *another* fifteen, from every possible angle and with every imaginable kind of shot: drives, jump shots, hooks, bank shots, you name it.

I think Gervin scored 70 points that day. With about five minutes left, he came down on a break. When a defender came out to pick him up, Gervin jumped over him and finger-rolled the ball into the net—*swish—from fifteen feet out*. The crowd went nuts, and people ran onto the court to embrace him. The game ended right there. I had never seen anything like Gervin's performance that day, and I still haven't. When I went back to Lansing that's all I talked about.

After the game, I was introduced to the Iceman. Gervin had heard that I was a high school star, and during the next few weeks we played a few one-on-one games in Detroit and Lansing. And I thought Furlow was tough! Gervin was impossible. I hated to play him because he never seemed to be working very hard. It's one thing when the other guy is huffing and puffing like you are. But Ice would walk out on the court and nonchalantly kill you.

He was devastating. But he also taught me a few tricks, including his specialties—the finger roll and the bank shot.

When people in Lansing heard that I was playing against George Gervin, I was the talk of the town. It didn't matter that I couldn't score a single point against him. It was an honor to be on the same court as Ice, even if he destroyed you.

The first time I played against Gervin in the NBA, he was at the height of his career. And I was assigned to guard him. He gave me a big hug before the game and welcomed me to the league. "You made it, kid," he said. "And I knew that you would." Then he introduced me to his teammates. "You see this young man?" he said. "I used to play against him in Michigan when he was just in high school. You watch him now, because Earvin Johnson is a real player."

I was beaming. Then Gervin went out and scored 40 points on me. Thanks, pal.

CHAPTER 4

DECISION TIME

One afternoon toward the end of my first year of high school, Coach Fox called me into his office. Uh-oh, I thought. What have I done wrong?

"Here, Earvin," he said, handing me four or five envelopes. "I've got some mail for you."

They were introductory letters from college coaches who wanted me to start thinking about attending their schools. According to the NCAA regulations, high school athletes can't actually be recruited until their senior year. So to get the ball rolling, colleges with basketball programs routinely send out preliminary letters to leading high school players around the country.

All of this was new to me. When those first letters arrived, I was elated. After all, I was only fifteen years old. And these colleges had actually heard of me? I ran home to show my parents, and I didn't get much sleep that night.

By my senior year, recruiters were all over me. Before long there were so many calls that we had to change our phone number. But even that didn't help much. The moment you'd hang up the phone, it would ring again, with another college on the line. The calls kept coming, from nine in the morning until eleven-thirty at night. What had started as a thrill soon became incredibly tedious. And since recruiters were always showing up on our doorstep, I spent a lot of time at other people's houses. Sometimes they would stand for hours outside our house or in front of the school building just so I'd know who they were. Will Jones, the assistant coach at Maryland, practically lived in Lansing. Every time I looked up, there he was. But he was only doing his job, and he was never unpleasant about it.

The recruiters seemed to believe that a boy's mother held the key to his heart. So they made sure to tell Mom all the right things—that Junior would eat right at their college, that he'd go to all his classes, and that he'd stay out of trouble. "Believe me, Mrs. Johnson, Earvin will be in excellent hands. We'll take good care of him, and you'll have nothing to worry about." A day or two later, they'd even send flowers.

But my parents are not easily fooled. Dad is a streetwise workingman, and Mom wasn't born yesterday. It was hard to dazzle them, even when recruiters came in with their fancy speeches and sales pitches.

All our visitors had to go through Coach Fox, who acted as my screening agent and traffic cop. Coach had never been in this position before, but he loved it. The two of us were like a couple of kids, excited by all these offers coming in.

Like everybody else, I've heard stories about the sleazy tactics used by some college recruiters. But we honestly didn't experience much of that. Sure, some of these guys were a little too aggressive, and two or three let it be known that if there was anything we wanted, we only had to ask. A couple of them offered money, too. But my father had decided in advance that we weren't going to play that game. "Nobody's going to turn you into a slave," he told me. "If anything goes wrong, I don't want them to come along later and say, 'We gave you all this money, so what's the problem?' "

The only nasty moment I can remember came when a recruiter mistakenly told my father that he was glad to hear I had decided to play for his school.

"Actually, I don't think he's going there," Dad replied.

"Mr. Johnson, it doesn't matter what *you* think," the recruiter said. "Earvin has already made up his mind."

"Don't talk to me like that," said Dad, and that was the end of *that* guy.

But this was the exception. The places I was seriously considering—North Carolina, Michigan, Notre Dame, and Maryland—were all great basketball schools. If they didn't bend the rules, maybe it's because they didn't have to.

Originally, UCLA was on my list, too. They invited me to visit, and I was interested in their program. Who wouldn't be? During the late sixties and early seventies, UCLA had the best college teams in history, winning one championship after another. But shortly before I was supposed to fly out to Los Angeles, their assistant coach called and asked if I would mind postponing my trip until they had seen Albert King and Gene Banks. At the time, King and Banks were said to be the best high school players in the country. "If they decide to play for us," he said, "we won't be needing you. But stay by the phone. We'll let you know."

I had no desire to play second fiddle to these guys, and I told UCLA to forget it. A couple of years later, I ran into the coach at an airport. "Well, Earvin," he said, looking a little embarrassed, "I guess you proved us wrong."

I smiled. "That's how it goes," I replied.

For me, the highlight of the recruitment process was a visit from Bobby Knight, the coach from Indiana University. He was a legend even then. When Indiana came to town to play Michigan State, Knight drove over to the high school to see me. I was honored to meet with him, but I had already decided that I didn't want to play for this guy. I had seen enough on TV, where he came across as angry and explosive. And this was *before* the famous chair-throwing incident.

But he was Bobby Knight, and I was a high school senior, so I couldn't very well refuse to see him. Besides, no matter what I thought of his personality, I knew that he was respected all around the world as a basketball genius.

In person, with just the two of us sitting in Coach Fox's office, he was nothing like I expected. Rather than being angry or volatile, he came across as calm, friendly, and funny. If I hadn't recognized that famous face, I could have sworn he had sent an impostor.

I liked his straightforward manner. Unlike some recruiters I had met, he didn't try to lure me to Indiana with fancy promises. He also didn't try to tell me what he thought I wanted to hear. "I guarantee you nothing," he said. "Not even a starting role. If you play for us, you'll have to earn that. I'll also expect you to go to class. No books, no basketball. Everybody in our program graduates. And I promise you this: No matter how good you may be, you'll get yelled at just like everybody else."

I'm sure I could have played for Knight. He's intense, and he wants to win, and I respond well to that kind of pressure. But even so, I knew that my talents didn't really suit Indiana's playing style. Bobby Knight likes to slow down the game. Indiana's well-known "motion offense" is essentially a half-court game with a lot of screens. I preferred a more open, spontaneous style. I was looking for a team that wanted to run.

After a few months I finally narrowed the field down to two choices, both of them close to home: the University of Michigan and Michigan State.

The University of Michigan was clearly the better option. Academically, they were one of the best schools in the country, and their basketball program was outstanding. They were winners, and they really ran with the ball. I was also friendly with Johnny Orr, their coach, and Bill Frieder, his assistant. Ann Arbor is only an hour from Lansing, and I had been going to most of the Wolverines' home games. They played on Saturday afternoons, so I could still attend the Michigan State games on Saturday night.

But when I drove to Ann Arbor for a recruiting visit, I got the feeling that some of their guys didn't want me around. Phil Hubbard, the star of the team, was nice to me, and it would have been great to play with him. He was so beautiful to watch that people talked about him as the next Dr. J. But some of his teammates must have figured that I would screw up their own plans.

I could understand why. This new guy comes in as a freshman. Everyone is making a big fuss over him, and right off the bat the coach makes him a starter. Where does that leave guys who've been sitting on the bench for two years, patiently waiting their turn, which now looks like it may *never* come? There were two or three guys in that situation at Michigan, and I could feel their resentment.

Even with all this, I was still leaning toward Ann Arbor. But State was like my second home, and I felt a strong attachment there, too. For years, I had played in pickup games and gone to basketball camps on campus. Both schools were recruiting me heavily, and both had made identical offers: tuition, room and board, and books. No extras, no strings attached. It was a real dilemma.

The whole town of Lansing got involved in trying to influence me in the direction of State. Black, white, it didn't matter. I'd be putting on a clinic at a local playground, but instead of basketball, all the kids wanted to talk about was where I would be going to college. In April of my senior year, when I returned from a basketball tour of Germany with other high school all-stars, a huge crowd was waiting for me at the Lansing airport. Most of them were cheering and carrying Michigan State signs. They presented me with a petition signed by five thousand kids in the Lansing school system, urging me to stay in Lansing.

My parents, too, were hoping I'd choose State, and so was Coach Fox. But they all made it clear that this was my decision, and that they would support me no matter where I went. Greta Dart, as I recall, was a little more direct. She and Jim were both graduates of Michigan State, but Greta let me know that even if I chose the University of Michigan, that was fine with her. "No, really, Earvin, that would be great. And we'd still come to see you, honest. It's just that you might find it a little difficult to play basketball with two broken kneecaps."

One of my concerns about State had to do with the coach

there. Gus Ganakas, by then the head coach, was fired before my senior year at Everett, and that changed everything. I'd been friendly with Gus and was looking forward to playing for him. The new coach was Jud Heathcote, a short, hot-tempered guy who reminded me of a bulldog. While Heathcote had been at MSU only a year, and I didn't really know him, I saw the way he yelled at his players, and I didn't like it.

As I was getting close to a decision, Heathcote came to see me. "I know that you've narrowed it down to Michigan and Michigan State," he said. "It seems to me that your head is saying Michigan, but your heart is saying State. Michigan is a great school, no question about that. And they have an outstanding team. But if you go there, you'll be one of several great players. And with your height, they'll probably have you playing center.

"You're not a center, Earvin. I've seen you play, and you're definitely a point guard. I want you to run our offense. I see you as the key to our fast break. Greg Kelser can really move. You've seen him play, so you know how good he is. I'm telling you, he'd be even better if you were running the plays. If you came to Michigan State, you'd make a tremendous difference."

When Heathcote left, I thought about what he had said. He was certainly right about the battle going on between my head and my heart. I had been going to games at Michigan State since I was ten—and not just basketball, but football games, too, watching the Spartans in the rain and the snow. I'd never had the chance to play for Sexton High, and I still regretted that. But now I had another chance to play for the home team. Maybe I should grab it.

That night, I dreamed that I was in Jenison Field House at Michigan State. The arena, which holds about ten thousand people, was filled with screaming fans. I had been to dozens of games at Jenison when the place was mostly empty. But in the dream, I was running down the court in a green-and-white uniform. And the whole crowd was on its feet cheering.

The next morning I had a visit from Vernon Payne, Jud Heathcote's assistant. Vernon had been at MSU for years, and I knew him well. I had hoped that he would take over as head coach when Gus was fired.

"The first thing I want to tell you," Vernon said to me that morning, "is that I'm leaving. Nobody knows it yet, but I've just accepted a job at Wayne State. So I have nothing to gain by trying to get you to come to MSU. But I think you should. And I've heard that you have reservations about Jud Heathcote."

"You heard right," I said. "But I don't really know him."

"Well, I do," he said. "And if I didn't like him, or I thought he was a bad coach, I would tell you. But he's good, Earvin. Really good. I think you should play for him. I know you've seen him yelling at the guys. But that's because he's intense, and he wants to win so badly. Behind all that yelling and screaming, Jud Heathcote is a terrific coach and an excellent teacher. I've known you for years, and I've seen how committed you are to improving your game. This is the guy who can help you do that. Besides, if you come to MSU it'll be a great team. We've got Greg Kelser and all the other guys from last year. And you know we've signed Jay Vincent."

After listening to Vernon Payne's description of Heathcote, I shocked myself—and him, too. "Let's do it," I said. "Give me the papers and I'll sign."

Vernon was taken aback. He had hoped to change my mind, but he didn't expect to convince me *that* fast. "Just a minute," he said. "Let me make a call." Jud came right over with the papers.

As soon as I made the decision, I felt good about it. My parents were overjoyed. Mom must have been relieved. Because of her religion, she couldn't have gone to any of the Saturday-afternoon games in Ann Arbor. But she could see me play at Michigan State on Saturday night, when the Sabbath that she observed so carefully was over.

I really liked the idea of choosing to play for the weaker team, of going with the underdog and trying to bring them into the upper echelon. That's what had happened at Everett; we had won the high school title with a team that nobody took seriously. My goal was to do the same thing in college.

I realized that this would be an enormous challenge. But Michigan State wasn't nearly as bad as Everett had been. True, during Jud Heathcote's first year as a coach the team had finished with a pretty dismal record, 10–17. But most of those losses had come by five points or less. Four of their starters were returning, and I knew that Greg Kelser really *was* something special. I had known Jay Vincent all my life, and he, too, would make a difference. The Spartans were a decent team that just needed another couple of pieces to complete the puzzle. Maybe Jay and I could do the trick.

The University of Michigan would be a contender with me or without me. But Michigan State would be a lot better with me.

I didn't tell anybody outside my family about my decision, and the news didn't leak, either. A couple of days later, Coach Fox organized a press conference in the Everett auditorium. When I got there I was shocked to see reporters and film crews from as far away as Chicago and even New York. I was even more surprised when somebody told me that the entire press conference would be carried live over the radio.

I was very nervous, but this was such an exciting moment that I was determined to enjoy myself. When I got up there to make the announcement, I started by saying, "Any questions?" That broke the ice. Then I said, "I have decided to attend Michigan State University." The auditorium exploded with cheers and applause.

"When it came down to making a decision," I said, "I don't think I could have gone anywhere else. I was born to be a Spartan."

More cheers and applause. A reporter asked why I had chosen Michigan State when everybody knew that the University of Michigan had a superior basketball team.

"I don't care about the past or about reputations," I said. "All I care about is the future. And I see an NCAA championship for Michigan State."

My decision was only two days old. And already there were promises to keep.

CHAPTER 5

COLLEGE KID

In my first game for Michigan State I really stunk up the gym. We were playing at home against Central Michigan, and all my family and friends were there to see my debut. But with so much advance press and all those expectations, I was just too fired up to play well. I had stomach cramps the whole night. I missed most of my shots and had a dozen turnovers.

All through my career, whenever I moved up to the next level, my first game was a real turkey. It happened in junior high, and again at Everett, and at Michigan State, and even with the Lakers.

But we won that game anyway, and the next few after that. Before long we were visiting the University of Detroit to play the only other undefeated team in the state. I knew most of their players, and so did my teammates. But before the game started, these guys refused to say a word to us. Sometimes our opponents would talk trash, but we had never been given the silent treatment before. We talked about it in the locker room and decided to go out there and teach them some manners.

The gym was packed with some ten thousand fans. The Detroit players were introduced with spotlights, just like in the pros. But when the game started they had us so riled up that we ripped them apart. We let them know that *we* were the boys from the state of Michigan.

* * *

I was already famous when I arrived at Michigan State. The media had made so much fuss about my decision to go there that just about everybody on campus knew who I was. On my way to class, I'd hear people whisper, "Hey, isn't that Magic Johnson?" And this was before the basketball season had even started.

I hadn't expected this much attention. All my life, the big sport at Michigan State had been football. Usually the attendance at basketball games was so bad that we could pretty well sit wherever we liked.

But a year or so before I arrived, Michigan State's football program had been put on probation for a violation. Suddenly, between that and all the press over my decision to stay in Lansing, it seemed like everybody on campus was a basketball fan. One of my first-semester classes used to meet at 8:00 A.M. in Jenison Field House, so I happened to be there the morning that basketball tickets went on sale. I couldn't believe how many students were lined up outside the building, many of them carrying sleeping bags. These people had spent the whole night outside just so they could see us play!

They're really up for this, I thought. We'd better be good.

When the season began, more people started showing up for our practices than used to attend *games* the year before. Practices had always been open to the public, but now they became so popular that Jud was forced to close the doors.

Unlike in high school, where I had plenty of doubts about my abilities, I came to the college game full of confidence. I *knew* these guys, since for years I had been playing with them in pickup games on campus. By the time I joined the Spartans, there was no question that I belonged.

Still, I had to make a few adjustments. Back in high school, I had pretty well been able to dominate in any game, whenever I felt like it, and I'd rarely run across a player who could really challenge me. But college was—well, a whole new ball game. Every team we played had two or three terrific athletes. And just about every guy on every team had been the star of his entire high school.

The college game was also more physical. These guys were big and strong, and the referees allowed plenty of banging and bruising. It took me about a year to get used to it.

I had to unlearn a few bad habits, too. In high school, when I had the ball, I would often jump without any real plan in mind. But Coach Heathcote showed me that our opponents actually *wanted* me to jump. They'd guard all my teammates, and I'd end up off-balance with nobody to pass to. Either I'd be tempted to put up a bad shot or my defender would stand right in front of me and force me to foul him. "Stay on the ground," Jud would say. "Nothing good can happen when you're in the air."

But the biggest adjustment of all was the quality and intensity of the play. Michigan State was part of the Big Ten, which had some of the best college players in the country. Minnesota had Mychal Thompson, who was simply unbelievable. And in case he wasn't enough, they also had Kevin McHale. Kevin was almost as dominating in college as he would be later with the Boston Celtics. Ohio State had players like Herb Williams, Kelvin Ransey, Jim Smith, and Clark Kellogg. There was Mike Woodson at Indiana, Eddie Johnson at Illinois, and Phil Hubbard and Mike McGee at Ann Arbor.

But the best of them all was Ronnie Lester of Iowa, one of the greatest guards who ever played the game. He could do almost anything. If he hadn't injured his knee before the end of his college career, I'm sure he would have become a household name. Ronnie went on to play in the NBA, and we were even teammates for a while, but he was just a shadow of the player he once was.

With so much talent lined up against us, it's a good thing we had a great coach. Despite my earlier doubts about him, Jud Heathcote turned out to be terrific. He was a perfectionist, and he expected no less from us. You missed a shot? Okay, these things happen. But if you didn't do your job, like setting a screen or boxing out, or if you didn't run the play properly—in other words, if you made a *mental* error, he showed no mercy. He'd point to his head and yell, *"You gotta think!"*

The only thing he hated more than mental errors were excuses. "Why didn't you box him out?" he'd ask. If you said, "I missed him because I was covering the other guy and I couldn't get over," Jud's face would turn red and his voice would go up high: *"I don't wanna hear that!"* It didn't take long to learn that the only acceptable response to a "Why didn't you" question was "I blew it, Coach. It won't happen again."

He yelled at us constantly. If you weren't executing the way he wanted, he'd explode. And it didn't matter whether you screwed up at practice or during a game. Some guys were affected by Jud's hollering, but it bothered me a lot less than I had expected. Sometimes it even helped—I'd get mad at Jud, and then I'd take out my anger on the other team.

I know a fierce competitor when I see one, and I respected his passion. He was burning to win, and yelling was the way he got there. All he cared about was winning, and I was the same way.

Our hearts were in sync, and so were our minds. The way we analyzed situations and players was often identical. When the game was close and time was running out, I always knew what play Jud would call—sometimes even before he did.

Off the court, Jud Heathcote was straight as an arrow. He followed the NCAA guidelines so strictly that we all thought he had written them. If you wanted a Coke from the soda machine and you didn't have any change, he wouldn't give you a nickel. If it was ten degrees below zero outside and you needed a ride back to your dorm, forget it. It's not that Jud was mean, because he wasn't. But he always obeyed the rules, even when they were ridiculous. He had built his reputation on integrity, and he wouldn't do anything to jeopardize it.

He was that way about everything. If you didn't show up to every class and every study hall, you couldn't play. We always had a curfew the night before a game, but I don't remember what the penalty was if you were late. As far as I recall, it never even came up.

Jud was the most impatient man I'd ever known. We traveled all over the country, but one thing never changed: No matter where we went, he couldn't wait to leave. Once, after a game in Minnesota, our return flight was canceled because of a snowstorm. There was another plane leaving the next morning, but Jud wouldn't wait. We rode home from that game on an old, cramped school bus. It took us the whole damn night to get back.

Another time, after we flew home from a game in Oregon, we had to wait quite a while for our luggage to appear. Jud couldn't stand the delay. When our suitcases didn't show up after ten minutes, he plunked himself down on the conveyor belt and rode it out to where the bags were. For a long time there was no sign of the bags—and no sign of the coach, either. Finally a door swung open. Out came Jud, escorted by two burly cops, one on each arm. This was just about the funniest sight we had ever seen. I still smile when I think of it.

He was always in a hurry. When we were on the road, he would usually order a steak for breakfast. "Don't bother cooking it," he'd tell the waitress. "Just slap it on the grill for ten seconds, turn it real fast, and bring it right over." That certainly got our attention.

Impatient people don't generally make good teachers, but Jud was an exception. He worked with each of us individually, and he made us all better players. He spent hours working with me on my outside shot, showing me that I had been taking a lot of my shots off-balance. He also worked with me on my free throws, and helped me become a better passer.

Although Jud improved my game a lot, he never tried to change it. He knew where my talents lay, and, as promised, he turned me into a point guard. He wanted me to be running the show, and I was thrilled to do it.

Anyone who played for Jud soon got used to hearing the same phrases again and again. If a guard screwed up on the court, you knew that he'd yell, "Be a guard, not a garbage!"

He'd talk about Double A, Double I, Double P, which stood for: Academics and Athletic excellence, Intensity and Intelligence, Poise and Patience. And the five keys to victory: teamwork, fast break, defense, percentage shooting, and offensive execution.

Another of his sayings was KYP, which stood for Know Your Personnel. This phrase came directly out of one of Jud's other rules, which at first I couldn't go along with. If a guy missed a pass, he used to say, it was the fault of the passer.

I disagreed. After all, I often made good passes that my teammates just couldn't handle. We'd be running down the court on the fast break and I'd pass to a teammate. If he wasn't expecting it, the ball might hit him in the chest or even in the head. Was that really my fault? Jud listened to me. He made it clear that everybody on the team had a responsibility to get used to my aggressive passing. Whenever I had the ball, which was most of the time, they had to be ready for a pass—even if I was looking in a completely different direction.

But I, too, had some responsibility: I had to learn what kind of pass each player could handle, and more than that, what each man could use to best advantage. One guy might not dribble very well. So if he got the ball too far from the basket, it wouldn't help. Another player might be unstoppable—but only when he was open for a jump shot from the top of the key. A third might do best with bounce passes, and so on. Jud worked with me to develop a careful analysis of each player's strengths, style, and ability to anticipate.

KYP sounds simple enough. But it takes observation and practice and months of playing together to get it exactly right. It's not enough to know every player on your team. You also have to be familiar with the players on all the other teams who will be guarding your men. If the defender has quick hands, you have to be especially careful with your passes. If he's slow going to his left or right, you'll want to exploit that, or any other weakness.

Jud's KYP principle helped me enormously, especially later, when I played with the Lakers. In the pros, I have had the luxury of working year after year with the same great players, including Kareem Abdul-Jabbar, James Worthy, Michael Cooper, Byron Scott, and Kurt Rambis. We knew each other's strengths so well that by 1987 we could have played together blindfolded.

Jud has always reminded me of the tough drill sergeant in old war movies; beneath that gruff exterior he had a soft heart. He truly cared about his players, and eventually most of them realized that. Just about every kid who plays for Jud improves while he's there. And there must be a reason why so many of us come back to visit him after we've left.

Although Jud and I got along well, we weren't all that close while I was playing for him. For many of my teammates, however, he served as a father figure. Living away from home for the first time in their lives, they needed him more than I did. I was fortunate enough to have my family—not to mention the Darts and most of my good friends—attending every game. Even though I no longer lived with my parents, as long as I played at Michigan State I didn't really leave home at all.

It's funny, but it wasn't until I left Lansing and moved to Los Angeles that Jud and I really became close. During my early years with the Lakers, we often spoke on the phone. He would critique my game and give me advice. When I came back to Lansing during the off-season, I always checked in with Jud and worked out with the guys on his team. He even gave me the keys to the gym so I could practice at any hour. It's been years since I played for him, but I still think of him as my coach.

Over the years, I tried to return some of the many favors Jud did for me. Sometimes he'd ask me to put in a call to a high school player he was trying to recruit. But despite my good intentions, these calls rarely worked out. Usually the kid I was looking for wasn't even home. In most cases, he was probably staying away for the same reason I did—to avoid all the phone calls. When the line wasn't busy, I usually ended up talking to the player's brother, or his mother. But when I introduced myself as Magic Johnson of the Los Angeles Lakers, they just laughed. "Come on," they'd say, "who is this *really*?"

One kid's younger brother just couldn't make up his mind as to whether or not I really was Magic Johnson. He wanted to believe me, so I tried to help him out. "I'm calling from Portland," I told him. "Get out the newspaper, and you'll see where the Lakers are playing tonight. Here's the number of my hotel, and you can call me right back." That seemed to do the trick. But I wonder: Was he able to convince his older brother?

I loved being at Michigan State. As soon as I got there I knew I had made the right decision. I moved into the dorms, where I shared a room with Jay Vincent. By living on campus, I got to meet all kinds of people, including some who had nothing to do with sports. Like the basketball team, our dorm was racially mixed.

The only thing I had trouble with was getting to meals on time. The cafeteria was open only during certain hours, so if you wanted to play ball or do anything else on your own time, you might miss lunch or dinner. But here I had a big advantage. Dad had given me a car, so I always had the option of going home for a meal. I took my laundry home, too. I'd always known how to wash my own clothes, but as soon as Mom saw me at the washing machine, she'd take over and finish the job. On weekends, I spent time with Dad. But because of my schoolwork and all the games and practices, I wasn't able to help him as much as I used to.

I majored in telecommunications, with a minor in education. As part of the education course, we had to observe and then teach a fourth-grade class in one of the Lansing schools. I had an advantage here, because most of the kids knew who I was. But even so, and although I loved being with kids, it was still a challenge. The first time I stood in front of that classroom and saw all those eyes staring right back at me, I was really nervous. But the lesson went well. And during recess I made some new friends by playing kickball with the boys and jump rope with the girls.

That experience helped me appreciate just how difficult teaching is. Like most kids, I grew up thinking that the teacher just walks into the classroom and starts talking. I knew nothing about lesson plans, correcting papers, and all the other invisible preparation that teaching involves.

In the telecommunications course, we spent time at a local TV station, learning about every job in the building. I've always had an interest in broadcasting, and this course came in handy in 1992, when I worked as a color commentator for NBA games on NBC.

Although we were there to play basketball, Michigan State was serious about our education. We had our own academic supervisor, who made sure we were going to class and kept a close eye on our progress. Every night after practice, the whole team would show up at study hall. Any player who didn't maintain a 2.0 grade-point average was not allowed to play. My own grades were never a problem, thanks to the teachers at Everett High who had put me on the right track and encouraged me to attend summer school. Not to mention John the Narc, who unwittingly inspired me to prove him wrong.

I'd always had a part-time job, and college was no exception. Two nights a week I was E.J. the DeeJay at Bonnie & Clyde's, a popular student disco just off campus. I loved blending the music and the lights, and getting the crowd on its feet. *Saturday Night Fever* had just been released, and the disco scene was hot.

Being a deejay is not all that different from being a point guard. They're both about finding the right mix of control and spontaneity, about picking up the feeling in the room and working with it. The deejay gets the crowd in his hands and holds them there for hours. Doing it live is very different from being a radio deejay, where you never really know who's still with you. In a disco, the deejay and the dancers can always see each other. If the crowd isn't having a good time, you get the message pretty fast.

The most important thing that happened to me at Michigan State was meeting Cookie. My mind was mostly on basketball, and besides, she probably has a better fix on that period than I do. So let me introduce you to Earleatha Kelly, who can certainly speak for herself. (But this is still my book, so I get to interrupt a couple of times.)

I grew up on the northwest side of Detroit. We lived in a middle-class black neighborhood like the one where Earvin grew up. My father was a factory worker at Ford, and he's still there. We had a nice home—not too big, but nice enough, with a yard.

I was born in January 1959, which makes me a few months older than Earvin. I'm the second of three kids, with an older sister and a younger brother. All three of us were born in Huntsville, Alabama. Our parents were born there, too. My father came to Detroit first, found a job, and then brought us up when I was seven, just before I started second grade.

It's hard to move a southern family to the north, especially for the kids. It wasn't easy for us to adjust to a new school and a new neighborhood. It sounds funny, but we were used to playing without shoes. We *had* shoes, but we just didn't wear them. For the first year or two, the other kids in our neighborhood and at school used to tease us about our southern accents, or because we sometimes went barefoot in warm weather. Huntsville is a lot smaller than Detroit, and we probably seemed like country bumpkins. It was hard to make friends.

At first we lived with my aunt in a two-family flat. Then, after a year or so, my father was able to buy a house. We were the first black family on the block, but we never had any problems with our neighbors. After a couple of years, a lot more black families started moving in.

I have a strong memory of the riots in Detroit, which were very close to where we lived. We had just moved, and the street we used to live on burned down. I remember curfews, and we always heard sirens. Whenever there was a big fire or the rioting got really bad, the sirens would go off and the National Guard would come in.

Once the sun went down, you had to be in the house. At night we kids had to sleep on the floor. My mother took the mattresses off the bed, because people might come down the street and start shooting through the windows. They actually said that on the news: Put all your kids in one room, on the floor, because if they're sleeping in a bed they might get hit by a bullet. I was going into third grade, and I was scared.

Nobody ever shot at our house, but there was shooting close by. These people were so violent, so angry, that they didn't care who they hurt. It started with looting, and then people went crazy and started terrorizing, burning, and shooting. Even during the day, my mother wouldn't let us play any farther than our driveway, because you never knew what could happen.

But no matter what was going on, my dad still had to work. He was the new man, so they assigned him to the night shift. During the violence, he needed a special pass to drive to work. We were scared to death that he wouldn't make it home.

Later on, he started going to school during the day, taking classes in special education at Eastern Michigan University in Ypsilanti. Meanwhile, he continued working nights. He became a teacher, and for a while he did both—teaching during the day, and factory work at night. But he couldn't do both jobs well, so he gave up teaching because he was making more money at the factory.

My real name is Earleatha, a girl's version of Earl. It was Mom who started calling me Cookie, and I was always Cookie at home. It wasn't until I went to kindergarten that I learned I had another name. Before I started school, my father had to teach me how to spell it. And then all through school, and later, when I worked in Ohio, I was Earleatha.

When I moved to Los Angeles, the scene was so casual that I stopped using Earleatha and went back to Cookie. I didn't mind, because I used to have to say my name about five hundred times before anybody got it right. And even then they'd sometimes turn around and call me Aretha.

Going to college was my idea. My parents never pushed me. As long as you had some ambition and didn't sit around the house, you could find your own way. But all of us were motivated. We could see how hard our parents worked, so there was no way we would just sit back.

When I was a teenager, rather than ask my parents for money for things I wanted, I got a job selling popcorn in a downtown movie theater. I ate so much popcorn there that it was about ten years before I wanted to have any again. When I met Earvin in college, I probably still smelled of popcorn. Popcorn is his favorite food, so maybe that's what he liked about me.

I've always been independent. Even dating Earvin, and knowing he had a lot of money, I never let myself be dependent on him—until now, with the baby. And I'll probably go back to work before too long.

I learned tailoring in high school, and I did pretty well. I chose Michigan State because they had a good retailing program. I got a grant to go there and worked my way through college.

I came to Michigan State with two cheerleader buddies from high school. One of them was Adrianne, my best friend who also became my roommate. After we got there, everyone was talking about this guy Earvin Johnson and the big fuss over which school he had picked. Adrianne had her eye on him. She said, "I'm going to meet Earvin Johnson and marry him." She started going to their practices.

I had just broken up with my high school boyfriend. He had decided to stay in Detroit and wanted me to stay, too. He said, "If you go to Michigan State, you're going to meet Earvin Johnson. I just know it." At the time, I didn't even know who he was talking about.

I met Earvin at the very end of the first semester. A friend of mine in the dorms wanted to go out, so we went to Dooley's, a restaurant and disco where everybody hung out on Saturday nights. Adrianne was upset about something, so she stayed home.

When we got there, Earvin and Jay Vincent were standing by the door. As usual, they were surrounded by a swarm of women. My friend knew Earvin, so we went over to say hello. She introduced me, and it was nothing more than Hi, nice to meet you. A guy I liked was there, so we went right in. The whole night went by, and I'm dancing with everybody and having a good time. Not once in all that time did Earvin ask me to dance or say one word to me.

On the way out I had to pass by him to leave. I looked up to say good-bye. He said, "Hey, come here. Why don't you give me your phone number? I'll call you when we get back."

This was right before the long Christmas break, and I just laughed. "Come on," I said. "You won't even remember my name when you get back." But I gave him my number. I said, "Okay, we'll see if you even remember me next month."

That's pretty accurate. We met at Dooley's, and Cookie was out there dancing all night. She was a beautiful dancer, and I just sat back and watched her. As she was leaving, I asked for her phone number. She said, "You won't even remember my name after the break."

"I'll remember," I said. In my mind, there was no doubt at all.

When we got back to campus in January, the first thing I did was call Cookie and ask her for a date. A real date. For the first time in my life, I put on a suit and tie and took a girl out for dinner and dancing.

Even though I didn't expect him to call, I kept thinking, How am I going to tell Adrianne? I waited until the next day. "Guess what?" I said. "A funny thing happened." I tried to make it sound like a joke, because it really was. We hadn't talked, we hadn't danced, and nothing had really happened. I told her he had asked for my phone number, and we both laughed about it.

Adrianne was great. She said, "Well, if I couldn't meet him, at least you did."

During the Christmas break, I told a few friends that Earvin Johnson had asked for my number. But I never thought I'd hear from him.

As soon as we got back to the dorms, he called to ask me out for Saturday night. In college we didn't usually go on real dates, where you actually dressed up and went out for dinner. There were so many girls around that there was no incentive for the guys to take them out. I was impressed. A date, wow!

We talked on the phone a little while, and he came over to see me the very next day. My dorm was near where the team used to eat, and he came to see me twice that week, on Thursday and again on Friday. And we hadn't even gone out yet.

On Saturday night, he wore a jacket and tie and I wore a dress. When he picked me up at the dorms, every girl on our hall was peeking around the corner to get a look at him. He didn't even notice it, but I sure did. He took me to a nice restaurant, and then to a disco.

The first thing that struck me about him was that he was down to earth. I had thought he might be a show-off, but he wasn't like that at all. We laughed and talked a lot that night—mostly we talked about school—getting to know each other. I asked him about his family, and he told me he spent a lot of time with them, and that he sometimes went home to sleep. His parents were only fifteen minutes away. Sometimes on a first date you really have to work to make conversation, but for us it was easy.

At the disco, people kept coming up to him. He spent a lot of time talking to them, but he didn't ignore me, either. I think he was impressed that I didn't need him to stand by my side all night. He was very nice to me, very polite.

When he took me home, he acted like a real gentleman. I was shocked. I didn't expect that this popular athlete would be so respectful. He was definitely the Big Man on Campus. Until I got to know him personally, that's all I knew.

The first time my mother met Earvin was when she and my sister came to Michigan State to visit me. I asked him to stop by, and he did. They just sat there with their mouths open. It was his height that they reacted to, not his fame. They had never seen anyone that tall before, and he was still a college player, so he wasn't that big a deal outside of Lansing. To see him come in the door of my little dorm room and have to bend his head—my mother was in shock.

Even though we started going out regularly, he was really Mr. Macho. I knew he liked me, but he didn't want to make a commitment. After a few weeks, I was still seeing other guys, and he was seeing other girls. One day he said, "You can't be doing that anymore."

I said, "I can't? And are you going to stop going out with other girls?"

"No." Okay, at least he's honest.

"Then how can you ask me to stop dating?"

He didn't have a good answer, and it turned into a fight. I said, "I'm not going to stop if you don't. That's not fair."

His attitude seems so old-fashioned today. I was willing to drop other guys, but he wasn't willing to do the same on his end. We broke up over it.

Not long after I met Cookie, I asked her if she'd stop going out with other guys. I probably did say that I wouldn't stop going out with other girls. Or else I evaded it. Like many men in those days, I operated under a double standard. I didn't see anything wrong with it. It's embarrassing by today's rules, but that's what happened. She didn't go for it, and we stopped seeing each other.

Then one day I got a call from Adrianne. "You two should really be together," she said. "I know she misses you, and you probably miss her, too. She's unhappy, and you should speak to her."

I agreed to see Cookie, because I really did miss her. She was different from other girls, and I knew that. She had class and style, and she was warm and smart and funny. After the first week with Cookie I just knew I would marry her. I never told her that, of course. I hid my feelings. But I knew in my heart that we would be together for a long time.

This was in February. I was miserable. "I can't live like this," I told Adrianne. "I really miss him."

I got her to call him. She told Earvin that I was very down, but that I was too bull-headed to call him myself, so maybe he should call me and we should sit down and talk about it. Earvin was sure she was making this call on her own. But I was sitting right there, telling her what to say. To this day he doesn't know that I talked Adrianne into doing this. I've tried to tell him, but he doesn't believe it. Or maybe he doesn't want to.

At our wedding, in a toast to her he said, "If it hadn't been for you, Adrianne, this day never would have happened."

The day after Adrianne called him, Earvin and I got together and talked. We decided that I would stop seeing other people, and supposedly he would, too.

But even when we were together, we weren't completely together. He belonged to the team, not to me. When we went to parties, most of the time we had to arrive separately. We could leave together, but he had to show up with the boys. When I'd ask him about it, he'd say, "Spartan rules." I hated that answer, so maybe he should explain.

Spartan rules. Cookie did not appreciate that, and she still teases me about it. But our team was like a fraternity. If the guys decided that we weren't bringing girls to a party, everybody followed that. If we decided to go to a football game, it would either be with dates or without. Or we might decide that we were all going to wear suits one night. We all did exactly the same thing, and nobody could deviate from the rules. Greg Kelser and I, the co-captains, made the decisions. But anybody could make a suggestion.

Cookie hated it. She'd say, "Why can't I go with you?"

And I'd respond, "Sorry, baby. Spartan rules. No dates tonight. Just the boys hanging out."

To this day, if she's going out with the girls, and I'm not invited, she'll say, "Sorry, Earvin. Spartan rules." We still talk a lot about what happened in college, and she still teases me about the guys she dated. We don't get upset about things in the past. We both know that our love is stronger than any of that.

We had another fight over the issue of sex. I hadn't slept with him yet. In those days, dating didn't necessarily mean sleeping with somebody. Anyway, I was an old-fashioned girl. He wanted to sleep with me, and I said, "If that's all you're interested in, you should leave."

He said, *"All I'm interested in? I've been with you for weeks."* He was right about that. We had already been on ten or fifteen dates. I thought he got mad because I was saying no. But he got mad because I was accusing him of being a certain way, and he wasn't that way.

There was a big fashion show and dance on campus that night. The Spartans were playing at the University of Michigan, and when they came back from their game in Ann Arbor, they all showed up at the dance. Earvin and I ignored each other the whole night. Finally, when it was ending, he found me and said, "Come with me. We need to talk."

We went back to my room and talked. He explained why what I had said had hurt him. And that's when he said he loved me.

For a long time I didn't even try to sleep with Cookie. Not that I didn't want to. But for some reason, I didn't need to. I loved just being with her, especially at parties. What a great dancer! Sometimes I wouldn't dance with her just so I could have the pleasure of watching her dance. Boy, could she move. She had so much grace.

We had been dating for about two months, and she thought I was trying to sleep with her. In all reality, I wasn't. We were physical with each other, but we hadn't been sexual. Not yet. It was a Saturday, and the Spartans were playing in Ann Arbor that afternoon. That morning, before the bus left, Cookie and I were fooling around on the bed. She grabbed my hand, but I had to get ready for the game. "I have to go," I told her. She thought that I wanted to make love, and that I was leaving because she wouldn't sleep with me.

Just before I left, we got into a big argument. She thought it was about sex, but that wasn't the issue. I had to leave for Ann Arbor. We beat Michigan that day, and I had a great game. I was really pissed at Cookie, and I took it out on Michigan.

When we got back, there was an event on campus called Showcase, a fashion show and party for the black students. Cookie was there, but I was so mad that I wouldn't even speak to her. I flirted and danced with other girls and had a good time. When she came over, I refused to talk to her. That made *her* mad.

Instead of being with Cookie, I danced with another girl I liked. But when it was time to leave, I grabbed Cookie and said, "Get your coat. You're coming with me." We went to her room and talked. I was coming down with the flu, and she took good care of me that night. But we still didn't sleep together.

That night I said to her, "Don't you understand? If this was just about sex, I would have left a long time ago." I was furious that she thought that. Girls were lining up to have sex with athletes. I had my share of opportunities, and I took them.

Cookie was entirely different. This was the first time I had ever been in a relationship like this, and I tried to explain that to her. "You saw all those girls tonight," I told her. "I could have gone home with any of them. But you're the one I care about, even if you're not ready to sleep with me."

When I explained all that, she was able to hear it. She made sure I was warm and bundled up, and that I had plenty of water to drink. She took care of me, and I knew I had found somebody special.

For a while we dated every week. But it was definitely an on-again, off-again relationship. Even when we were together, I was never a one-woman man.

I had girlfriends on campus, but that's about it. Nothing ever happened when the Spartans traveled to play other schools. In college, you didn't even get a chance to talk to girls on the road. We played the game and got back on the bus. Sometimes we didn't even stay the night. Occasionally we'd meet some cheerleaders, but it was nothing more than "Hi, what's your name?" As soon as we started a conversation, it was time to leave.

His main focus was basketball and nothing else. Basketball came first, and I had to understand that. I didn't understand it right away. All the other players had one major girlfriend, but Earvin didn't. I was important to him, but there always seemed to be other women around. Exactly what was going on with them, I didn't know.

We broke up a few times, and some of these breakups were pretty traumatic. And yet we always remained friends. Even after we broke up, and even when we were nothing more than friends, there was always some contact. He'd still call me, although there were times when I just wasn't sure whether he was calling me as my friend or my boyfriend. It was a roller-coaster relationship.

In those days, when something was bothering him, he just wouldn't talk about it. Sometimes he kept away for weeks at a time. He just didn't know how to talk about things. The problem wasn't necessarily in our relationship—there might be something wrong in his basketball life. Later on, when he was having problems with Coach Westhead, he wouldn't speak to me for months. I never even knew why. I thought it was me. Or us. Whenever something bad happened in basketball, I suffered.

But the older we got, the better he got. Every time something happened, I'd say, "You've got to talk to me. You can't just shut me out. You've got to learn to open up and talk."

Gradually, things changed. He finally let down his guard, and that's why we were able to get married. He realized that I wasn't the enemy, that he could trust and confide in somebody else. He never knew he could trust anybody other than his father.

From the start, Cookie accepted the fact that my main interest in life was basketball. She herself was a fan. She was a member of the Spartan Spirits, a group of enthusiastic supporters who sat together in Jenison and led the home crowd in cheers and songs. Sometimes she came to our practices, because Jud allowed special friends of the players to sit in— as long as they sat high up, far from the floor, and kept quiet. Every time I came into the gym, I used to look up to see if Cookie was there. And if she was, I would say hello by throwing her the ball.

In my first season at Michigan State, the Spartans finished with a 25-5 record. That was a big turnaround from the previous year. The biggest reason, I think, is that Greg Kelser and I had terrific chemistry on the court. Greg was known as Special K. He was such a great jumper that people said he had pogo sticks built into his legs. The two of us read each other so well that I knew just what he was going to do— and when. We'd make eye contact, he'd drive to the basket, and then I'd hit him with a high lob for an alley-oop dunk.

What Greg and I had was an early version of Showtime. We'd run the fast break, and one way or another I'd get him the ball. When he caught it near the basket, he was Mr. Excitement. Even on the road, the fans loved to see Greg score. If the defense tried to pressure him on one side, he would go the other way and dunk it.

This was the first time I had ever played with anybody that good. And each of us made the other a better player. I had watched Greg the previous year, of course, so I knew what he could do. But that didn't necessarily mean that we'd be a good combination. You can never assume something like that until you actually get out on the court and try it. But once we started practicing, it was like we had been playing together for years.

Often, after one of Greg's baskets, we would give each other a high five. That may not sound unusual today, but back then nobody else was doing it. I just held my hand up one day, Greg slapped it, and from then on we did that in every game. Before long, the high five was all over college basketball as well as the NBA.

I'm still in touch with Greg, who went on to become a broadcaster for the Detroit Pistons. After I turned pro, I even had the pleasure of being interviewed by him. He's a smart, classy guy, one of the most intelligent and articulate players I've ever known. You can bet on it: No matter what Greg does in the future, he'll be successful.

In my first season at Michigan State, we came within half a game of going all the way to the Final Four. Kentucky was the number one team in the country, and in a postseason game against them we were actually leading by nine points at the half. Then we made a big mistake: We slowed down our game to protect the lead. If we had stayed with our running offense, we probably would have beaten them. But once we allowed Kentucky to go into their half-court game, they were impossible to stop.

We learned an important lesson that day: Stick with what you do best. Jud had done everything just right until then, so nobody questioned his decision at the time. But in retrospect, all of us, including Jud, realized what had gone wrong. It was one thing if Kentucky had deserved to win. But what made that game so painful is not that they had won the game, but that we had lost it.

Still, winning 25 games out of 30 was pretty good for a team that nobody took seriously when the season began. And we were only getting better.

CHAPTER 6

THAT CHAMPIONSHIP SEASON

Any serious athlete will tell you that winning a championship is the greatest thrill in the game. Being acknowledged by everybody as the undisputed number one, better than any of your competition—that's the ultimate measure of success. In high school, we won the state. But in college, it was the whole damn country. There's no thrill quite like the first one, and my first national championship came with the Michigan State team in 1979.

To this day, wherever I go, people still want to talk about that incredible season. I feel the same way. Despite all the victories and the titles I've been part of since then, nothing else can match it.

My second year at Michigan State followed a busy and unusual summer. First came a trip to the Soviet Union with a team of American college all-stars. Our Russian opponents were big and very strong and terrific outside shooters, the best I've ever seen. But they had no running game, and they moved without spirit or spontaneity. Playing against these guys was like going up against a team of robots. No wonder their fans cheered us every time we ran the break and dunked the ball.

For a black kid, going to Russia was weird. Basketball players are used to being stared at in airports and hotel lobbies, but what we went through over there was ridiculous. Every time we left the hotel we were on display. It wasn't that I felt any hostility from the people on the street, but all of their gawking and pointing gave me the chills. We felt like visitors from outer space, and we couldn't wait to get home.

I won't even mention the food, which was the same every meal. I don't ever remember enjoying pizza and hamburgers more than when we got home from Moscow.

But the biggest thing that happened to me that summer was when I got back to campus and Coach Heathcote told me that *Sports Illustrated* was planning their annual issue on college basketball and wanted a picture of *me* on the cover! Man, oh man! When Jud told me that, I couldn't sleep for three days. They had run a small item about me back in high school, and I'd thought *that* was exciting. But a cover? Unbelievable.

They came to campus and shot the photograph in our gym. In the picture, I was up in the air, putting in a lay-up with my back to the basket. Only instead of my uniform, they had me dressed in a tuxedo, complete with a top hat, white tie, and patent-leather shoes. The caption read: MICHIGAN STATE'S CLASSY EARVIN JOHNSON.

The article was a profile of the top ten sophomore players in the country. I was described exactly how I like to see myself—as a winner. "Opponents have learned that they may be able to outrun, outjump, outmuscle or outshoot Johnson," it said. "But it is almost impossible to beat him."

When that cover appeared on the November 27, 1978, issue I was so excited that I actually walked into stores just to see how it looked on the racks. The picture came out great, and I still think it's the best cover shot I've ever had.

It also changed my life. Within weeks, I went from being known throughout Michigan to being recognized all over the country. Fans started lining up for autographs—I must have signed thousands of that cover alone.

I enjoyed the attention, but I was afraid it would lead to problems with my teammates. I had been worried about this even before I arrived on campus, and early in my freshman year I had talked to the guys about all the press I was getting. I found myself almost apologizing for the publicity that came my way. I wanted them to know that I hadn't gone looking for it, that I wasn't some hot-dog rookie who only cared about his clippings. I liked these guys, and I didn't want them to resent me.

I had nothing to worry about. My teammates understood that the more attention I received, the more they would get, too. I was grateful that nobody seemed to be jealous of or angry at me. And I knew I had picked the right college. At some other places, I could have run into big problems with egos, or my teammates might have resented me because they weren't getting much attention from the media, or a starting role from the coach.

At Michigan State we were all working toward the same two goals—first, to make it to the Final Four, and then to win the NCAA championship. The Spartans had reached the Final Four only once, back in 1957, when they lost to North Carolina in the semifinals in triple overtime. My freshman year we had come within one game of getting there; this time we intended to go the distance.

Who knew when we might get another chance? Greg Kelser was now a senior, and players with his talent didn't come around too often. And I, too, was thinking of turning pro when the season was over. After my freshman year, I had flown out for talks with the management of the Kansas City Kings (who have since moved to Sacramento). It was nice to be considered, but I knew in my heart that I wasn't ready for the NBA, either physically or mentally. There would be time for that, but right now I wanted at least one more season at Michigan State—especially since we had a chance to win it all.

The season got off to a great start. We won our first few games easily, including a big 20-point victory over Bobby Knight's Indiana team. Everything was going smoothly when, in early January, Minnesota came to town. They were tough, and at the half they were ahead by 13. Forget this one, I thought. These guys are hot, and we're not hitting anything. We'll get them next time.

But our fans had a different idea, and when the second half

began they took over the game. I'd never experienced anything like it. Jenison Field House was always loud, but that night the crowd was so noisy that they actually forced us to make a comeback. They kept up a steady roar, and it echoed louder and louder, demanding that we play harder. With the crowd refusing to let us lose, we ended up beating Minnesota by seven points.

The victory belonged to the fans. If that game had been played anywhere else in the country, Minnesota would have killed us.

A few days later, we were named the number one team in the country by the Associated Press. But instead of being inspired by that, now, instead of playing to win, we were playing not to lose. A week after the Minnesota game, Illinois beat us with a shot at the buzzer. Two days later, against Purdue, another buzzer-beater, another loss. The following week we beat Indiana and Iowa at home. But then we lost to Michigan, our third defeat in two weeks. This one, too, slipped away from us in the final seconds.

All of these losses were painful, but at least they were close games against good teams. Who could imagine that something worse was right around the corner? Northwestern was easily the weakest team in our conference, and we should have beaten them by 20 points. But instead of us blowing them out, they beat us by 18. The other losses had been painful; this one was humiliating.

The bus ride home from Evanston felt like a funeral. All that proud talk about making it to the Final Four, which had sounded so realistic only two weeks earlier, now seemed ridiculous. We had now lost four of our last six games. That didn't exactly sound like the record of the best team in college basketball. And to get crushed by Northwestern, which hadn't won against a Big Ten team all season? That was unthinkable.

Two months earlier, with the *Sports Illustrated* cover, I had been on top of the world. Now I wondered: Is this the notorious *Sports Illustrated* jinx? Whatever it was, the press was all over us, and especially me. What was wrong with Michigan State? What had happened to Magic Johnson?

I had some ideas on this subject. As I saw it, our mistake was in giving up our high-scoring running game in favor of a set offense. Ever since we were ranked number one, Jud had been overcoaching the team. He was slowing us down, not letting us run and gun.

After our loss to Northwestern, Coach Heathcote called an emergency meeting. Beforehand, he spoke with us individually. "The problem is our offense," I told him. "You've got us playing a half-court game, but we're a fast-break team. We need to go back to what we do best."

"No," he said, "that's not it."

"Coach, that's *exactly* it," I said, "and the other guys feel the same way." We had been talking about this for quite a while, but nobody had had the guts to say it in front of Jud.

At the meeting, Jud gave his own version of what I told him: "Earvin here thinks that I'm the problem. He tells me that the rest of you guys agree. Well, if anybody has something to say about it, this is your chance."

Gee, Coach, when you put it *that* way . . . My teammates had been complaining to me for weeks about Jud's overcoaching, but now, when I needed them, the room was quiet. I looked around in disbelief. What's going on? I wondered. Am I nuts? Why is everyone so quiet?

Finally Greg spoke up: "Coach, we're not playing well because you're slowing the game down. We need to run more, like we used to."

Jud turned to Mike Longaker. Mike was just a lowly reserve, and he rarely got to play. But he was a top pre-med student and a Rhodes scholar, and we all respected his judgment. "I think Earvin and Greg are right," he said. "We've got to go back to our running game. But there's another problem here. We're not playing as hard as we should. This team has great potential, but we're not living up to it."

Before the meeting was over, we made a pledge to push ourselves much harder during the rest of the season. Maybe it was too late, but if we could put together a long winning streak, we might still finish with a good enough record to sneak into the tournament.

Jud could be stubborn, but what made him a great leader was that he knew how to listen. We had presented the problem, and now he came up with a solution. After that meeting, he took Ron Charles out of the starting lineup and replaced him with Mike Brkovich. This was a gutsy move because Ron was more talented than Mike. But Mike was better at running the fast break, and that's what we needed to win.

Our next game was at home against Ohio State, one of the two or three best teams in the country. They were 8-0 in conference play. We were stuck at 4-4. If we had any hope of turning things around, this game was an absolute must.

We started out great. Near the end of the first half we were ahead by 14. Then I sprained my ankle so badly that two of my teammates had to carry me off the court. As I sat in the training room in agony, I listened to the game on the radio. The pain was bad, but it felt even worse as Ohio State fought back to tie it up.

The doctor and the trainer had already agreed that I had to sit out for at least a week. But when Ohio State took the lead with just a few minutes remaining in the game, I had to respond. It was now or never. We couldn't afford to lose this one, not after all we had been through. "Wrap me up tight," I said. "I'm going back in."

I came limping back as somebody was shooting a free throw. When the crowd spotted me, they went absolutely crazy. Greg Kelser had been on the bench with foul trouble, and he was just getting ready to come back in. His back was to me, so Greg figured all the applause was for him. He waved to the crowd to thank them for the rousing ovation.

The fans were so excited that I stopped feeling the pain. It was incredible. A sportswriter who covered that game wrote that my reappearance at that moment was like something out of an old Hollywood movie. I couldn't run too well, but that didn't matter. The crowd and their emotion carried me through. As ten thousand fans screamed their heads off,

I scored nine points in the last four minutes, enough to win the game.

Then came Northwestern, this time at home. There was no way on earth they could beat us again, but they sure put up a good fight. The following week we played Kansas. This was our first time ever on national television, and Dick Enberg, Al McGuire, and Billy Packer did the broadcast for NBC. We dominated from start to finish. Even Mike Brkovich dunked in that one, and Mike wasn't a dunker.

Now we were back on track, playing our running game and racking up the points. In the next few games we took our revenge on all the teams who had beaten us earlier. Maybe the Northwestern disaster was a blessing in disguise, because after Jud's emergency meeting we went on to win 10 in a row. Our only loss came at the very end of the regular season, when Wes Matthews of Wisconsin hit a fifty-five-foot desperation shot at the buzzer. Of our five defeats that season, four had come during the final seconds of play.

Now came the second season, the NCAA tournament. We had to be at our best, because a single loss meant instant elimination. First we played Lamar, a small school in Texas. Although Lamar had surprised everybody with a big upset over the University of Detroit, we beat them easily when Special K scored 31 points.

But what everybody would remember from the Lamar game was not Greg's brilliant play, but Jaimie Huffman's shoe. Jaimie was a sub who had been on our team back at Everett High. He came into the game near the end, after we had rung up a big lead. And almost as soon as he started playing, he lost his left shoe. The poor guy had a terrible time trying to put it back on while the game continued around him. Finally he just threw it away and played without it.

NBC ate it up. With the outcome no longer in doubt, the cameras focused on every embarrassing detail of Jaimie's little adventure. Al McGuire started referring to him as ''Shoes'' Huffman, and the name stuck. When Jaimie finally got his shoe on again, he went in for a basket. It was the first hoop of his college career.

Next came Louisiana State. We had to play them without Jay Vincent, who had injured his foot in the Lamar game. The guys from Louisiana were big trash talkers. I went in for a shot, and when one of their guys blocked it, he said, "Don't be coming in here with that weak stuff, man." They had some real leapers, and I shot poorly that day. But my teammates pulled us through, and we beat them without much trouble.

Our next game, against Notre Dame, was shaping up as the biggest battle of the year. Notre Dame and Michigan State had a long, bitter rivalry, not only in basketball, but also in football. They had a history of beating us in both sports, and we were itching to get even. Their coach was the legendary Digger Phelps, and they had several players who went on to the NBA, including Kelly Tripucka, Bill Laimbeer, and Orlando Woolridge.

The winner of this game would go on to the Final Four. This was where we had been stopped the previous year, against Kentucky. But we were determined that it wasn't going to happen again.

The game was played in Indianapolis. I had a good feeling about it when I saw thousands of Michigan State fans walking along Market Street in their green-and-white. When we got to the locker room, we turned on the music, as always. Then Jud would come in, write the matchups on the board, and give us last-minute reminders.

So when Jud appeared, I turned off the music. But he just looked at me. "What are you doing?" he asked.

"Well, Coach, I know you're getting ready to talk."

"No, that's all right," he said. "Turn the music back on."

We all stared at him. Was something wrong? "It's all right," he repeated. "I don't have anything to tell you that you don't know. You know what to do. Just go out there and kick their butts."

And we did, right from the start. In this case, the *very* start. In studying the films, Jud had noticed that Notre Dame didn't have anyone hanging back on defense when they lined up for the opening tap. We were ready for that. Greg jumped center and tapped the ball to me. Without looking, I batted it over my head to Mike Brkovich, who was streaking down-court for the slam dunk. The game had barely started and already we were ahead. Special K was absolutely brilliant that day, and he finished with a season-high 34 points, including six dunks. I'll never forget the sight of Greg running down the lane and dunking over three Fighting Irish with his left hand.

We beat Notre Dame by 12. When the game was over, we were almost delirious with excitement. Just a few weeks ear-lier, after the loss to Northwestern, it had looked like our season was finished. Then came the meeting with Jud, when we promised ourselves that we'd live up to our potential. From then on, before each game, Greg led us in a chant as we spelled out the word *potential* in the locker room. When the Notre Dame game was over we sang our song loudly and proudly, right there on the floor of the arena. The promise had been kept.

On the bus back to Lansing, the atmosphere was electric. When I got home, I couldn't sleep. All I could think about was playing in the Final Four. I had watched these champi-onship games ever since I was a little kid, and now I was going to be part of it all. Looking ahead to the next weekend, we were all pumped up like kids at a carnival.

I had never seen our guys so motivated. Our practices became more intense than ever. The whole team was work-ing so hard that for the first time, we didn't hear any yelling from Jud. Everybody was on the same page and everything was clicking. We'd go at it for three hours, but it seemed like the practice was over almost before it began.

During the Final Four weekend, the semifinals are played on Saturday afternoon. Then, on Monday night, the two win-ners from Saturday play for the championship. We would be going against Penn on Saturday while Indiana State played DePaul. Everybody expected that the two finalists would be Indiana State and us. Indiana State hadn't lost a single game all season, thanks to a certain blond superstar named Larry Bird.

The games were to be played in Salt Lake City. We weren't scheduled to fly in until Thursday, but Jud decided to take us out there two days early. The whole state of Michigan had rallied behind us, and the level of excitement was sky-high. There were too many distractions, too many well-wishers telling us how great we were, and endless requests for interviews and for tickets, all of which diverted our attention from the mission at hand.

Michigan State University includes a major hotel school. When we arrived in Salt Lake City, we were contacted by a graduate of that program who was now the head chef at an elegant ski resort. He invited the whole team over for dinner.

That evening, we enjoyed a magnificent buffet in front of a huge picture window overlooking the slopes. The food was terrific, and we all ran back for seconds. But it was the view that blew us away. Most of us had come from urban black neighborhoods. Nobody on our team had ever been skiing. We had never seen anything remotely like the majestic snow-capped mountains that stretched out right in front of us. If not for that one dinner, we might not have known that places like this even existed.

What did all of this have to do with basketball and the Final Four? I can't say exactly, but I believe that somehow the splendor of that place set the tone for our stay in Utah. Maybe it inspired us. In any case, I'll always remember what it was like to look out and watch the skiers whizzing right by us. When the sun went down over the mountains and the lights came on, it took your breath away.

At Friday's practice, we prepared for Saturday's game against Penn. Jud was worried that we weren't taking them seriously enough, and he kept telling us that they were a better team than we realized.

"But, Coach, they're from the Ivy League!" The ultimate put-down.

"That's true," he said. "But they beat some good teams to get here."

As it turned out, Jud had nothing to worry about. Al-

though Penn attacked our matchup zone defense more effectively than any team we had played, they kept missing their
shots. We made most of ours, and the game was essentially
over at halftime. Some of our reserves played more minutes
in the second half against Penn than in any other game that
season. We won by 34 points.

By the second half, our fans were looking ahead to Monday's game against Indiana State. "We want the Bird," they
chanted. "We want the Bird!"

Indiana State's fans, who were waiting for their team to
play DePaul, responded with: "You'll get the Bird! You'll
get the Bird!"

When our game was over, we went into the stands to watch
Indiana State and DePaul. It looked like a great game, but it
was impossible to concentrate because the crowd wouldn't
leave us alone. Everybody wanted autographs, and all the
Michigan State fans wanted to congratulate us. We needed a
good look at our next opponent, whoever it would be, so we
got out of there fast and ran back to the hotel to watch the
rest of the game on television.

DePaul had knocked off UCLA to get to the Final Four,
and they had a hot freshman named Mark Aguirre. They
were good, but we were all pulling for Indiana State. Since
they were unbeaten that season, we wanted to be the team
that finally stopped them.

I had another goal: I wanted to be the guy who stopped
Larry Bird.

Although Bird and I were the two best-known college
players in the country, our two teams had never played each
other. In fact, it wasn't until that Saturday against DePaul
that I saw him play. But believe me, once was enough. It
wasn't just that he went 16 for 19 against DePaul, with 35
points, 16 rebounds, and nine assists. What impressed me
even more was the way he refused to let his team lose. As
my teammates and I watched his incredible performance, we
all wondered the same thing: How on earth are we going to
shut this guy down on Monday night?

"Okay," Jud told us when we got to practice on Sunday.

"You've seen what Larry Bird can do. Today you're going to practice against him."

Earlier that morning, he had asked me to play on our second team during practice. "Gentlemen," Jud said, pointing to me, "meet Larry Bird. Double-team him as soon as he puts the ball on the floor. When he gets the ball, cut off all the passing lanes. Whatever you do, don't leave him open."

I had seen the real thing only once, but that morning I did the greatest Larry Bird imitation you ever saw. I made impossible passes. I knocked down shots from all over the court. I was tossing them in from twenty-five, even thirty feet out, hitting nothing but net. Our guys were playing me like Earvin Johnson, leaving me open because I didn't have that kind of range. But Bird could hit the long ones, and that day I *was* Bird.

I must have hit eight or nine in a row from out there. Jud was boiling mad. "Goddamn it!" he said. "That's Larry Bird. Get *on* him!" He was really cursing that morning, and my teammates were pissed. They couldn't believe what I was doing, and neither could I. I was laughing, and talking trash, too, although at the time I didn't even know that Bird did that. "Don't you know who I *am*?" I said. "I'm Larry Bird. Try and stop me."

I had the time of my life at that practice. Bird had the green light to do anything he wanted, so I did, too. And for that one morning, just about everything I tried was working. When the practice was over, one thing was clear: No matter how good the real Larry Bird was, he couldn't be any better than the imitation we had just seen.

Salt Lake City was swarming with reporters, and on Sunday afternoon Greg and I had to attend a press conference. We drove over there with Jud, and in the car he warned us what to expect: "They're gonna ask you again and again about Earvin and Bird. Greg, they'll ask you which one you think is the better player. Earvin, they'll ask if you think you're better than Bird. Be careful, and watch every word you say. Believe me, whatever you tell these guys will be magnified a thousand times over in the press."

Greg and I had met with reporters before, but we had never seen anything like this. There must have been three hundred people in that room from just about every newspaper and TV station in the country. Jud's predictions turned out to be right on target.

"Greg, who's better, Bird or Magic?"

"I don't know how you could compare them," Greg said. "They're the two best players in the tournament."

"Earvin, how about you? Do you think you're better than Bird?"

"I watched Larry Bird yesterday against DePaul, and he was incredible. He's older, he's more mature than I am, and at this stage he's probably a better player."

Yes, I was being diplomatic. But it was also the truth.

The championship game against Indiana State was almost an anticlimax. There were no locker-room speeches and no theatrics. This was business, pure and simple. We had a plan, and now it was time to execute it. But I still remember every shot from that game, every move.

Although we had only one day to prepare for Bird, Jud had figured out a way to contain him. Instead of playing our normal zone defense, we put a man on Bird wherever he was. Every time he got the ball, we shaded a second defender toward him. When he put it on the floor, we double-teamed him. We kept tabs on him the whole game, almost like police cars chasing down a criminal: "Okay, I've got him now. Jay, he's coming over to you."

Bird had never seen anything like it, and there wasn't much he could do. You could see how frustrated he was, how he kept calling to his teammates to get him the ball. But even when he had it, he just wasn't the same player we had seen on Saturday. He ended up shooting only 7 for 21 against us, and his teammates couldn't make up the difference.

At the half we were up by 10. Five minutes later we were ahead by 16. But with Greg on the bench with four fouls, Indiana State started to come back. With ten minutes left to play, they had closed to within six.

Now the pressure was enormous. Every moment was intense, and every play huge. Every move you made, you knew the entire country was watching. Later, we were told that this was the most widely watched game in the history of college basketball.

When Greg came back, we were able to increase our lead. And well before the game was over, we knew we had it won. It ended perfectly, with a full-court pass from me to Greg. Slam dunk! We won it, 75–64.

While we were celebrating and cutting down the net, I looked over at the Indiana State bench. I'll never forget what I saw. While half the arena was screaming with joy, Larry Bird was sitting there with his face buried in a towel. He was obviously crying, and my heart went out to him. As happy as I was, I knew that if things had gone just a little differently, *I* would have been the one sitting there with his face in a towel. I take losses the same way.

As I turned back to join the celebration, I knew in my gut that this wasn't the end of the story. Somewhere, somehow, Larry Bird and I would be seeing each other again.

PART TWO

THE LAKER YEARS

CHAPTER 7

THE NEXT LEVEL

Basketball has always been a joy to me, but the most fun I ever had playing the game was in college. The level of play is a lot higher in the pros, but the NBA is a business, with big money, big stakes, and big egos.

When I was finishing high school, I could have chosen to play for any college in the country, and when I arrived at Michigan State, the applause was ringing in my ears. But when I decided to turn pro, the situation was very different. Although I was a big college star, and Michigan State had won the NCAA title, the decision of who I would play for in the NBA wasn't really mine at all. My career with the Lakers turned out great, but the beginning wasn't all that promising. I wasn't sure about the Lakers, and the Lakers weren't sure about me.

I ended up in Los Angeles for two reasons: first, because of a trade that had been made back when I was in high school; and second, because a man named Larry O'Brien flipped a coin that came up tails.

Larry O'Brien was then commissioner of the NBA. In the spring of 1979, shortly after Michigan State won the NCAA title, he flipped a coin to determine which NBA team would get first pick in the upcoming college draft. Larry Bird was already committed to the Celtics, so he wasn't a factor. Most people expected that the first player selected in the draft would be Earvin Johnson from Michigan State.

Two teams were in the running for the right to make that first choice. The Chicago Bulls were involved because they had come in last in their division. And here it gets a little complicated. The second team should have been the New Orleans Jazz, who had finished their season with the worst record in the entire NBA.

But back in 1976, when New Orleans had acquired Gail Goodrich from the Lakers, the Jazz had traded away their 1979 first-round draft pick. So now the Lakers, with a season record of 47 wins and 35 losses, were vying with Chicago for first pick in the college draft.

Chicago wanted me badly, but the feeling wasn't mutual. If that coin had come up heads, I probably would have gone back to Michigan State for another year, or even two. For one thing, the Bulls already had a big guard, Reggie Theus. For another, five years before Michael Jordan, it was hard to imagine Chicago as a winner.

Now, it's true that I had played for an underdog team in high school, and again in college. But the NBA was a different story. Every basketball fan in America could rattle off the names of highly touted college stars who had come into the league and promptly disappeared. I thought I was good enough to make it in the pros. But it would take a lot more than one college star to resuscitate the Bulls. Even after Michael Jordan came along, for example, it took the Bulls three years to finish with a winning record.

The Lakers, however, were already pretty good. And they had Kareem Abdul-Jabbar, the foremost player in all of basketball. If he and I could develop some chemistry on the court, and I could feed the ball to Kareem as I had done with Greg Kelser in college, the results could be very interesting.

All things being equal, I preferred to play in the Midwest, where I would be closer to my family. But all things were not equal. Assuming they picked me first, the Lakers were my only option. If they came up with the money I was looking for, that's where I would go.

Back in Lansing, a lot of people were disappointed when I decided to leave college after only two years.

Several sportswriters were convinced I was about to make the biggest mistake of my life. As they saw it, This guy can't jump, can't run, and isn't much of an outside shooter. He may be exciting, but he isn't really ready to play in the NBA. His best move would be to stay in school for another year or two.

Nobody wants to admit it today, but the Lakers' top brass had reservations, too. They knew I had talent, and they were definitely interested in me. But they were leaning toward Sidney Moncrief, a shooting guard from the University of Arkansas, and David Greenwood, a power forward from UCLA. They worried that I was a flash in the pan, a college showpiece with no outside shot who wouldn't survive in the pros. They also wondered about my size. At the time, all the experts agreed that a big man couldn't be an effective point guard. Besides, the Lakers already had a good ball-handling guard in Norm Nixon.

I learned later that the team's decision to draft me was actually made by Dr. Jerry Buss, a real estate developer who was about to buy the team from Jack Kent Cooke. Buss had watched Michigan State on TV during the recent NCAA tournament and decided that I was the man who could help the Lakers improve their break. He liked my style and enthusiasm and believed that bringing me to Los Angeles would help put fans in the seats.

But Jerry Buss was in the minority. Just before he bought the team, Cooke told him that the Lakers' management had recommended drafting Sidney Moncrief.

No way, said Buss. Magic Johnson is the guy, or the deal's off.

When the owner speaks, the executives listen. He's the boss, after all. Some players look forward to becoming a coach after they retire, but I've always dreamed of being an owner.

Now it was time to talk turkey with Jack Kent Cooke, and I flew to Los Angeles with my father and two business advisers, George Andrews, a Chicago lawyer, and Dr. Charles Tucker, a psychologist in the Lansing school system. Tucker had played briefly in the ABA, and he used to play in pickup games around town. He helped me a lot during my teenage years by taking me to NBA games and introducing me to some of the players. When I decided to turn pro, he became my agent.

Later on, our relationship soured, the way business ties sometimes do. I subsequently teamed up with Lon Rosen, who has represented me ever since.

When our little group arrived at the Forum, Cooke invited us to join him for lunch in the Trophy Room. We sat at a long wooden table, and the walls around us were decorated with photographs of Cooke posing with various celebrities. He was a handsome man in his mid-sixties, and he wore an expensive, elegant suit. I am rich and powerful, he seemed to be saying, and I want everybody to know it.

"What would you like to eat?" he asked me.

I was nineteen, and wasn't used to private dining rooms. When I hesitated, he said, "Never mind. I'll order for both of us."

He ordered sand dabs, which I had never even heard of. "These are great," he said. "You're going to love them."

When lunch arrived, he turned to me and said, "Well, Earvin, how do you like your sand dabs?"

I didn't like fish, and I definitely didn't like *these* fish. "They're all right," I said, trying to be polite.

A hush fell over the room. I had no idea that Cooke took lunch so seriously. He looked like somebody close to him had just died.

"All *right*?" he said. "These are *delicious*."

Maybe so, but not to me. "Would you mind if I ordered something else?" I asked.

"Like what?"

"A hamburger? Or a pizza? Or maybe a roast beef sandwich?"

I was a kid then, but even today I prefer simple food. Although Cooke was hurt, he asked the kitchen to rustle up a couple of burgers for me.

After lunch we got down to business. When Cooke asked

me how much I was looking for, I told him I was thinking of $600,000 a year for five years. We knew that the Lakers were paying Kareem around $650,000, and that I would get substantially less. What I had in mind was half a million dollars, along with a signing bonus and a car. I also wanted an education allowance. I intended to continue taking courses at Michigan State during the summers, and for the first few years, I did.

"Let's get one thing straight right off," Cooke said. "I'm not paying for your education. I put myself through school, and if I can do it, you *certainly* can. Now, we can offer you four hundred thousand. It's not what you're asking for, but it's a hell of a lot of money. And let me remind you that the Lakers have made the playoffs seventeen times in the last nineteen years. We'd love to have you, Earvin, and I hope you'll play here. But the team has done just fine without you."

"I understand," I said. "But in that case, I guess I'll be going back to school." I was serious. I was happy at Michigan State, and I wasn't all that eager to move to a large city so far away from home. If the Lakers' offer wasn't good enough, I was prepared to wait another year or two before turning pro.

Cooke seemed surprised. "Well, let's just hold on a minute," he said. "Why don't we all go back and think about this overnight?"

I explained that we were planning to fly back home that same afternoon.

"Please don't do that," he said. "I'd like you all to stay overnight as my guests. I'm sure we can wrap this up in the morning in a way that will satisfy everybody."

As we drove back to the hotel, my father let me have it. "Mr. Cooke made you a generous offer," he said. "I've worked in a factory my whole life for what he's offering you for one year! And for something you love doing! Don't be greedy, son."

But I hadn't forgotten my childhood dreams. If I couldn't be a businessman, at least not yet, I still wanted to be rich.

I had already made up my mind that I wanted half a million dollars a year.

The next morning, Cooke raised his offer to $460,000. Not good enough, I told him. Finally he came up with a package that was equivalent to $500,000 a year. Now, at last, we had a deal.

We celebrated over lunch. This time he let me order. It was pizza for everybody. Cooke told me he had never tasted pizza before. When it arrived, he said, "Actually, this stuff is pretty good."

"Who knows?" I replied. "Maybe it'll catch on."

When I left Los Angeles that day I was the highest-paid rookie in the history of the NBA. That lasted for about a month. Then the Celtics signed Larry Bird for $600,000.

The first time I drove up to the Forum, I loved the way those big, beautiful white pillars surrounded the whole building. And it only got better when I went inside. I had been to NBA arenas in two or three other cities, but this place was unbelievable.

And clean! People in Los Angeles cared a lot about cleanliness, and the place was spotless. Down on the court, the lighting was just right for basketball. I've never liked playing in domes, because it's hard to measure your shot. But the Forum, like Madison Square Garden and Boston Garden, is a shooter's paradise.

At the beginning of each season, just before training camp, the Lakers have a media day, when all the players get together and meet with the press. I got there early, and asked Jack Curran, the trainer, if I could sit by myself in the stands. As I sat there, looking down at the polished hardwood floor, a little film started running in my mind—a documentary of some of the moments in my life that had led up to this one. There I was watching the games on television with my father on Sunday afternoon. Now I was Wilt Chamberlain at the Main Street courts, and my brother was pressuring me all the way. Then I was with Jim Dart in fifth grade. And in junior high, wearing my first uniform. And now Everett High

School, where I was given a warm-up suit with my name on it. Then Reggie and I were shooting jump shots after school. Now Everett was playing Brother Rice, and we were into overtime. There I was at Michigan State, playing at Jenison Field House in the noisiest game of the season against Minnesota. Now we were beating Notre Dame, and here came Indiana State, with Larry Bird.

But the show didn't end there. It actually continued into the future. I saw myself in a Laker uniform, running up and down the court. Now I was throwing no-look passes to Kareem, and the crowd cheered each one as the big guy tossed in one skyhook after another.

Finally Jack came up to get me. He had been calling me for five minutes, he said, but I never heard a word—I was having too much fun at the movies.

He took me downstairs to the Lakers' locker room. It was clean and spacious, but surprisingly modest. There were no actual lockers, just a stall to hang your clothes in, and a little safe on top for your valuables.

But one of those stalls had my name on it. And hanging there was my brand-new Laker uniform, number 32, the same as in high school. When I saw it, my smile was a mile wide.

"Would it be all right if I tried it on?"

"Sure. Take as long as you want. I'll come back later."

As I put on the uniform, I looked over at the other stalls and read the names. ABDUL-JABBAR. NIXON. WILKES. When I looked at myself in the mirror, a member of the Los Angeles Lakers, my eyes filled with tears. That's when it really hit me that I had actually made it.

A lot of people thought I'd never get this far. Not because they didn't support me, but because almost nobody back in Lansing had big dreams. There were times when I, too, had doubts. But here I was, wearing this beautiful uniform. And now, finally, I could begin to give something back to my parents for all they had given me.

I was grateful to be in the NBA, and doubly grateful to be playing for the Lakers. It isn't often that a winning team has the number one draft pick. And in the next few years, I would come to appreciate that even more. Think of the Bulls when Michael Jordan came along. Or the Pistons when Isiah was drafted. Or Cleveland in 1986, when Brad Daugherty arrived. Or the Knicks in '85, when Patrick Ewing was a rookie.

As Jack Kent Cooke had reminded me, the Lakers usually made the playoffs. And there, on the far wall, was their 1972 championship banner. For all their victories, this was the only title the Lakers had won since they moved here from Minneapolis back in 1960. But there was a lot of empty space along that wall, plenty of room for more banners.

Later that day, there was a press conference at the Forum. Somebody asked about my enthusiasm. It was one thing to show that much excitement in college, but wasn't I going to cool down now that I was playing with the big boys?

"No," I replied. "I've always been this way."

As I expected, there were several questions about how I would get along with Kareem. Some of the press was trying to create antagonism between us, but I refused to let that happen.

After the press conference, two television reporters, Jim Hill and Stu Nahan, took me aside. They were both former pro athletes—Stu had played hockey, and Jim football—and they wanted to give me some advice. Always take your time before answering a question, they told me. And be especially careful with the print media, because it's easier for print reporters to misquote you. They warned me that some of their colleagues might try to put me on the spot, or that they'd try to twist what I said in order to create some conflict.

It was good advice. As I soon learned, the big-city media types were a lot rougher than the handful of reporters I'd known back in Lansing. But I got along with everybody, and I stayed friends with Stu and Jim. When Jim used to interview me on the air, he would often say, "Magic, there will eventually come a time when you won't play anymore. What do you see yourself doing when your playing career is over?"

And I would look at him and say, "Actually, Jim, I'd like *your* job."

The first time I ever saw my dad cry was the day I left Lansing to move to Los Angeles in the summer of 1979. Mom was crying, too, of course. I was a wreck. I managed to hold back my tears because I didn't want to break down in front of my parents. But as soon as I got on that plane the tears started flowing.

Although I was thrilled to be playing for the Lakers, my last few weeks in Lansing were very painful. I had left town many times before, on all kinds of trips, domestic and foreign, but this was different. Now, for the first time, I was leaving home.

Two years before, I had been able to delay this painful moment by going to school at Michigan State. But now it was unavoidable. Some kids can't wait to leave home and live on their own. But I was just the opposite. It was hard enough to leave my friends and my community, but the thought of moving away from my family just tore me up. My father had always been my best friend, and Mom had always been there with that hot meal or that big hug. My sisters and brothers had watched my whole career. . . . I just didn't want to think about it.

When I moved to Los Angeles I was the loneliest guy in town. Here I was, playing in the NBA and making more money than I ever dreamed of. I should have been the happiest guy on earth. But for the first few months I was miserable. It wasn't like college, where everybody on the team is in the same situation, and you're like a closed, tight fraternity. The Lakers had their own lives and their own friends, and some of them were married. And veterans are always slow to warm up to rookies anyway, because so many new guys don't work out.

Sunday nights were the hardest. Even when I was in college, our family always sat down to Sunday dinner together to enjoy fried chicken, black-eyed peas, rice, and apple and sweet-potato pie. Living in California, I missed those dinners more than anything else. I called home every day, but especially on Sunday nights, because I knew everybody would be there.

It wasn't just the conversation I missed, but the contact, the touch. I missed being in the room together and sitting in my favorite chair. I missed Mom knowing what I loved to eat. I missed the whole family together, all of us laughing and talking.

There were other adjustments I had to make. I had a good income, but the money didn't feel real to me yet. I was used to the prices in Lansing, and I was shocked by how expensive it was to live in Los Angeles. Dr. Buss helped me out by telling me about a vacant apartment in a three-story building he owned in Culver City. It was nothing special, but it looked pretty good to me. There was a park across the street and a supermarket on the corner, and it was close to the only three places I ever had to drive to: the Forum, the airport, and Loyola Marymount University, where the Lakers practiced.

For that first year I didn't go anywhere else. I found the city overwhelming and was afraid of getting lost. In Lansing we had one highway and three main streets. Los Angeles had more freeways than I could imagine, and everything was miles apart. I watched a lot of television that year. I listened to music, cooked my own meals, and ran up an incredible phone bill. Sometimes I called the same people three or four times a day.

When I did go out, I was often recognized. "You look like Magic Johnson," people would say.

"Oh yeah?" I would reply. "I wish I was. That guy is really something."

Or I'd walk by a group of people and overhear their conversation:

"Hey, who was that?"

"Who?"

"Over there. I didn't get a good look at him. He's gotta play ball."

"He looks like Magic Johnson."

"No, that's not Magic Johnson."

"Sure it is."

Sometimes I'd be sitting at the movies before the lights went out, and a fan would notice me, say hi, and keep going. A few seconds later, he'd suddenly do a double take. Once, just before the movie started, somebody pointed to me and yelled, "Look, there's Magic Johnson!" Everybody turned around to see, and I started slinking down in my seat. But when you're as tall as I am, you can only slink so far.

One of my first friends in Los Angeles was the new owner, Jerry Buss. We were like a couple of kids, both of us full of energy and new ideas. People thought my enthusiasm wouldn't last, and they said the same about Jerry. But then, he wasn't exactly your typical franchise owner.

Jerry Buss grew up poor in Wyoming, but he managed to earn a doctorate in chemistry at USC in Los Angeles. He then made a fortune in real estate, and by 1979 had put away enough money to buy the Lakers, the Los Angeles Kings, and the Forum in a package that cost him $67.5 million.

Jerry used to invite me over to his house, where we'd eat chocolate doughnuts and play pool. He was divorced, and he dated the most beautiful women in town. Sometimes we would double-date, going out for dinner or dancing. A couple of times I went with him to Las Vegas, were he would win (and sometimes lose) as much as $50,000 in five minutes. Some of my teammates were jealous because I was friends with the owner, but Jerry extended the same invitation to everybody on the team. I was the only one who accepted. He did treat me especially well, however.

Jerry Buss made the Lakers into a real show, and in doing that, he had a big impact on the entire league. Take the Laker Girls. Other teams had cheerleaders, but Jerry put together a group of girls who could really dance. It wasn't enough to look good. This was Los Angeles, where there were plenty of beautiful people in the stands. Other teams used canned music, but Jerry hated that. He put in a whole band, because live music is so much more exciting.

He saw the Lakers as more than a sports team. He understood Los Angeles, and he knew that people wouldn't drive to the Forum just to watch a game; they wanted to be entertained.

The Forum Club, a restaurant and bar, was already there. But Jerry started inviting television and movie stars. He wanted the public to associate the Lakers with glamour and prestige, and before long they did. He raised the price of courtside seats, which now sell for $500 a ticket—assuming you can find one. But he didn't abandon the real fans, either. To this day, the Forum still has tickets that sell for as little as $8.50. That's where Jerry sits: He installed a sky box up in the cheap seats for himself and about sixty of his closest friends.

When I first came along, the Laker fans had a reputation for showing up late and leaving early. But winning makes a big difference, and Los Angeles deserves an award for the most improved fans. We had the highest ticket prices in the league, but once the team improved and we gave people a *reason* to come on time, they did. Before long the Lakers were leading the league in attendance. The Forum was a happening place, and everybody in town wanted to be part of it.

But that was Showtime, which was still some years in the future. For now, Earvin Johnson, with butterflies in his stomach, was getting ready to play his first season of big-league ball.

CHAPTER 8

ROOKIE

When I showed up at my first Laker training camp in Palm Springs, my teammates thought I was crazy. Although the formal start of the season was still a few weeks off, I jumped right in with my usual exuberance. Some guys don't go into overdrive until the playoffs, so I stuck out like a sore thumb.

I could see right off that my intensity was very different from the cool, laid-back style of the NBA. Most professional athletes try to conserve their energy, especially before the season begins. My teammates were shocked to see me diving for loose balls in a meaningless practice, dishing out high fives, and smacking everybody's hand after a little 10-point scrimmage.

"Earvin's running around like a young buck," said Norm Nixon. The name stuck, and from then on my teammates and coaches always called me Buck.

I could see that some of the older guys were rolling their eyes and waiting for me to settle down. They had seen rookies come and go, and I'm sure they expected that my high spirits would fizzle out within a few weeks. But then the Lakers of the late 1970s were not exactly famous for their sparkle and personality. It took a lot to get this team excited. As columnist Jim Murray put it in the *Los Angeles Times* a few weeks before the season began, "I've seen happier faces on guys carrying a casket."

* * *

We opened the season in San Diego against the Clippers. Naturally, I maintained my perfect record of screwing up in my first game with every new team. This time, however, I outdid myself: I actually managed to make a fool of myself even before the opening tap.

As the hot new rookie, I was given the honor of leading the Lakers onto the court for the pregame warm-ups. I was supposed to take the ball, dribble to the basket, and dunk it for the first hoop of the new season. That wasn't hard, but I was still nervous. After all, this was the first game of my professional career. The last official game I had played in was back in the spring, against Indiana State. That was only seven months earlier, but it already seemed like another era.

When it was time for the Lakers to come out on the floor, I took the ball, drove to the basket, and—boom!—fell flat on my face. I had tripped over my warm-up pants. I was so anxious that I hadn't bothered to tie them right. They slipped down just enough to send me sprawling onto the floor. My teammates found this absolutely hysterical, and so did the crowd. As I pulled myself up, I did my best to put on a smile. That's because CBS had picked *this* game to kick off their weekly national broadcasts.

Things could only improve from there. At least, that's what I thought. But I played so badly during the first quarter that Coach Jack McKinney took me out after about nine minutes. He brought me back later on, and this time I held my own, and was still on the floor during the final minutes of a very close game.

With eight seconds left, and the Lakers down by one, McKinney called a time-out to set up our final shot. There was only one conceivable play in that situation, and everybody in the building knew exactly what it was: get it to the big guy, and let him shoot. And that's what we did. When Kareem caught the ball at the free-throw line, he put up a long, elegant skyhook that won the game at the buzzer.

As he was running off the court, I was so excited that I leaped into his arms and hugged him. But when I looked up at his face, he clearly wasn't sharing my excitement. What's the big deal? he seemed to be saying. Hitting shots like that is my *job*.

When we got to the locker room he said, "Calm down, Earvin—we've got eighty-one more games to play." But I wasn't about to change my style. I'd always played with passion, and eventually my teammates would get used to it.

Later that same week, in Seattle, I experienced another emotion on the court: fear. Early in the third period, when I was going up for a rebound, somehow my feet got tangled up in Jack Sikma's legs, and I came crashing down to the floor. My knee hurt like hell, and I had to be helped off the court. In the locker room, an orthopedic surgeon gave me a quick exam. "I'm only guessing," he said, "and you'll definitely need X rays. But it doesn't look good. My guess is torn ligaments."

I was devastated. This was only our third game of the season, and if I needed knee surgery I would be out for months—possibly the whole season. It's a good thing I wasn't listening to the radio. When I went down, Chick Hearn, the Lakers' longtime play-by-play announcer, told his listeners that he hoped this wouldn't mean the end of Magic Johnson's career.

Early the next morning, Jerry Buss sent a private jet to fly me back to L.A. for X rays and medical attention. After a long, careful exam, the doctor said, "I'm sorry, Earvin, but we might have to amputate your leg."

I looked up, and he was grinning. It turned out to be nothing worse than a bad sprain. A week later I was back in action.

What happened in Seattle was a real wake-up call about how physical the pro game really was. I had heard about that, but it took some getting used to. And for me there was an even bigger problem—the NBA's intense, one-on-one type of defense. In college we played a zone, and I didn't have much experience guarding individual players. Now, suddenly, I was expected to stop some of the most explosive scorers in the league.

It wasn't fun. In that first game against San Diego, World

Free scored something like 40 points against me. The next
night, Paul Westphal did the same. In the Seattle game it was
Dennis Johnson who killed me. Then came George Gervin.
Before long I started to wonder, Can I guard *anyone* in this
league? My teammates were probably wondering the same
thing.

Coach McKinney helped me understand that my biggest
mistake was trying to play every guy the same way. World
Free was a one-on-one player who didn't use any picks. He
could shoot the ball from anywhere, and he often did. I tried
to play Paul Westphal the same way, but Westphal used picks
constantly. He never stopped moving without the ball. I had
to learn how to fight through a pick and stay with my man,
which wasn't easy. In college I had always held my own on
defense, but the pro game was a real challenge.

To some extent this problem took care of itself. In that
respect it's a little like baseball, where a new pitcher generally has the advantage until the hitters get used to his motion.
My first game against just about every team in the NBA was
a real struggle. And for the first time in my career I was
getting into foul trouble.

A lot of these fouls were called simply because I was new
in the league. The officials will never admit it, but every
rookie has to pay his dues, just as every star gets a few breaks.
When you've got a veteran who makes great moves and ex-
cites the fans, the refs go easy on him. After all, nobody pays
good money to see Michael Jordan or Larry Bird foul out.
By my third year in the league I was making some of the
same defensive plays that had gotten me in trouble when I
was a rookie, but now I was getting away with them.

I improved a lot just from practicing with my teammates.
And the more I played, the better I became. I learned how
to get around a pick, how to shade a guy toward his weaker
hand, how to get up on a man who shot the jumper well, and
how to guard somebody who was quicker than I was.

The guy who really taught me about defense was my teammate Michael Cooper. Coop was my first real friend on the
team, and over the years I was closer to him than to anyone

else on the Lakers. Although he had arrived a year before me, he tore a ligament in his knee a few weeks before that season started and played in only three games all year, so when I met him he was essentially a second-year rookie.

We became friends during training camp, when Coop was fighting to make the team. I loved his aggressive style and the way he didn't back down from anyone. He reminded me a little of Reggie Chastine, and I quickly became his personal cheerleader. Michael not only made the team; he became our all-important sixth man, the first guy off the bench.

"How do I get more playing time?" he asked Coach McKinney.

"Defense is the ticket," McKinney replied.

"Okay," said Coop. "Then that's how I'm going to make my living."

And he did. The only other guy in the league who was as good on defense was Dennis Johnson, who drove us crazy every time we played against him.

Coop taught me that the key to good defense was mental preparation. After a game at the Forum, he would drive home and watch the videotape—*twice*. Before the game, he'd think about the last time we played that team, and how he could be even more effective against them. He would even think about the officials, because some referees will let you play tighter than others. But mostly he'd focus on the man he was guarding, who was usually the other team's high scorer. Night after night, Coop would come off the bench and shut that guy down.

He was constantly working to make himself better—and not just on defense, either. Coop came into the league without a strong outside shot, and in his early years our opponents used to leave him wide open. He worked his butt off in practice, and he later made himself into one of the best three-point shooters in the league. He still holds the record for the most three-pointers during the playoffs.

Coop could also drive to the hoop. We had a play where I would throw it high above the basket and Coop would slam it down for two points. A classic alley-oop. Only we called it a Coop-a-Loop.

Michael had always been a worker. Back in high school, he built a seven-foot defender out of wood and dragged him around the court so he could pretend somebody was always guarding him.

One reason I had so much success in the NBA was that Coop guarded me in every practice and gave me no slack. The next night, when we played in an actual game, I felt like a prisoner who had just been let out of jail. Nothing an opponent could do could be worse than the moves Coop had already put on me during practice.

The two of us played our hearts out in those scrimmage games, and Coop was all over me. He would pressure me full-court, pushing me and elbowing me all morning. Michael was so skinny and wiry that he could really hurt you. When I went home to take a nap, I'd be feeling Coop all afternoon.

That was another thing I had to get used to as a rookie—taking an afternoon nap whenever I could. It's impossible to fall asleep right after a game, so you end up having a lot of late nights. But there are always morning practices, or early wake-up calls so you can get on the bus to the airport and fly on to the next city. The only way to survive in the NBA is to learn to sleep in the afternoons.

And on airplanes. It took me most of my rookie year to get that right. I finally found a system: I would take a window seat and get myself two pillows. I've been flying that way ever since.

One of the hardest things for a rookie to get used to is the incredibly long and draining NBA season. The college schedule is only 30 games long, but in the pros you play 82—and that's not counting the preseason exhibition games and the playoffs. These days, a team can end up playing as many as 26 postseason games, and every single one is intense and exhausting. The travel and the schedule take their toll on you, and by the middle of January most rookies are ready for their summer vacation. It's depressing when you've already played the equivalent of a full college season and you're not even halfway to the playoffs.

In college there are games where you can coast, but the NBA is a constant battle. Even when your opponent is an expansion team, you're up against men who are playing basketball for their livelihood and are trying to keep their jobs. It's not just a question of talent; these guys are hungry.

It's a good thing I don't mind getting knocked down. I took a real beating that first year, but I played hard, and missed only five games due to injuries. I loved being a member of the Lakers, and I couldn't wait for the games. We were supposed to show up at six o'clock for a seven-thirty home game, but I was always in the locker room by five.

Some rookies have trouble adjusting to the pro game, and I can understand why. You come out of college as a big star, and suddenly you're at the bottom again. You have to learn to be humble. In addition to doing little chores for the veterans, the rookies help carry the equipment on the road, such as the ball bag and the video machine. Some guys mind that, but I didn't. To me it was one more way of being accepted.

As we traveled around the country during my rookie year, I got to play in every arena in the league. One thing I noticed was that the nets were slightly different from one place to the next. If the net is tight, the ball comes out a little slower, which makes the fast break more difficult. New York was that way, because over the years the Knicks had not been a running team. But I never minded too much, because the fans in New York were so great. They really understood the game.

The Boston fans were the same way. Boston Garden had loose rims, where you got a shooter's bounce. That's why most teams loved to play there—the basket would be good to you.

But what really affects the arenas are the crowds. The Capital Centre in Maryland was dark, and it could feel very empty there when the fans didn't come out. New Jersey was the same way. In both those places, there were times when we had more fans there than the home team did. That sounds like an advantage, but I never liked it. I preferred loud, antagonistic fans on the road, because they motivated me to play harder.

Dallas was great. Whoever designed Reunion Arena did a wonderful job. We had a special rivalry with the Mavericks, and it was very tough to beat them at home. They had a wonderful crowd that really got behind the team.

Chicago Stadium was another terrific arena. The building might have been falling apart, but it was built for basketball. The lighting was great, and the fans were right on top of you. It was the noisiest place in the league. When the Bulls got going, these folks went crazy. They were so loud that nineteen thousand fans could sound like a hundred thousand. I loved going into places like that because they really got my juices flowing.

All through the early weeks of my rookie season I looked forward to January, when the Lakers would be making their annual trip to Detroit, and I could finally see my family and friends. Unfortunately, the Pistons were no longer playing in Cobo Arena—they had moved out to the Silverdome, an immense football arena in the middle of nowhere that seated over fifty thousand fans. The place was so big that for basketball games they used to pull down a huge blue curtain to block off some of the empty seats and provide some background. These days the Pistons play in the Palace in Auburn Hills, a beautiful state-of-the-art arena that seats over twenty thousand.

I had recently pulled a hamstring muscle, and if we had been playing anywhere else, I would have sat this one out. But it was my first NBA appearance in front of my own people, and I would have played in a wheelchair if I had to. I was so happy to be back in Michigan that this one little visit carried me through the rest of the season. I even managed to sneak in a quick visit to Lansing when a TV station flew me over in a helicopter.

The Lakers always drew well in Detroit, and twenty-eight thousand fans came to see us. At the time, this was the largest crowd the Pistons had ever drawn, which was all the more remarkable when you consider what a terrible season they were having. Detroit had won only 10 games by the time we arrived, and they finished the year with a record of 16-66. That translates to a winning percentage of .195, which couldn't have been much fun for my friends Greg Kelser and Phil Hubbard, both of whom were now playing for the Pistons.

The whole evening was like a huge welcome-home party. When the Pistons came out they were greeted with boos, but when the Lakers appeared, the whole place just erupted. Mom and Dad drove down from Lansing with dinner for the entire team. They warmed it up in the kitchen and set it up in the locker room after the game: chicken, collard greens, corn bread, green salad, macaroni salad, home-baked rolls, and Mom's specialty, sweet-potato pie. She had been cooking all month, and my teammates just loved it. From then on, Mom's homemade cooking was a part of every Laker visit to Detroit.

That night was also the first time I ever played in front of Leon the Barber, the funniest, meanest, and best-known fan in the entire league. I had heard that voice as a kid, and now I was one of the players he was yelling at. Even in that gigantic arena, we could hear him loud and clear. Leon was no ordinary heckler; he really knew the game, and he never complained about the officials. But he always let you know when you weren't playing well. He wasn't too tough on me unless the Lakers were losing, and that didn't happen too often.

People who didn't know any better thought Leon was just an older guy with an attitude. But that was only part of the story. After the race riots in the late 1960s, he had given up being a barber to get involved in community work. He was responsible for the city's opening up basketball courts in vacant lots all over town. And he worked with hundreds of young people, organizing neighborhood games and coaching young players.

Just before my third season in the league, and just after I

had signed a huge new contract, the Lakers came to Detroit for an exhibition game. It was widely reported that Kareem wasn't too pleased about my new deal, and during a time-out Leon let him have it: "Ka-reem! Ka-reem! I *told* you that attitude wasn't going to get you nowhere! I *told* you to smile! You see! Look at Magic. He just smiled his ass up on twenty-five million!"

Leon was especially rough on Bob McAdoo, who had joined our team after an unsuccessful couple of years with the Pistons. Maybe that's why McAdoo always seemed to come up with an injury whenever we played in Detroit. Leon would yell at Pat Riley, too, and he loved to make fun of Riley's hair.

Leon wasn't the loudest fan in the league, but you could always hear him because he made his comments during time-outs, when most other fans were quiet. He sat about four rows behind the visiting team's bench, so we could hear every word clearly. In the old days he used to sit behind Detroit's bench, but they moved his seat when the Piston coaches started getting thrown out of games for remarks that had actually come from Leon.

He could be equally tough on the home players. When Cliff Levingston shot an air ball, Leon let him have it. "No, Cliff, no. They don't pay you to *shoot*. Rebound, Cliff. Rebound! *That's* what they pay you for!"

Isiah was his favorite. "Don't hurt my baby Isiah. Byron, you can't guard him. Nobody in this *league* can guard Isiah. Don't worry, Byron, it's not just you. Isiah does that to *everybody*."

There were times when Leon made us laugh so hard that we could barely control ourselves. He always reminded us that whatever else basketball had become, it was also a game. And if we weren't enjoying ourselves, we were missing out on something.

The Lakers won 60 games during my rookie season, and you can't ask for more than that. Okay, maybe a *little* more. The Celtics, with brand-new you-know-who, won 61 games, but who's counting? Besides, Boston lost to Philadelphia in the Eastern Conference Finals. We won our playoff series against Phoenix and Seattle, so it was the Lakers and the 76ers in the championship series.

If my first few minutes as a Laker were a total disaster, the last game of my rookie year more than made up for it. In fact, that final playoff game against Philadelphia was probably the best performance of my life. It was certainly the most dramatic.

Kareem was usually at his best during the playoffs, and he absolutely dominated that series. In the first five games he averaged over 33 points, and his performance in Game Five was just incredible. Both teams had won twice. But during the fifth game, Kareem was forced to leave with a badly sprained ankle. A few minutes later he made a dramatic return, and in the final quarter he scored 14 points to lead us to victory. That gave us a 3–2 lead in the series. Game Six was set for Friday in Philadelphia. The seventh game, if necessary, would be played on Sunday in the Forum.

We were about to board the flight to Philadelphia when Jack Curran told us that Cap, as Kareem was known, would not be making the trip. His ankle was in bad shape, and he couldn't play on it. The hope was that if Cap stayed home and rested, he'd be able to come back for Game Seven. As Curran was handing out the boarding passes, Coach Paul Westhead, who had taken over the team early in the season after McKinney was injured, took me aside. "We'll need you to take over at center," he said.

"I'd love to," I said. "I played some center in high school."

Coach didn't ask me to take over Kareem's leadership role, but that came naturally. I was still a rookie, but I no longer felt like one.

On the plane, I went straight to Kareem's regular spot— the first aisle seat on the left, the bulkhead seat with the most leg room. Then I turned around and announced to the team, "Never fear, E.J. is here." Everybody laughed, but I wasn't kidding.

As soon as we landed in Philadelphia, reporters started asking us about Game Seven in Los Angeles. Without Kareem, nobody thought we had a prayer in Game Six.

That night, we had a team meeting at the hotel. After watching the videotape of Game Five, we all spoke. "I'll be guarding Dawkins," said Jim Chones, our backup center. "I intend to shut down the middle, and you guys can count on it."

That was quite a promise. Darryl Dawkins, who was known as Chocolate Thunder, was one of the most forceful and electrifying players in all of basketball. He was famous for his explosive dunks, and there were so many in his repertoire that he actually gave them names: Earthquake Shaker, Go-Rilla, In Your Face Disgrace, and Rim Wrecker. And then, of course, there was the dunk that he modestly referred to as Chocolate Thunder Flying, Robinzine Crying, Teeth Shaking, Glass Breaking, Rump Roasting, Bun Toasting, Wham Bam, Glass Breaker I Am Jam.

If Jim could do the job on Dawkins, that would go a long way.

"Philadelphia thinks this game is already over," I told my teammates. "But we can use that to our advantage. We can beat them because they'll have a problem matching up against us. But only if we go into this game believing we can win."

Philadelphia was used to trying to deal with Kareem in the low post. But now we had Michael Cooper coming in, which gave us a smaller, faster lineup. Philadelphia had a big size advantage, but we were fast enough to run right by them.

Up until game time, half the population of Pennsylvania still expected Kareem to show up. People were sure that all the talk of his ankle injury was just an elaborate deception. They thought the big guy would suddenly appear at the last minute to drive them crazy.

On the day of the game, there were Kareem sightings all over Philadelphia. A taxi driver told a radio station that he had picked up Kareem at the airport. A woman reported that she had seen him at the Philadelphia Museum of Art. Although Kareem wasn't at our morning shootaround, people still believed he would make a dramatic eleventh-hour appearance at the Spectrum. We didn't invent these stories, but once they started flying we did nothing to discourage them, either. Let people wonder.

The night before the game, I called my dad in Lansing. "Kareem can't be there," I told him. "They've asked me to play center."

"You'll do great," he said. "All you have to do is go back to the kind of game you played in high school." Back at Everett I had been a scorer, shooting the ball from all over the court. It was hard to believe, but that was only three years before.

On Friday night, when I walked out to center court for the opening tap, I was grinning from ear to ear. I had a good feeling about this game. Maybe it was because everybody expected a blowout, and we had nothing to lose. Before the game, people kept saying, "See you in L.A. for Game Seven." They weren't even trying to psyche us out; it just seemed obvious to them.

I smiled when I heard that. But in the back of my mind I was thinking, No way. It's all over tonight.

I felt like we had a terrific joke up our sleeves that the 76ers weren't prepared for. We were going to whip that ball around so fast that they wouldn't know what hit them. Without Kareem, we couldn't afford to play the half-court game and think defensively. Tonight we had to play full-court and take our chances.

I lost the opening tap against Caldwell Jones, but that was no surprise. He was six-eleven, with incredibly long arms. I had already decided that I'd just jump up and down at the start and then go to work on the rest of my game.

We came out smoking and jumped out to a 7–0 lead. Then Philadelphia pulled ahead by eight in the second quarter. At the half, the game was tied, 60–60. Given the expectations, that was already a big psychological edge. I was shooting the lights out, and Philadelphia just couldn't shut me down. They didn't know whether to put a big man on me or a smaller guard, but nothing they tried seemed to work. Caldwell Jones was guarding me, and it seemed like every time he gave me the outside shot, I managed to hit it.

But it wasn't just me. Kareem's absence confused the 76ers, and they never did find the right matchups to cover our guys.

All season long we had dominated teams in the third quarter, and this game was no exception. Before the 76ers even knew what hit them, we ran off 14 straight points. Finally Bobby Jones tapped one in to break the spell. But by then we were just carving up Philadelphia, and getting most of the rebounds. We took their fans right out of the game. Philadelphia knew they were in trouble when their own crowd started booing them after they missed seven shots in a row.

When the third quarter ended we were up by 10. Now we could taste the title.

We knew that Philadelphia would attempt a comeback in the fourth quarter, and of course they did. But each time they came close, we stepped on the gas and pulled away. Three times they closed to within two points. But despite the heroic efforts of Julius Erving, we kept gunning the engine and leaving them behind. The final score was 123–107. For the first time since 1972, the Los Angeles Lakers were world champions.

I had the game of my life. I played forty-seven minutes out of forty-eight, and finished with 42 points, 15 rebounds, and seven assists. I shot 14 free throws and hit every one. "He has played center, forward, and guard in this game," said Brent Musburger on CBS. "He'll pack the uniforms afterward."

I did a lot, but I didn't do it alone. Almost nobody noticed that Jamaal Wilkes finished with 37 points, the most he had scored since high school, and 10 more than Dr. J. Cooper, off the bench, hit for 16. Norm Nixon finished with only four points, but he had nine assists, a game high.

Jim Chones had 10 rebounds, and he kept his promise by holding Darryl Dawkins to 14 points and four rebounds. Dawkins saved his energy for Cooper. In the fourth quarter, he knocked Coop down so hard that we practically had to scrape him off the floor.

"Michael, do you know where you are?" asked the trainer.

"I'm at home, right?" Cooper replied.

Not exactly, Coop. Somehow, Michael stumbled over to the free-throw line and hit both shots.

Usually the winning team's locker room is a wild scene with champagne flying. But ours was strangely quiet, and even I was reserved. We were exhausted. With two minutes left in the game, I had called a time-out just to catch my breath. It was the first time in my career that I had ever done something like that.

We were also stunned. Nobody had expected us to win that game. We knew we could do it, and we were up for the game. But to actually have it happen without the greatest player in the league—that was hard to believe.

But most of all, it just didn't feel right to celebrate this victory without Kareem. Yes, we had won this game without him, but he was still our leader, and we all knew that he was the one who had carried us to this point.

I knew that he was watching us on TV. "Big Fella," I told him during a postgame interview, "I did it for you."

Kareem had watched the game at home with his sprained left ankle propped up on a coffee table. It was so frustrating for him not to be with us that he had to turn off the sound and chew on a pillow. When Wilkes dunked the ball to give us a 12-point lead in the fourth quarter, Kareem limped out to the backyard and started yelling.

As soon as we got back to the hotel I collapsed on the bed and called my dad. They had let him leave work early to watch the game, which was on tape delay in most of the country. He already knew the outcome, but when I reached him he was still watching it.

When Jim Dart heard that the game wouldn't be shown live, he flew to Philadelphia, took a cab to our hotel, and demanded that I get him a ticket. Jim came into our locker room after the game, and it was great to see him at that moment.

But it's pretty amazing, when you think about it, that as recently as 1980 the Lakers could win the world championship and most fans couldn't see it until the wee hours of the morning. And these were two famous teams with plenty of media appeal! You would have thought that a matchup of Dr. J. and his boys against Kareem's team would have rated a prime-time audience. Could anyone imagine a World Series game on tape delay at 11:30 P.M.? The NBA has come a long way, baby.

I've probably watched that tape a thousand times, and it's always in one or another of the VCRs in my house. Normally, I'm very critical of my own play. But I don't have too many complaints about that incredible night in Philadelphia, when, as Pete Vescey cleverly phrased it, I played center "in Lew of Alcindor."

Lionel Hollins, a guard for Philadelphia, paid me the ultimate compliment after the game. "Magic," he said, shaking his head. "He is his name."

CHAPTER 9

BIG FELLA

Of all the exciting things that happened to me when I joined the Lakers, thinking of myself as a teammate of Kareem Abdul-Jabbar was the most amazing. For the first few weeks, I just couldn't get over it: I, Earvin Johnson, twenty years old, from Lansing, Michigan, was actually playing on the same team as Kareem. He was one of the great legends of the game, and he had been one ever since I could remember. He already had an amazing career in the NBA. But when I came along, nobody even imagined that it would continue for another decade.

Kareem *was* the Lakers. He was also the dominant figure in professional basketball. He was so important to the team, to the game, and certainly to me, that I want to tell you all about him. But that won't be easy. In addition to being the most intelligent athlete I've ever known, he's also the most mysterious. I've never fully understood Kareem, and I guess I never will. But maybe that's not surprising for a guy who barely spoke to me during my first five years on his team.

At least I wasn't the only one. When I first came to the Lakers, Kareem was so aloof, so distant, and so completely *different* from the other players that some of the guys referred to him as the "brother from another planet." And these were his teammates! If you were a newcomer, you might as well not exist. You could be standing right in Kareem's face and

123

he wouldn't even acknowledge you. Whenever I was around him, I felt like Casper the Friendly Ghost.

Every rookie is assigned to help out one of the veterans. When I got to training camp I was teamed up with Kareem. I had to make sure that the *Times* and the *Herald-Examiner* were outside his door by 7:00 A.M. Whenever there was a break in the practice, I had to bring him a drink. If Kareem needed something at the store, I was expected to pick it up.

It was a match made in hell—especially for Kareem. I was barely out of my teens, and I showed up in camp lugging a tape player the size of a Volkswagen. That machine had enough switches and gadgets to operate a spaceship. The first time Kareem saw it, he said, "Don't tell me—I bet you can pick up the weather on Mars with that thing. But that's all right. You won't be carrying it when the season starts."

"Why not?" I asked.

"Because your arms will get tired."

He was right about that. A few months later, one of our teammates developed a mysterious sore shoulder. The doctors were stumped, but it was eventually traced to the weight of his boom box. Right after our first road trip, I decided to switch to a smaller model. Score one for the captain.

What really drove Kareem crazy was a tape I used to play over and over by the acid-funk group P-Funk, or Parliament-Funkadelic. Kareem just hated them. He was a serious jazz fan, and he had no use for disco, rhythm and blues, or hard rock. Every time he saw my boom box or heard it from the next room, he made a face. But if he was waiting for me to outgrow that kind of music, he must have been very disappointed.

All the rookies in camp had to get up early so we could get our ankles taped for practice before the veterans came in. One morning on my way to get taped, as I walked past Kareem's door, he came out and yelled, "Earvin! Turn that damn thing down!"

Well, at least he knew my name! But from then on, whenever I passed Kareem's room I turned off the music until I was well out of earshot.

I was Kareem's rookie all through that first year. Whenever we were at the airport, he would ask me to pick him up a hot dog and nachos. I had to make sure the hot dog was all beef, because Kareem is a devout Muslim and won't touch pork. When you're a rookie, one job quickly leads to another. When the other guys see you going over to that dog stand, you might as well get out your pencil and start taking orders.

I knew in advance that Kareem wasn't a guy I would make friends with right away. When I first moved to Los Angeles, everybody had warned me that he never smiled. There had also been some speculation in the press that Cap was going to resent this flashy young rookie. L.A. had been Kareem's town for a long time, and now a new cowboy was coming in.

But that was never a problem. He understood that I wasn't there to win the town. I was just there to win.

And even during the early years, when we had no relationship at all, I never sensed any jealousy from him. Our styles complemented each other, and we worked well together from the start. Unlike many superstars, Kareem never wanted to be treated like a prima donna. He just wanted to be left alone.

The gap between us wasn't personal, because Kareem was distant from everybody. The public saw the mask he wore on the court—the protective goggles that became his trademark. But beneath the goggles was another mask—his face, which rarely showed any emotion. In that respect, the two of us couldn't have been more different.

There was also the age difference. I was only ten when Kareem first came into the NBA. But he had also been famous all through college, and even in high school. I grew up watching him on television with my dad, and I thought of him as one of the gods, up there with Wilt Chamberlain, Oscar Robertson, and Bill Russell. He was a legendary player from another era. And now he was also my teammate.

I was in awe of him. But then, so were guys who had been in the league for years.

Until I played on Kareem's team, I didn't appreciate just how great a player he really was. Everybody knew he had been amazing back in college, and that the NCAA had actually outlawed the dunk for a few years because Kareem was dominating the game. But what I hadn't understood was that this rule had actually backfired. Instead of restricting Kareem, it made him even better. It forced him to develop his other skills—like his all-powerful hook shot.

There was nobody like Kareem—when he wanted to play. What a beautiful basketball player! He could dominate a game almost at will. And when that happened, the rest of us could pretty well stand back and watch the show. Hook shots, blocked shots, rebounds—he did it all.

A lot of people have pointed out that I made his life a little easier, and I'm sure that's true. He's the first to acknowledge that I made it possible for him to play much longer than he had planned. Instead of having to come out to get the ball, he could stay in the low post, where I would hit him for an easy basket. And with both of us playing our game, the Lakers kept winning.

But what often gets overlooked is that Kareem made it easier for me, too. And not just me, but all the Lakers. He was so dangerous inside that our opponents had to double-team him, which, of course, left one of us open for the outside shot. And he was great at getting us the ball. Kareem scored so many baskets that people didn't realize that he was also one of the best passers in the game. Or else he'd force the defense to sag toward the middle, which allowed our guys to blow right by them on the wing.

At first I didn't talk to Kareem on the court, but after a year or two, when the game was close, I could give him a look that said, Okay, Big Fella, quit messing around. There's five minutes left and we need you to take over.

Even after Kareem embraced me as a player, off the court we were practically strangers. During my early years with the Lakers, he was actually closer to my parents than he was to me. I didn't know this at the time, but as soon as I moved to Los Angeles my mother sought him out and asked him to keep an eye on me. It wasn't long before he and Mom had more or less adopted each other, and they talked often on the phone.

He was a great fan of her cooking, especially her sweet-potato pies. Because Mom was a Seventh-Day Adventist, Kareem could be confident that nothing she cooked or baked contained pork. That meant a lot to him, and at one point, when he needed to hire a cook, he called Mom for advice. It wasn't long before Kareem, too, began looking forward to our annual trip to Michigan.

Finally, in the summer of 1984, he let me into his world. The Celtics had just beaten us and won the championship, and I had taken a lot of heat in the media for some bad plays I had made in that series. Kareem called me up to see how I was doing. I was grateful that he cared, but I was shocked to hear from him. Kareem was calling *me*? I was even more surprised when he invited me over to his house in Bel Air. We just started talking—not only about basketball, but about our families, too. From then on, everything was different.

With Kareem, it's not a matter of words. Even when you're his friend, he might not talk to you every day. But once you form that bond, you're his friend for life.

When I first came to the Lakers, I didn't know all the team's traditions. If a few of us were going out for dinner, I might say, "Come on, Cap, why don't you join us?" He usually declined, but sometimes he came along. And he definitely appreciated being asked. He was a loner, and over the years the other guys had stopped inviting him. Now, after a couple of us tried to change that a little, he even went dancing with us a few times. We'd have to encourage him, but he did come.

And he always showed up at team parties. He wouldn't stay very long, and he usually left early. But he always showed up, and that meant a lot.

Among the people he knew and trusted, he might even talk about himself. When his son Amir was born, he brought the baby into the locker room. I had never seen him so joyful before, but he was giggling and laughing and sharing his happiness with the whole team.

I learned a lot just from being his teammate. More than any other player, Kareem taught me what it meant to be a professional. By watching him, I learned how to focus in on the game, how to prepare myself mentally.

He had his own unique way of doing that. Most guys would listen to music in the locker room or watch tapes of the team we were about to play. Kareem would sit there in his underwear and read. He had an incredible ability to shut out all the extraneous noise and music and just concentrate. In the locker room, on a bus, on the plane, or in a hotel lobby, we rarely saw him without a book. He read just about everything—from black history to biography, from Asian history to the novels of Raymond Chandler and Dashiell Hammett. He also wrote two good books of his own—*Giant Steps,* an autobiography, and *Kareem,* a diary of his final season.

Even when he wasn't reading, he had a way of blocking out everything except the game. He would just sit there and concentrate. When that happened, nobody could enter his zone. If you talked to him, there was nobody home. If you called his name, he wouldn't answer. He was off in his own world, getting ready to play basketball.

One time he noticed that I was giving interviews right up until 6:45, which was forty-five minutes before game time and when members of the press had to leave the locker room. "You shouldn't be doing that," he told me. "You need more time to prepare. If you talk to these guys that close to the game, you'll lose your concentration." He was right, and I stopped doing it.

But mostly he taught by example. Twice during our years together Kareem suffered a major personal loss. And yet his teammates couldn't help but notice that he never took out his frustrations on us. And he never allowed his problems to influence his play on the court. Early in 1983, we were playing on the road when the news came in that Kareem's house had burned to the ground. He lost *everything*—his clothes, his photo albums, his trophies, his Oriental rugs, and his enormous collection of jazz albums. He never let us see the hurt and pain he must have felt, but we all knew it was there. He didn't let it affect his game, either.

A couple of years later, he woke up one morning to find that virtually all his money was gone. There had been some big problem with his business manager, and the situation was so bad that it looked like he would have to declare bankruptcy.

Kareem was our leader, and he certainly knew how to take care of himself. We wondered how something like this could happen to him.

That incident had a big effect on me. Later, when we talked about it, he didn't show much anger or bitterness. Instead, he wanted to make sure that nothing like this ever happened to us. Kareem's situation was my wake-up call. That's when I brought in Lon Rosen to handle my business affairs.

Every professional athlete should have learned from Kareem's disaster, but many guys didn't. A lot of players have ended up close to broke when they retired from the game. Some of them never bothered to check on their finances; others just preferred not to know.

When I decided to develop a hook shot, I went straight to Kareem. He was the best in the business. In fact, he had been using the skyhook for so long that some people thought he had invented it. His shot was impossible to block, and people joked that the only way to shut him down was to get up real close and breathe on his goggles.

For as long as anybody could remember, the hook shot had been the major weapon in Kareem's arsenal. By now it was part of his identity. He had perfected it at UCLA during the 1960s, where Coach John Wooden made him shoot it hundreds of times every day. It was also one of the reasons he had stayed in the game so long. Normally, a guy who plays that close to the basket takes a beating every time he puts up the ball. But the skyhook allows you to avoid that contact. And Kareem's agility let him slide away from the two guys who were usually guarding him.

When I first approached him for help with the hook, he looked a little surprised. And no wonder. He had been in the league for about fifteen years, and in all that time nobody had ever come to him to learn it. But he was happy to have a student, and we started working together every day after practice. Kareem would shoot one, and I would have to match it. He showed me that the key to the hook shot was in the release and the follow-through, which had to be the same every time you put it up.

Working with Kareem was like studying with the master. It took a while, but eventually I developed a decent hook shot of my own. I called it the junior, junior skyhook.

If Kareem helped me improve my game, I helped him enjoy his. During his first decade in the league, he never seemed to be very happy on the court. It wasn't easy, but eventually I was able to show him that basketball was fun, and that he could let loose a little.

During my first few years with the Lakers, he didn't want to be involved in any high-fiving. That aloof expression he wore after his game-winning shot in San Diego was typical of the man. Eventually, though, Coop and I helped him realize that he could show his feelings without being embarrassed. After a few years it got to the point where he'd make a great play and his hands would already be out, as if to say, Hey, where *are* you guys?

The best moment of all was the night he shot the three-pointer. We were playing in Phoenix, and there was about a minute left in the first half. Coop missed a jump shot, and the rebound ended up right in front of our bench. Kareem got to it first. Larry Nance, who was guarding him, stayed well back, because if there was ever a sure bet in the NBA, it's that Kareem Abdul-Jabbar would never shoot the ball from downtown. I was taking a breather on the bench, and a couple of us started yelling, "Shoot it, Cap! Shoot it!" Kareem looked at the basket, considered it for a moment, and then reared back and let it fly. The ball went right through the net for the only three-pointer of his entire career.

The moment he hit that shot, Kareem turned from a serious grown-up into a little kid. He was smiling, cheering, and holding up his hands. Suddenly we had a glimpse of the child in him that we had always wanted to see.

The boys on the bench were so excited that we stood up and started dancing. We could see how happy he was, and that made *us* happy. Sometimes in practice Kareem would fool around with a long jumper, but he had never done anything like this during a game. I bet it was his longtime secret fantasy to go out there just once and hit the long bomb.

But that was Kareem. Just when you thought you had him figured out at least a little, he'd do something you never expected. In the spring of 1985 we were playing Denver in the Western Conference Finals. We had won the opener, but in the second game they were beating us badly. We were down by something like 20 points in the fourth quarter when I went in for a lay-up. I made the shot, but Danny Schayes hit me on the head with his elbow. Denver had been roughing us up all game, and I was mad. "Don't do that again!" I yelled at him. He yelled something back, and soon we were jawing at each other.

Suddenly Kareem appeared out of nowhere and tackled Danny, getting him in a headlock and wrestling him to the floor. "Don't say another word," Kareem warned him, "or I'll gouge your eyes out."

Danny cried to the press, and when the series moved on to Denver, the fans booed Kareem every time he touched the ball. But the more they booed, the harder Kareem played. I had seen him dominate a lot of games, but this was something else. He was shooting left-handed, right-handed, hook shots, jump shots, and dunks. He was blocking shots. And every time he did something, he'd yell to the crowd: "Booing me, huh? Take *this*, then." And after he scored: "I don't hear any booing *now.*" He kept turning around and talking to all sections of the arena, and he put on a hell of a show.

All of this was completely out of character, but that's Kareem.

After we became friends, we could say almost anything to each other. I even told him about the time I'd asked for his autograph in Cobo Arena when I was a kid, and how he had brushed right past me without even making eye contact. After all these years, he was still doing that to people.

"You know," I told him, "you could be a lot nicer to the fans. It wouldn't cost you anything. Even if you can't sign every autograph, you can acknowledge people, or just say hi. The autograph itself isn't that important. It's the contact. Whatever happens during those five seconds is what the other person will remember for the rest of their life."

I don't give autographs every time I'm asked, especially when I'm on vacation. But whenever I say no, I try to do it nicely. A smile, a word, a high five—these little things make people feel good.

I also suggested to Kareem that he might pay a little more attention to the people we saw every night in the Forum— not just the fans, but the ball boys, ushers, and vendors. I always said hello to the ushers, and I could see they appreciated it. Nobody's asking you to be close friends with them, I said. But to know somebody's name, and to acknowledge their existence—that's all most people want.

People don't change overnight, but Kareem did warm up a little. And he certainly surprised a lot of fans when he appeared in the movie *Airplane!* There's a scene where Kareem is the co-pilot, and a young boy comes into the cockpit and recognizes him. Then the kid lets him have it: "My dad says you don't work hard enough on defense and he says that, lot of times, you don't even run downcourt and that you don't really try, except during the playoffs."

In the movie, Kareem blows his stack. He grabs the kid by the neck and says, "The hell I don't. Listen kid, I've been hearing that crap ever since I was at UCLA: I'm out there busting my buns every night. Tell your old man to drag Walton and Lanier up and down the court for 48 minutes!"

A lot of people saw that movie, and it certainly didn't hurt

Kareem's image to appear in a goofy comedy—and to show some emotion.

But when it came to his dealing with the media, I could only sit back and shake my head. Back in New York, his high school coach had kept him away from the press. So had John Wooden at UCLA. To Kareem, reporters were, depending on his mood, either flies or buzzards. He tried to avoid them whenever he could. If a reporter got him mad, he would never speak to the guy again. But that wasn't much of a punishment, really, because he didn't speak to most of the press anyway.

Coop and I would be sitting in the locker room, right across from Kareem, when some innocent young writer from another city would start walking toward him. Cap was usually engrossed in a book. Coop and I would look at each other.

"What do you think?" one of us would ask the other. "One or none?" We were betting on how many words Kareem would say to the guy.

The reporter would go up to Cap and say, "Excuse me, Kareem, could I get an interview with you?"

Kareem wouldn't even raise his head.

Sometimes the reporter would put his hand on Kareem. Big mistake. Kareem would look up with those eyes. His book wouldn't move, but his face would. He'd look right *through* the guy. The next thing you'd see was the reporter backing up in fear.

There were other times when Kareem was positively effusive. He'd look at the guy and actually say, "No." It all depended on his mood.

When he had no choice and had to do an interview, he'd drive the network guys crazy: They'd ask a series of questions and he'd give them a string of one-word answers. They hated it even more a few minutes later, when they'd see Kareem talking to some TV crew from Yugoslavia, holding forth in great detail about his childhood, his religious development, and his philosophy of basketball.

Once, when he was forced to be on the radio, the technician attached a little microphone to his shirt. Another big mistake. Kareem read a newspaper during the entire conversation, and practically all you could hear was the loud rustling of paper.

He didn't talk all that much when the team was together. But whenever he did, I always paid attention. He's sophisticated and worldly, and he pays attention to the news. If two guys were arguing about some political event that happened twenty years before, Kareem would always know who had said what, and when, and what it all meant.

He had a strong sense of history, although he rarely spoke about his own militant past. Young people who followed him in his final years as a player might not even know how controversial he used to be, especially when he became a Muslim and changed his name. But his past was private. He rarely mentioned it.

Kareem grew up in New York as an only child, and he was still close to his parents. But he was so tall as a youngster that he lost his privacy very early. Maybe that's why as an adult he worked so hard to get it back.

The public saw Kareem as sullen, closed, and detached, and usually he was. Although it's hard to believe, he was also the Lakers' number one practical joker—but some of his jokes weren't all that funny.

When Larry Spriggs and Mike McGee wore the same blue silk shirt one night, Kareem snuck back into the locker room during warm-ups and switched them. Larry was a lot bigger than Mike, and Kareem laughed his head off as Larry got dressed. Sometimes he would hide your shoe, which could be incredibly annoying. Or he'd come out of the shower before anybody else and switch people's underwear.

But his nastiest tricks were on the road. If you were sleeping on the plane and your mouth was open, Kareem would fill it with paper. One writer had a ponytail—until Kareem walked up to him on the bus one day and cut it off. Once, when he was mad at Coop, he took some hair remover and rubbed it on Michael's head. The bald spot is still there. Coop was furious, and he planned to get back at Kareem by pouring some India ink on Kareem's bald head—until a couple of us convinced him that maybe this wasn't such a great idea after all.

Kareem could read lips. He was also a gifted pickpocket. Most of the time, he picked on the same victim—Byron Scott. Byron was a dapper dresser who used to wear a pocket handkerchief, but Kareem stole so many of them that Byron gave it up. One time Kareem got a key to Byron's hotel room, stole his pants, and left them on the bus next to Byron's regular seat. We carried pouches instead of wallets, and Kareem loved to steal your pouch and watch you sweat. We were boarding a bus at some airport when poor Mike McGee had to run all the way back to the plane because he was sure he had left his pouch there. Kareem had it all along.

When Brad Holland was a rookie, we were at a morning shootaround when a pair of women's panties fell out of the leg of his sweatpants. His wife had done the wash the day before, and her underwear had gotten tangled up in his pants.

When Kareem saw the panties lying on the floor, he got this crazy look in his eye. "Hey, where did *these* come from?" he asked loudly. Brad was totally embarrassed, but when he tried to grab the panties, Kareem pulled them away. Then Cap put them on his head like a face mask, and continued practicing. Poor Brad was hiding his face in his hands. He was an innocent, clean-cut kid who had just come out of UCLA. Kareem was usually nice to him, but that morning, Cap was having the time of his life. "She smells *good,* Brad," Kareem said as he danced around the court. This went on for a good five minutes, and nobody who was at that practice will ever forget it.

Or you'd be sitting there peacefully, reading a newspaper, and suddenly Kareem would sneak up on you and give it a sharp karate chop. To be fair, he wasn't the only one; Coop and Byron did the same thing. Believe me, there's nothing like sitting there quietly at six in the morning, waiting for the airport bus and reading about last night's game, when suddenly, *snap!* If the paper was torn all the way through, it was considered a home run.

We finally got back at Cap on the day he retired, Sunday, April 23, 1989. It was the last game of the regular season, and Kareem was saying good-bye to the fans at the Forum. His parents were introduced, his son Amir sang the national anthem, and when the Lakers came out on the court, we were all wearing goggles. With two minutes left in the game, Kareem scored his final two points when I passed him the ball and he dunked it.

Kareem received several gifts that day, including a beautiful white Rolls-Royce from his teammates and coaches. Nothing like that had ever been done before. But then, nobody like Kareem had ever existed before, either. The car was Pat Riley's idea, and everybody on the team made a generous contribution. "Since you've been carrying *us* on your back for all these years," I told him at the presentation, "we decided to get you something that would carry *you.*"

It wasn't cheap, but we all knew how much Kareem had done for us over the years. We also knew how much extra money he had put in our pockets because of all those playoff victories.

After all the hoopla, Kareem was the last one out of the shower. Meanwhile, Gary Vitti, our trainer, brought out twelve pairs of scissors so we could go to work on Kareem's jeans. He had come to the Forum in his favorite ones, an old pair of bell bottoms from the early seventies. Not only was it time to put those jeans to sleep, it was also payback time for all the pranks that Kareem had pulled on us.

It says a lot about Kareem's mystique that a couple of our guys were afraid to pick up the scissors. But this could only work as a team effort. "We need everybody's participation," I announced. "Anybody who doesn't help out won't get his share of the playoff money." Then we cut those old jeans into shreds.

Some guys can dish it out better than they can take it. When Kareem saw what had happened to his jeans, he was really mad. He tried to laugh about it, but you could see he was burning. Never mind that we had bought him a new

Rolls-Royce and had paid for it out of our own pockets. Kareem was pissed, and he had to go home in his warm-ups.

Just about everywhere we went during that 1988–89 season, there was a special farewell for Kareem. The ceremony in New York was particularly moving, because Kareem had grown up there. Seven of his high school teammates were on hand from his days at Power Memorial in Manhattan, and they presented Kareem with a stat sheet from one of their games, back when he was still Lew Alcindor.

Then it was time to play ball. The Knicks were tough that night, but after such an emotional ceremony we just couldn't allow Kareem to lose this game. We were down by one when the fourth quarter started. The crowd was chanting, "Beat L.A." Then Coop said to me, "Okay, Buck, time to go to work." I hit a few hoops, and set up a few more. That was enough, and we came out of there with a win. It was my first triple-double of the season.

Largely because of Kareem, I had the joy of playing on one of the great winning teams in the history of basketball. I was accustomed to winning even before I came into the NBA. But I was also used to being the main man. And that change took a little getting used to.

When I first arrived, the Lakers consisted of Kareem and eleven other guys. I accepted that, and I never tried to rock the boat. But because of Kareem, I could never really let loose on the court. I always knew I was capable of more, and sometimes I was frustrated because I *knew* I was a better player than I was able to demonstrate. That's what Larry Bird had over me—that some people thought I couldn't score and couldn't shoot. I could do both, of course. But on the Lakers, shooting and scoring weren't my role.

We were successful because each of us knew and accepted his job on the team. Mine was to feed the other shooters—especially Kareem, but also Jamaal Wilkes, Norm Nixon, and, later, James Worthy. For everything to click, I had to take a backseat and play at a level that was slightly below my talent.

It's not that I felt unappreciated—not at all. I kept making the All-Star team, and fans all over the country were singing my praises. As for my ego, that was satisfied in the best possible way—by winning. Wherever we went, people said, "Here come the Lakers. They're the champs." I loved hearing that, and winning had always come first.

Even so, I wasn't playing the way I had, for example, in that championship game in Philadelphia when Kareem was injured. The fans and the sportswriters didn't know the full story. They hadn't seen me at my best. "Just wait," I used to say. "Someday you'll see the *real* Magic Johnson."

Whenever I talked that way, people just smiled. There's a lot of bragging in the NBA, and they probably thought I was shooting my mouth off. But I always knew that eventually my turn would come; I just assumed it would happen after Kareem retired.

As things turned out, I didn't have to wait that long.

In 1986, the Lakers finished the season with a record of 62-20. That was a great start, but we were only warming up. As always, we came into the playoffs with high hopes and expectations. For five of the previous six years we had gone all the way to the championship series. In 1980, and again in 1982, we had defeated Philadelphia to win the title. We had lost to Boston in 1984, but the following year we came back to beat them. Now, as the defending champions, we were looking forward to another title series against the Celtics.

As everyone expected, we breezed past San Antonio and Dallas in the first two rounds. Then came Houston. The winner of this series would advance to the finals. It looked like a third-consecutive Celtics-Lakers series was just around the corner.

We won the opening game in the Forum. But Houston shocked us by winning the next four to take the series. The Rockets, with their "twin towers" offense of Ralph Sampson (seven feet four) and Hakeem Olajuwon (seven feet), were simply more than we could handle. The two of them closed down the middle against Kareem and James Worthy, and our outside game wasn't strong enough to beat them.

We could see that our offense had become too predictable, and that the time had come to shake things up. That summer, Coach Riley sent me a letter, saying he wanted me to become more of a scoring threat. When I read these words, I practically jumped out of the room. Yes! Now I could play *my* game. But before I allowed myself to get too excited, I wondered how Kareem would accept this change.

Kareem had just completed his seventeenth season in the NBA. During every one of those seasons, his team's offense had been built around him. Before that, the same thing had been true in college and high school. In the entire history of basketball, no one player had ever dominated for that long.

In the fall, when we started training camp, Riley told me again that he was planning a more balanced offense that would rely on all five players. And he repeated that he had a special role in mind for me. "It's time the Lakers became your team," he said. "We need you to start scoring more."

"I'm ready, Coach," I told him. "But have you talked to the Big Fella about this?"

"Not yet," he said. "But I will."

"Well, let's wait until then," I said. "Because I don't want any problems."

It's not that Kareem had an unusually large ego, or that I expected him to object. But all good athletes have a lot of pride. I wanted to avoid doing any damage to my relationship with Kareem or the unity of our team. We were having one great season after another, and I didn't want to screw that up.

It wasn't just Kareem I was concerned about. For seven years I had been the setup man, getting the ball to the other players so they could score. If my role was going to change, that would affect everybody.

The next day, Riley told me that Kareem and James Worthy had both agreed to the new plan. But I felt a lot better when Kareem came over to me and said, "Okay, Buck, it's all yours." Then I felt free to go out there and play the way I'd always wanted to.

But it's hard to change old habits, and it didn't happen all at once. I was still holding back a little when, in late December, Kareem was forced to miss three games. Then I went to town. I scored 34 against Dallas, 38 against Houston, and a career-high 46 against Sacramento. In my first seven seasons, I had scored 40 points or more only twice. In 1986–87, I hit that mark in three different games. Not only was I hitting more shots from outside, but, more than ever before, I was also taking the ball to the basket.

That season is still my best as a pro. It was also the most fun I've ever had in the NBA. I averaged close to 24 points a game, which was five points higher than my previous average. It was hard to get used to looking for my own shot instead of taking it as a last resort. But after seven years of shooting well in practice, I was certainly prepared. I was also able to increase my assists, rebounds, steals, and blocked shots.

I couldn't have done this without Kareem's support. He was great about the team's new look. And he may have been relieved that he no longer had to carry us on his back. He became less dominant, but he still drew the double team inside, which now helped us more than ever. Some big men can't bring themselves to pass the ball back out, but Kareem did it often and easily. With less pressure on him, he started having more fun. And that loosened everybody up.

In addition to becoming the go-to guy, I took more of a leadership role on the team. I started talking more on the court, encouraging guys, and yelling at them when it was called for. This, too, came naturally to me, but I had held back as long as Kareem was running the show.

At the end of the 1986–87 season, I received the one prize that had always eluded me—the MVP. It felt so good to win it, because finally, after all these years, I had been able to show my best stuff. Now everybody knew what kind of player I was, and what I might have been able to accomplish under different circumstances.

And the Lakers didn't do too badly, either. The team was more balanced and less predictable than ever. We finished the season with 65 wins. And we beat Boston in six games to win another title.

Kareem was his own man, and he didn't always appreciate Pat Riley's coaching style. The two of them got along on the surface, but you could feel the tension between them. I always had the sense that Kareem hadn't respected Pat during the brief period when they were teammates in the mid-1970s. But the problem might have gone back farther, because Riley loved to remind Kareem that his team had beaten Kareem's in high school.

Whatever it was, Riley always dealt with Kareem separately from the rest of us. And Cap made it clear that he didn't have much use for Riley's motivational techniques. With most of us, Riley was very effective, but Kareem always thought of it as manipulation. He was against the whole idea of being motivated, because he motivated himself. When he wanted to. He decided when it was time to play, and when it wasn't.

Basketball was never Kareem's life the way it was with the rest of us. To him it was a job; he had all sorts of other interests, including literature, music, politics, art, and religion. He never took the game home with him. When he wanted to dominate, he usually would. But when he was tired or bored or didn't feel like working hard, his teammates had to pick up the slack.

It was depressing to see his powers decline. He had such a long career, and he had stayed on top for so long. He's a proud man, and that's what he was playing on in the end—pride. When a new center came into the league, Kareem, in his own quiet way, made sure the guy knew who was still king of the mountain. Even when Kareem was well past his prime, he would still shoot down every new gunslinger who came into town. He never bragged, but he let you know in other ways that he was the man.

If his decline was hard on us, it had to be much harder on him. When he finally left the game, there was no question that an era had ended. Today, a team doesn't need a great center. Guys like Larry Bird, Michael Jordan, and me have changed the game. These days it's possible to dominate from anywhere on the court.

In the end Kareem was like an old lion. He rested a lot, but every now and then he would show you a flash of his former self. And if you didn't leave him alone when he wanted some peace, you'd get swatted.

But even when he was well past his prime, Kareem was still a major force on the team. In 1984, when Elvin Hayes retired, Kareem became the oldest player in the league. By the time he retired in 1989, he was no longer a factor in every game, and we were usually able to win without him. But there was no way we could have won championships without him. During Kareem's last five years in the NBA the Lakers won three world championships, including two consecutive titles. He was a genius at conserving his energy and then elevating his game by another notch or two in the spring, when it was pressure time.

In a sport where most players last only a few years, it's hard to conceive of what it means to stay around for twenty seasons, or to score in double figures in 787 straight games. In the spring of 1984, Kareem was closing in on the all-time scoring record of 31,419 points that had been held since 1973 by Wilt Chamberlain. He finally broke it in a game against the Utah Jazz. We were in Las Vegas, where the Jazz played some of their home games. I had already told the guys that I intended to throw the pass that allowed Kareem to break the record. "Does everybody understand?" I said. "Nobody is throwing him that ball but *me.*"

The tension was building. Every time Kareem hit another one, the crowd would explode. Finally there was just one basket left. During a time-out, Coach Riley drew up a play for him. I had the ball outside. I passed it in to Kareem in the low post just the way he liked it. "Throw it up where he lives," assistant coach Bill Berkta had told me years ago. I usually did, because nobody else could reach it.

Kareem faked a couple of times and then spun around for a fifteen-foot skyhook. When he hit it, the whole place went wild. The officials stopped the game and gave him the ball. His parents came onto the court. We were all so happy for him—especially with the devastating fire still fresh in our minds, and everything we had gone through together. After the game, the whole team went out and partied in his honor. I don't know how Kareem celebrated, or even if. As usual, he stayed in the hotel.

Years later, somebody pointed out that Kareem's record-breaking basket wasn't 100 percent legal. Apparently the guy who threw him that pass was so excited that he had forgotten to check in at the scorer's table before coming into the game. I can understand why.

CHAPTER 10

Sophomore Blues

My second season with the Lakers was the worst year I've ever had in basketball. And the first couple of months of the following season were even worse. It all started when I got injured early in my second season. This turned out to be as difficult emotionally as it was physically. Then, when I finally came back in late February, there was terrible tension on the team. On top of all that, early in my third year, I found myself in the middle of a huge public controversy, where everybody saw me as the villain. That's a lot of baggage for a young player to carry, and there were times when I wondered how long I was going to last in the NBA.

When the Lakers won the championship in my rookie year, our next goal was obvious—to do it all over again. We did win a second title, but it took a year longer than we wanted. And for me in particular, the road to that next title was very, very difficult.

The injury happened in November. We were playing in Atlanta, and Tom Burleson, the Hawks' seven-foot-two-inch center, fell on me as we were both going after a loose ball. Burleson was wearing a big iron knee brace, which banged into my left knee. It hurt pretty bad when I got up, but there didn't seem to be anything wrong, so I kept playing.

A few nights later I collided with Tom LaGarde of Dallas, and the next day my left knee was stiff. The team doctor, Dr. Kerlan, looked at it and found no damage. But the following night, when we played Kansas City in the Forum, I heard something snap. This time I couldn't even get up, and I had to come out of the game.

I didn't know what it was, but it hurt like hell. I prayed that it was nothing more than a sprain, like the one I had had early in my rookie year. But the arthrogram exam showed torn cartilage. (Today they would have used an MRI.) I needed an operation right away to repair the knee.

I was devastated. "But it could have been worse," Dr. Kerlan said. "At least you didn't tear a ligament. I'm sure we'll have you back in time for the playoffs."

The *playoffs*? We were still in November!

This was my worst nightmare. I had been playing ball my whole life, but I had never been seriously hurt before. It's amazing when I think about it, but until I got to the NBA, I had never missed a single game because of an injury—not even that time I sprained my ankle in Jenison Field House against Ohio State. Until I joined the Lakers, the only time I'd had to sit one out was after my run-in with Mrs. Dart back in the fifth grade.

My parents flew out to be with me in the hospital, and to help me after the operation. As soon as it was over, the doctors wanted me up and walking again to get the blood circulating in my leg. I put my right leg down, and then slowly, carefully, I started to move my left leg, which was now in an enormous cast. When I stood up, I was sweating like crazy. Then I fainted. They put me back in the bed, and we tried again the next day. It wasn't until the third day that I could finally stand up.

It was awful. I hate losing, and I was losing big time with this.

The cast stayed on about three weeks, and I hobbled around on crutches. I went to the Forum to watch our home games, but I couldn't travel with the team because I had to be at the hospital twice a day, six days a week, for physical therapy. Even before they took off the cast I was doing special toe exercises to keep the blood moving. All the exercises were painful, and I was so down about the injury that I often found it hard to get motivated.

When they finally took off the cast, my left leg was all shriveled and weak. The muscles had deteriorated, and I had to work incredibly hard to build up my strength again. The pain was terrible. I kept trying to focus on the image of myself back in uniform. But that seemed so far away.

The hardest part was being alone. It had taken a while, but I had finally started to feel at home with the guys. And now, suddenly, all that was gone. I no longer felt a part of the team. When I watched the Lakers play at the Forum or on television, it just tore me up that I couldn't be out there on the court. I'd see a loose ball or an open shot, and I'd think, I could have had that!

But even more than missing basketball, I missed being around the guys: singing on the bus, jiving in the locker room, kidding around on the plane, working together in practice, watching tapes of our opponents. Giving up all that was incredibly difficult.

You take so much for granted when you're healthy. And when you're playing in the NBA, you don't even realize how busy you are. Maybe it's because so much of your time is regulated. At almost every moment, you know where you're supposed to be: at practice, getting ready for a game, taking a nap, on the bus, on the plane, at the hotel.

Now I had all this free time that I didn't want. And it was passing so *slowly*. I had nowhere to go and no way to release my frustration. I could work out with weights, but that was about it. No running, no shooting, and certainly no basketball.

Everybody kept telling me not to worry, but I worried anyway. I expected my leg would get better with time. But how could I be sure it would heal completely? And when I finally came back, would I ever be as good as I once was? I had been having a great season when I went down, averaging 21.4 points a game. Not too shabby for a point guard whose main role was passing the ball, and who had averaged 18 his rookie year. I was also leading the league in assists and steals, and had more rebounds than any other guard.

Questions, doubts, and more questions. Would I be able to continue at the same pace when I came back? And how could I be sure I wouldn't hurt myself all over again? How long would my knee hold out? Another year? Three years? Five?

In my darkest moments, I wondered what would happen if I couldn't come back at all. What if I turned out to be one of those guys who played in the NBA for just one season? In that case, maybe I should be thankful that my rookie year had ended on such a high. But I didn't *feel* thankful. I felt ripped off. And very angry.

That was my biggest fear—that I'd never play again. After a few weeks of staying home all day, I was feeling pretty sorry for myself. Coop came to see me, and he reminded me that he had gone through the same thing two years earlier. That helped a little.

For the first few weeks, all I did was sit around the apartment and watch TV. I knew the schedule by heart. *Ironside* was on at 2:00. At 3:00 there was *The Wild Wild World of Animals*. Then came *Barnaby Jones* at 3:30, and *M*A*S*H* at 4:30. The Scooby Doo show came on at 5:00. Then *All in the Family* at 5:30. At 6:00 was the news, and then another episode of *M*A*S*H* at 6:30.

It may not sound that bad, but believe me, for an athlete this was hell. I'd never been the type to lie around the house all day, and there were times when I just wanted to put my fist through the wall. At least I could travel, and I spent a lot of my recovery back in Lansing with my parents. But I still shudder when I think about that awful winter. It's the most down I've ever been.

Being injured really opened my eyes. Now, for the first time, I felt vulnerable. I began to understand that all the good things that had come my way could just as easily disappear. One minute you're the hottest property in basketball, the next you're wearing a cast and watching TV all day. Although I was still new in the NBA, I realized that sooner or later the day would come when I could no longer play. For the rest of my career, no matter how strong I was feeling, I always reminded myself that I was only one knee injury away from retirement.

As soon as I was allowed to practice again, I worked my butt off on drills. Pat Riley, our assistant coach at the time, volunteered to help me out. He worked me hard on just about everything—wind sprints, sliding drills, rebounds, dunks. There were times when I hated his guts, but I kept working.

Dr. Kerlan said I could start playing again on February 20. That was earlier than I expected, and I was thrilled. But Jerry Buss was so worried about me, and so afraid that I'd come back too early, that he was even more conservative than the doctors. "Convince me," he said. "Show me beyond a shadow of a doubt that Earvin is ready, and then I'll consider it." They compromised—I came back a week later than planned.

It wasn't an easy adjustment. I had missed 45 consecutive games, the equivalent of one and a half college seasons. And while I was gone, everybody had had plenty of time to get used to the team's new configuration. My teammates were doing fine without me, winning most of their games. Now that I was coming back, a couple of players would have to cut down on their minutes and take lesser roles. The guy most affected was Norm Nixon, who had been the starting point guard during my absence. He was having a good season and didn't see why he should have to step aside just because I was ready to come back.

The media was making a huge fuss over me, and several of the guys apparently resented this as well. And no wonder: I was getting more attention for being injured than my teammates were for winning. Ten games before I was due to come back, the Laker organization started a big countdown to my return. The night I finally played, there was a huge welcome-back ceremony, with tons of media and a huge swarm of photographers. There were T-shirts and buttons saying THE MAGIC IS BACK. And all over town you could see my face looking down from big billboards advertising 7UP. I was so anxious about coming back that I wasn't even aware of how my teammates were feeling about all of this hype.

Before the game, Coach Westhead took me aside and said, "There's a Spanish word for what I want you to be tonight. *Suave, suave.* Easy, easy. Take it easy tonight, okay?"

Sure, Coach. But I had my usual opening-night jitters. The first time I touched the ball, I made a great pass—right to Maurice Lucas of New Jersey. Then I missed my first two shots. Things did improve a little in the second quarter. I played decently, and, most important, my knee felt fine.

But I had lost a lot of confidence during the long layoff. And for a long time after I returned, I still held back. I didn't play my usual aggressive style, and I was afraid to explode to the basket. All I could think about was protecting my knee from another injury. We made it to the playoffs, which began with a best-of-three miniseries against Houston. But that's as far as we got. Although we won the first game, Houston took the next two. Moses Malone was at his peak, and he just destroyed Kareem on the boards.

I played terribly, especially in the deciding game. With about fifteen seconds left, Houston was ahead by one. I brought the ball down-court. As you would expect, the play was designed to get the ball to Kareem. But I couldn't find an opening, so I started driving to the hoop. Then I ran into Malone. I put up a shot that could have won the game. It missed. Completely. Air ball. Malone caught it, Houston scored, and we lost by three. End of season. Only a year after we had beaten Philadelphia for the title, Houston sent us home for a longer-than-usual summer.

That was probably the worst game of my career. I took only 13 shots, and I missed 11 of them. But the worst part of all was that last shot. I was trying to be the hero and ended up the goat.

The Rockets, who had finished the regular season with a mediocre record of 40-42, didn't stop there. They went on to beat San Antonio in seven games, and Kansas City in five. But even Moses couldn't take his people to the promised land. Boston won the 1981 title in six games.

Meanwhile, the resentment had built among my teammates. By the time the playoffs had started, Norm Nixon and I were having a quarrel in the papers.

A lot of it was my fault. People were grumbling, but I shouldn't have responded in the press. Reporters love feuds, and their stories help keep the trouble going. I should have kept my feelings to myself, or shared them only with Norm.

We were friends, after all, and I owed him a lot. During my rookie year, Norm had taken me under his wing. When the team was on the road, I'd often be sitting alone in my hotel room, not knowing what to do or where to go in Cleveland or San Antonio or Portland, when Norm would knock on my door and say, "Come on out with me, Buck, it's time for dinner." He was a friend when I needed one.

In my rookie year, Norm and I were the starting guards. We didn't really establish which one of us was the point guard, because our team offense was geared to whichever guy had the ball. Until I was injured, everything had worked fine.

But when it became Norm's show again, he felt he wasn't getting the respect he deserved. Kareem, Jamaal Wilkes, and I were getting all the publicity. And when Michael came off the bench, the crowd would start hollering, *"Coop, Coop, Coop!"* Norm missed being the main man, the way he'd been before I came along.

"I'm not one of the chosen people," the paper quoted him as saying after my return. "I thought Magic would come in and have to adjust to our game, but we had to adjust to his."

I should have let it go. But during the playoffs I told Rich Levin of the *Herald-Examiner* that some of my teammates were ungrateful, that they were jealous of my commercial endorsements. Maybe it was true, but that doesn't mean I was right to say it.

As soon as the season was over, Jerry Buss asked me to ride down with him to Palm Springs. He was angry at the media for focusing on the tension between Norm and me, and he wanted my take on the situation. "What about you and Norm?'' he asked. "Is this something you two can work out, or should we be thinking about a trade?''

"I know we can get along,'' I replied. "We just need to talk it out.''

The following week, Jerry met with both of us in Las Vegas. Normally an owner doesn't get involved in this sort of thing, but Jerry has always put a premium on team harmony. It felt like Norm and I were brothers who were going through a bad spell, and Jerry was our dad.

I told them both exactly what I thought: that Norm and I were the best guard combination in the league, that we could work out our problems, and that the best thing Jerry could do for the team was to keep both of us. He did, and the following year Norm and I even played together on the All-Star team. Norm spent another two years with the Lakers. Then he was traded to the San Diego Clippers, where he finished out his career.

Norm and I stayed friends, even after the problem between us. But things were never quite as smooth between us as they'd been when I was a rookie.

It wasn't until the summer that I finally felt like my old self. As usual, I went back to Lansing, where I kept in shape by playing in pickup games at Jenison Field House. In one of those games, as I was driving to the basket, the guy defending me was giving me the lane and his eyes were telling me to come on in, so I drove to the hoop, jumped off my left leg, and dunked it on him.

Yes! This was the moment. Suddenly I just knew I was all right again.

I only wished it had happened a month earlier.

Since the end of my rookie year, Jerry Buss had wanted to extend my contract. He had already done that with some of the other players, and all during the time I was injured he was working with my agents to come up with a new deal. In the summer of 1981 he offered me what was then the longest and most lucrative contract in the history of sports: twenty-five years, $25 million.

Obviously, this deal would extend well beyond my playing days. Jerry explained that he wanted me to have a good income even after I retired. He also wanted to guarantee me a job with the Lakers. It was a very generous contract, although it has since been renegotiated more than once.

The terms of the deal leaked out, as these things always do, and some of my teammates were unhappy. Nobody, not even Kareem, had ever had a twenty-five-year contract. So what did this mean? Was I now part of management? Kareem asked for a meeting with Jerry. I've always assumed that he wanted to know if I was now making more money than he was.

He had nothing to worry about. As long as Kareem was around, it was understood that he would be the highest-paid player on the team. In fact, one of the first things Jerry Buss had done when he came in was improve Kareem's contract.

The biggest problem arising from my contract didn't come from my teammates, however; it came early the next season, when I found myself in the middle of a nasty dispute. The media and much of the public thought I was wrong, and they blamed it on that long-term, big-money deal.

First, some background. When I came to the Lakers in 1979, our coach was Jack McKinney. I liked Jack and learned a lot from him, especially in adapting to the NBA's style of one-on-one defense. He also worked with me to improve my passing. Back in college I had sometimes thrown lazy passes, but that didn't work in the NBA. McKinney got me to put a little more zip on the ball, which made my passes more difficult to intercept.

Thirteen games into my rookie season, I was at home in my apartment when the news flashed across the television that Coach McKinney had been badly hurt in a bicycle accident. He was on his way to play tennis with Paul Westhead, his assistant, when something went wrong with his bike as he was going down a hill. When we showed up at the shootaround the next day, we were told that Westhead would take over as coach.

For *his* assistant, Westhead chose Pat Riley, the color commentator for the Lakers' radio and TV broadcasts. Riley wasn't sure he was cut out for coaching, but he decided to give it a try. If this didn't work out, he could always go back to broadcasting.

In his first year as a coach, Westhead basically threw out the ball and said, "Play." He stuck with McKinney's system, which involved plenty of running and a great motion offense. We were running the fast break, although not as much as we would later, under Pat Riley. We played well enough that year under Westhead to win the title.

A lot of NBA coaches are former players, which gives them a certain advantage in talking to the guys. Paul Westhead was a former English professor who'd specialized in Shakespeare. He had coached at La Salle College before coming to the Lakers, but he didn't have much experience in the pros. Although he tried to motivate us, he wasn't a very good communicator. He spoke in such a complicated manner that there were times when nobody really understood what he was talking about.

At one point during Westhead's first season with the Lakers, we were down by a point or two with just a few seconds left. During the time-out he looked at me and recited a line from *Macbeth*: "If it were done when 'tis done, then 'twere well / It were done quickly."

Say *what*? But we had been here before, so I made an educated guess: "Coach, are you saying that you want me to get it in to the Big Fella?"

He nodded. While Westhead didn't usually go around quoting Shakespeare, there were plenty of times when we didn't have a clue as to what he was saying.

But the problem wasn't Paul Westhead's language. The problem was that he violated one of the fundamental rules of sports, politics, business, and just about everything else: If it ain't broke, don't fix it.

Westhead kept us loose and improvising for two seasons. But when we arrived at training camp before the 1981–82 season, he introduced a whole new system. Instead of having us run, he moved us into a planned-out, deliberate, half-court offense. Our whole game was now predicated on getting the ball to Kareem, while the other four guys were supposed to stay in specific areas of the floor. As systems go, it wasn't bad. But it wasn't Laker basketball, and it definitely wasn't a good use of our talent. Instead of Showtime, he gave us *Slow*time.

Back when McKinney was our coach, Kareem had been more than a scorer; he was also an effective decoy. Whenever he was double-teamed, which was most of the time, we would think about other scoring options. First we'd look for Jamaal Wilkes to take a jumper. If Silk was tied up, we'd set a screen for Norm Nixon. And if that didn't work, we'd get the ball in to Kareem in the low post.

Westhead wanted us to go to Kareem first. But when you start doing that, it doesn't take long before everyone in the building knows what to expect. Under Westhead we became predictable.

The key to winning basketball lies in *not* being predictable. The trick is to score easy baskets whenever you can. The lay-up is a high-percentage shot, and the fast break is what gets you there. Sometimes the half-court game is necessary, especially if you don't have a running team. But in most cases, it shouldn't be your first choice. It can easily lead to a mechanical game that isn't very effective—or fun.

Westhead's new system had a major impact on the team's morale. Now there were fewer high fives and less camaraderie. Previously, we had been five guys running all over the court. Now we were four guys looking to pass in to one. The ball moved, but the bodies didn't.

A lot of us were upset, but nobody wanted to complain. Kareem, loyal to Westhead, didn't see a problem; he was getting the ball and dominating more than ever.

We had plenty of talent, but we weren't blowing teams out. And we certainly weren't taking advantage of our strengths.

Even my dad was upset. He watched all the Laker games on a satellite dish hookup back in Lansing, and he would call me to complain. "How come you guys aren't running?" he'd say. "This isn't the team I know."

When Westhead put in his new system, the Lakers got off to a terrible start. We lost four of our first six games, including a blowout against San Antonio. With most teams, a 2-4 record means only that you got off to a bad start. But when the Lakers open that way, you know something is wrong.

I tried to tell Westhead that I thought he was on the wrong track, but he didn't want to hear it. When he told me I wasn't getting enough rebounds, I asked him how he expected me to do that when he had me playing thirty feet from the basket.

The situation came to a head in Utah on November 18. We were in a huddle during a time-out when I asked for water.

"Earvin, shut up!" he said. "Get your ass in this huddle and pay attention!"

"I *am* paying attention," I said.

"You should be looking at *me*," he said.

I held my temper.

Right after the game he pulled me into a little equipment area just down the hall from the locker room. Both of us were pissed.

"I'm tired of your horseshit attitude," he said. "And I'm not going to put up with it anymore. Either you start listening to me, or you don't have to play."

"I'm tired of it, too," I said. "So maybe you shouldn't play me at all. I'm not doing much anyway, so why don't you send me somewhere else?"

This was the first time we had ever fought like this. He was in my face, and when that happens, I don't back down.

When I got back to the locker room, I said, "I've got to leave. It's been great, fellas, but I'm going to ask the Man to trade me."

My teammates didn't respond. They shared my frustration, but they didn't really think I was serious about wanting to leave. After all, I wasn't exactly the first ballplayer to bitch and moan in a locker room.

When the reporters came in, they already knew something was up. They came right at me, and I was blunt. "I can't play here anymore,'' I told them. ''I've got to leave. I want to be traded.'' They were stunned. Did I mean these things? Was I really serious? ''Definitely,'' I said. ''I haven't been happy all season. It's nothing toward the guys. I love them and everybody. But I'm not happy. I'm just showing up. I play as hard as I can, but I'm not having any fun.''

The next morning the *Los Angeles Times* ran a front-page headline: MAGIC'S BOMBSHELL: HE WANTS TO BE TRADED. LAKER STAR SAYS HE AND WESTHEAD ''DON'T SEE EYE TO EYE.''

As soon as we got back to Los Angeles, I met with Jerry Buss and Jerry West, the general manager. Both told me the same thing: that I should have come to them first before shooting off my mouth. And both of them were right.

Paul Westhead was fired the next day.

Was I responsible for that? No. But I wasn't blameless, either. Jerry Buss had already made up his mind to let Westhead go. But none of us knew that at the time. And my comments certainly didn't help.

Did I *mean* to get him fired?

Not at all.

I was young and naïve, and I really didn't understand how much power I had. When I told the press I wanted to be traded, I wasn't trying to send a message about the coach. I meant what I said: I thought I'd be happier with another team. Playing in Westhead's walk-the-ball system, I felt like I was being wasted. What I was doing, anybody could do. It wasn't fun, we weren't playing our game, and there was a lot of bad feeling on the team. (Of course, nothing is black and white. We *were* winning: When Westhead was fired, the Lakers were 7-4, with a five-game winning streak.)

Others saw it differently. The entire city of Los Angeles, and just about every sports fan in the country, was convinced that Magic Johnson had just fired his coach. My comments in the press about being traded were taken as an ultimatum. Today, looking back on it, I can understand why. But I certainly hadn't meant them that way.

* * *

After a little uncertainty in the front office, Pat Riley took over as our coach. Several years later, after a stint with the Chicago Bulls, Paul Westhead took a coaching job at Loyola Marymount, where the Lakers practice. That made it awkward for a while, because Loyola took the floor right after us. When Paul and I couldn't avoid each other completely, we'd say a quick hello. It was a couple of years before we started talking, but eventually the anger faded.

Over the years, I came to respect Paul Westhead. He became a better coach. And I hope I've become a more responsible person.

At the time, though, I was the bad guy. It was a new role for me, and I hated it. All around the league the fans started booing me. I had been booed before, but only because I was one of the stars of the visiting team; that kind of booing was an honor.

Now they were booing me for the kind of person they thought I was. In Seattle, the crowd jeered every time I touched the ball. I'd love to pretend that it didn't affect my play, but it did. This was in the Kingdome, with a crowd of more than twenty thousand. Believe me, that's a lot of booing. It was a rough night, one of the worst of my life.

The crowds were down on me in other cities, too, but Seattle was the worst for some reason. At the Forum they booed me only once—the first game after Westhead was fired. Though I was prepared for it, it was still horrible to be booed by your own fans. I had to bite the inside of my cheek to fight back the tears.

I was sure that the boos in the Forum wouldn't last. I expected that as soon as the fans saw us going back to our run-and-gun offense, all would be forgiven. That's exactly what happened. By the second quarter of that first game they were cheering again.

But it took a while for things to get back to normal on the road. And until they did, I was really down. I had trouble sleeping. I lost my appetite. I talked to my dad every day, and he told me to keep my head together and keep going. For a couple of weeks I avoided everybody and gave no interviews. But I knew in my heart that I hadn't done anything wrong.

During that time I thought a lot about Reggie Jackson. He was booed everywhere, all around the league, but that didn't stop him from hitting home runs. I didn't know how it would happen, but I took some comfort in the idea that somehow this controversy would make me a better person.

My biggest disappointment was that my teammates didn't come to my defense. I know that they agreed with me, because we had all been complaining to each other about Westhead's system. I was speaking for them, too, when I blabbed to the press, and they knew it. But when they saw how I was being treated, they decided to keep quiet. As soon as Westhead was fired, the press came running to Kareem and Norm. But they were far too smart and experienced to get involved in this one.

Timing is everything. One reason people were so angry at me is that Westhead was fired shortly after my new contract was made public. Again and again, I was portrayed as spoiled, overpaid, inconsiderate, and selfish.

Jim Murray in the *Los Angeles Times* was relentless: "The man they thought belonged on a shelf as a stuffed toy alongside Yogi Bear and Bambi turned out to be a guy who would bait a trap for Mickey Mouse."

And: "Now we know why they call him Magic. He made the boss disappear."

And: "Anybody who thinks Magic Johnson wanted to go to Milwaukee or Indianapolis or Detroit, go stand in a corner. Magic doesn't want to do sauerkraut commercials. He just wanted to fake the owner into the popcorn machine. Jerry Buss went for the fake, and—slam, dunk!—there went Westhead."

The fans were angry, too. The *Times* received so many letters that they added a special section just to air all the criticisms. Magic Johnson is a crybaby. He's not an All-Star. He's a spoiled brat. His next contract should be with Gerber's baby food. Somebody should give this kid a spanking.

"Find a new nickname," one fan wrote. "Yours no longer fits."

Some people were mad at the owner, too. "If a spoiled prima donna can get a quality coach fired, the ultimate bosses, the fans, should take the situation into their own hands. Boycott the games until Jerry Buss, the real culprit, sells the team."

And: "Jerry Buss has lost the faith and confidence of thousands. He has given in to one of sport's all-time great crybabies, 'Glory-Hog' Johnson."

And: "I can't believe it. A winning coach is fired because an overpaid, spoiled-rotten superstar has a temper tantrum."

Am I just being sensitive, or do I detect a certain pattern here?

You can't be as intense as I am, with as much of a will to win, and not have a boiling point. People sometimes think that because I have an easy smile, I never get mad. But I do. When the intensity of the game means that much to you, you can't keep your feelings inside forever. I never had another eruption like the one I had with Westhead. But fans should not underestimate how high-strung you can get when you're playing your heart out night after night and it's still not working.

If I had known that Westhead was actually about to be fired, I wouldn't have said a word. Instead, I said what I was feeling, and I paid the price. I should have realized that I wouldn't be traded, but I didn't understand that. And I was definitely ready for a change.

The change turned out to be Pat Riley. He kept parts of Westhead's system, but he was happy to see us run. Under Westhead, when we got the defensive rebound, everyone was supposed to go to his preassigned spot. Riley did away with that. He kept Kareem in the low post, which every coach did. We ran the same plays for Kareem as we used to, but we added new options for everybody else.

At first, Riley was cautious, even a little intimidated. And who wouldn't be? We were a good veteran team on a winning streak, so he had little to gain and everything to lose. He also had twelve pairs of eyes on him, waiting to see if he would command our respect. He did. He didn't assert himself much during that first year, but there was no doubt as to who was running the show. And he must have been doing something right, because our record under Riley was 50-21. Then, in the playoffs, we knocked off Phoenix and San Antonio without a single loss.

Once again, the Finals came down to Los Angeles and Philadelphia. And in 1982, just like in 1980, we beat the 76ers in six games to win the championships. Despite everything that had happened, we were the Lakers again. And under Pat Riley we only got better.

On top of everything else that hit me during that period, there was one other challenge I had to face. But this one had nothing to do with basketball. It was personal, and for a few years only a handful of people knew about it.

During a time when Cookie and I were broken up, I had gotten together with Melissa Mitchell, a friend from high school. In the summer of 1980, Melissa called me from Lansing to say she was pregnant. This was not good news. I was twenty-one years old, and I wasn't ready to be a father.

The baby was born on February 20, 1981, and I flew into Lansing to see him the next day. It was an awkward scene at the hospital, because here was this beautiful little boy who was my son—except that we didn't really belong to the same family. At the time, Melissa and her people saw me as a villain, and there was bad blood in the air.

But I would see Andre every summer when I came back to Lansing, and we'd spend time together. When he was old enough, I started taking him places—to the circus, the movies, or just to get a haircut—and he spent a lot of time with me and my parents. It was tough on all of us—on Andre, on Melissa, and on me. I was very young, and I didn't know how to be the father I wanted to be.

Even when Melissa and I were fighting—and we often did when Andre was little—he was a happy kid. As he grew older, he started asking why his mom and I couldn't get married. The honest answer to that question was that we didn't love each other, but I didn't want to tell him that. So I told him a different truth—that his mom lived in Lansing and that I lived far away, in California.

By the time Andre was five, Melissa and I were able to put the tensions of the past behind us. And ever since, we've talked regularly about Andre's development and his progress at school. It's not easy to be a single mother, and Melissa has done a great job.

· Once Andre was old enough to travel, he began visiting me in Los Angeles during his vacations. Sometimes we go places, like Disneyland. And sometimes we just hang around the house. Either way, we always have a good time. In addition to being his dad, I've tried to be his friend, too, just like my own dad has been to me. And I think I've succeeded at that.

CHAPTER 11

THE BOYS ON THE BUS

It was during my third year with the Lakers, when Pat Riley took over as coach, that the Lakers started coming together as the great team of the 1980s. Along with the Celtics, we dominated the league. Those years were also the core of my NBA experience. I was now a full veteran on a championship team. We had a coach with staying power and the greatest bunch of teammates you could ever ask for. These guys had what it took: talent *and* character. They were winners.

Of all the players who were there when Pat Riley arrived in 1981, only Michael Cooper and I were still around when he left in 1990. Kareem had retired a year earlier. Kurt Rambis was traded in 1988. James Worthy came along in 1982, so he was there through almost all of the Riley era. Byron Scott joined us in 1983. Other guys came and went, but the character of the team remained the same: hardworking, motivated, and close-knit.

Soon after Riley came in, the Lakers started becoming a family. On some teams you'd have twelve players arriving at the airport and getting into twelve different cabs. With us, it got to the point where if you were going to pick up a sandwich, you practically had to ask eleven other guys what they wanted for lunch.

We genuinely liked each other, and it showed. Whenever we had a team function, everybody showed up. If you couldn't stay long, that was okay—at least you were there. A

162

lot of the guys were married, and Riley made sure the wives were involved, too.

We knew all of this togetherness was a little unusual around the league because guys who were traded to us all said that no team they had been on had as much unity and rapport as the Lakers.

Within the team there were several smaller groups. Coop and I always hung out together, and I don't think I've spent more time with anybody in my adult life. Whenever we had to ride the bus, take a plane, or walk down a corridor, we were inseparable. Whether we were winning championships or losing big games, we always found something in each other to get us through.

Norm Nixon usually hung around with us on the road. After Norm was traded in 1983, Byron Scott moved right in. Coop, Byron, and I called ourselves the Three Musketeers. On road trips we would go to dinner and the movies together.

Kurt Rambis and Mitch Kupchak were close. James Worthy and Mike McGee hung out together, and sometimes Kareem joined them. We all had our individual friendships. But the moment we hit the floor, we were one team.

There wasn't much jealousy, either. If Kareem needed a day off from practice, we might kid him about it. But nobody really objected. If a little rest helped the big guy play better, we were all for it.

One reason the team was harmonious was that we were winning. Or maybe it was the other way around.

It also helped that our bench players knew and accepted their roles. I've never been in their situation, so I can only imagine how frustrating it must be. You spend years trying to make it to the NBA. Then, when you finally arrive, the only time you get to play is when the game is practically over and the fans are heading for the parking lot. Even the bench players were stars in high school and college, so the change in their status is very dramatic. Any guy who can maintain a positive attitude without much playing time certainly earns my respect.

Sometimes fans get the impression that the bench players

don't work very hard for their money. But that's not true at all. It's just that most of their work gets done during practice, when nobody is around to see it except their teammates and coaches. I can't speak for other teams, but the Laker bench players worked enormously hard. For them, every practice was like an actual game. These guys were always fighting for more playing time or a starting role. And sometimes they were fighting for their jobs.

If a bench player is going full-steam against you three mornings a week, it makes a tremendous difference in your performance when game time comes. It's the continued intensity of the bench players that keeps the regulars sharp.

To me, the epitome of a great bench player was Wes Matthews. Wes was with us for only two seasons, but he certainly picked the right two. During that time, 1986–88, we won back-to-back championships. Wes always played his heart out in practice, and he cheered us on during games. The fans barely knew him, but the guys on the team were all aware of how much he contributed. If he was angry or frustrated about not playing, he kept it to himself.

I've seen teams where the eleventh or twelfth man caused trouble, moaning about how he wasn't getting a fair shot or enough playing time. In my opinion, management has no choice but to dump these guys. I don't care how talented they might be; one or two players with a bad attitude can easily infect one or two others. Before you know it, you've got three or four complainers on the bench. Even one unhappy guy is too many, and more than one is a disaster. When players start to focus on whining instead of winning, it's all over.

Somebody once asked Jerry Buss if it was true that when the Lakers were considering a new player, Buss paid as much attention to the guy's character as he did to his talent.

"You're close," said Buss. "Actually, there's a lot of talent out there, so character is the *first* thing we look for."

The team had a different feel at home than it did on the road. When we played at the Forum, after the game everybody went back to his own house and his own life. On the road, we were much more of a unit. I loved the way people in other cities responded when the Lakers came to town. Walking through an airport we could always hear them telling one another, "It's the Lakers!" Usually they said it with excitement. Even if you weren't much of a basketball fan, you knew about Showtime. And you also knew that the Lakers were champions.

We'd sign a few autographs when we came into an airport, especially if one of us wanted to stop for ice cream or popcorn. But the real mob scene usually came a day or two later, when we were waiting in the terminal to board our flight. Then we had autographs, pictures, the works. Even if we had beaten the home team the night before, the fans were always nice to us.

But those days are pretty much gone now. Today, most teams use chartered planes. The Lakers were one of the first to do that, and we really appreciated the difference. It's a lot more expensive, but it's great when you can fly out right after a game. Most of us wouldn't fall asleep until two or three in the morning anyway, which is no fun when you then have to get up early for the next day's flight. Between the charter and the different time zones, we could fly back from places like Utah, Denver, Houston, Dallas, and San Antonio and still get to sleep in our own beds at a fairly decent hour.

No matter where we were going, we always had the same seats. Kareem sat in 1B. Behind him were Cooper and me. Behind us were Byron Scott and Mychal Thompson. Across from Kareem, on the right-hand aisle seat, was James Worthy, who sat there so he could stretch out his left knee. Before Worthy joined the team, Mitch Kupchak had the same seat for the same reason.

Most guys tried to sleep on the plane, but the bus was a whole different scene. Here, too, we had our regular seats. Riley always sat up front in the first seat on the right, with the other coaches just behind him. Across the aisle from Riley was our trainer, Gary Vitti, who was responsible for getting us wherever we were going and sat right behind the driver. Chick Hearn, the Lakers' radio and TV announcer, sat behind Gary. He was always the first one on the bus.

Then came the reporters. If a writer ever tried to move to the back, where the players sat, we'd kick him back up. The second half of the bus was reserved for players only. If somebody needed to talk, or to complain about Riley, or just to let off steam, he had the privacy and the freedom to do that.

The black players always sat in the rear. That's the way we liked it, and we had fun back there, singing, listening to music, and clowning around. E.J. the Deejay served as master of ceremonies. "Good morning, this is E.J. the Deejay, from Lansing, Michigan, Little L.A. Today we're coming to you from the back of the bus in San Antonio. The sky is blue, the temperature is seventy-seven, and the Laker show is on its way to Indianapolis. My man Cooper had a great night. And Pat Riley, a.k.a. Michael Douglas, is the man of the hour in his fine Italian suit. But Norm Nixon hit five jumpers in a row, so we're gonna send this song out to Stormin' Norman, Mr. Savoir Faire."

My tape player and I always sat on the last seat on the left. Coop was across the aisle. Sometimes Kareem sat in front of us, but usually he liked the very back seat, which went all the way across. Sometimes he'd be part of the fun. But most of the time he'd tune us out by putting on his headphones and playing his own music.

There was a lot of laughing on the bus, and plenty of teasing, too. If your shot was blocked two or three times or somebody dunked on you, you'd definitely hear about it— sometimes for days. But it never got out of hand. We were blessed to have such good guys and such a strong bond.

One of the great things about the NBA is the large number of good friendships that develop between blacks and whites. But usually the closest friendships are between men of the same race. Nobody was surprised, for example, that Kurt Rambis and Mitch Kupchak hung out together, although both of them had black friends, too. There's rarely a problem unless a white player tries to act black, or a black player tries to act white.

The only time that happened on our team was with Mychal Thompson. He used to insist that he wasn't really black, because he was from the Bahamas. That didn't sit too well with us, and we always let him know he was wrong. "Man," we told him, "when you're done playing, there will be situations where you'll just *know* you're black."

It didn't take too long. One time in Portland he was accused of taking some golf balls from a golf course. He got into some trouble, and I believe he was even arrested. "You see," I told him. "That's just what we're talking about. If something like that happened to Kurt or Mitch, do you think they would have called the cops?"

But Mychal still didn't get it. He kept trying to separate himself from the rest of us and act more educated. We teased him constantly. "Hey, Mychal, why don't you go up to that cop over there and tell *him* you're not black?"

Guys were always bragging about their skill in Ping-Pong, tennis, and other sports, and we had plenty of friendly arguments about who was better at this or that. But there was one area where nobody disputed Mychal: He had *definitely* killed the most sharks.

If we were on the road and there was no game that night, the first thing I would do was pick up the local newspaper and look up the movie times. Coop and I always went to movies on the road, and sometimes other guys would join us. Even Kareem came along once or twice. We saw only action and adventure films, which got us motivated for the upcoming game. Comedies and love stories were not helpful.

But most cities are not like L.A. or New York, where you have dozens of choices. The same movies would be playing in every city we went to, and we ended up seeing them again and again. If something we wanted to see was playing in a comfortable theater, we didn't care how far away it was. Sometimes we ended up miles away from the hotel in a suburban shopping mall. Coop would arrange for the cab, and we'd always have another one waiting for us when the movie was over.

We usually went in the late afternoon. But in some of the smaller cities you couldn't find anything playing that early. Often we were the only ones in the theater. Occasionally we were recognized, and somebody would ask for an autograph. Sometimes a fan would actually ask for an autograph during the movie. That always amazed me, and we'd ask them to please wait until it was over.

Back home, Coop and I went to comedy clubs. Our favorite was Regency West, a club in South-Central Los Angeles where a number of fine black comedians got their start. The emcee was a very funny man named Robin Harris, who died in 1990 of a heart attack at the age of thirty-six. He had appeared in several movies, including Spike Lee's *Do the Right Thing*, and he was on the verge of becoming a star. Whenever Coop and I walked in, Robin would start in on us. He'd say, "Smile, Coop, so we can see you." (Coop's skin is so black that his nickname on the team was Dark Gable.)

"Hey, there's Magic. Nice to see you, man. You know, Magic got me tickets to the Lakers game the other night. My seat was so high up that when I yelled to the peanut man, there was an echo!" Then he made fun of the way I ran down the court.

Coop is as solid a guy as you'll ever see. He's a family man with an enormous heart, and all through his career he went back to the community to help underprivileged kids.

As a group, the Lakers were pretty good about giving back to the community. But Coop didn't wait to be asked. He was always the first one to say, "What can I do? How can I help?"

He was the same way on the team. He and Wanda, his wife, were the social and emotional anchors of the Lakers. Their relationship was inspiring to see. Every time Michael scored a big basket, he would look up at Wanda in the stands and point.

Wanda welcomed the new players and their families coming in. She and Michael would always invite the new guys and the rookies over for dinner and make them feel welcome.

Twice a year the Coopers would have the entire team over for a big gumbo dinner. And when the Lakers were on the road, the wives often went over to Wanda's to watch the games. She used to videotape every Laker game, and she'd sit there with the remote in her hand to edit out the commercials.

Michael had many talents, but he didn't have much self-confidence. You need a thick skin to be a professional athlete, and sometimes Coop read the papers a little too closely. Even if the article was generally positive, he might take offense at a critical quotation or a negative phrase. If he had had a bad game, he would stay in the shower forever to avoid the press.

It was wonderful to watch him get better, season after season. In the early years our opponents used to embarrass him by leaving him open for the long jumper. Coop didn't like that, and just about every day before practice, he, Byron, and I would work on three-point shots together. Sometimes we'd take crazy shots from behind the visitor's bench. Often we made them. That sort of thing really helps your confidence. When you make a shot like that, a regular three-pointer starts to look easy.

Coop had some good moves to the basket, too. My favorite was one where, as the defender reached in, he'd scoop it under the guy's arm and glide in for the lay-up. I called it Cooper's Scooper Looper to the Hooper.

And Coop and I had a defensive play that we ran together. Our opponent would be coming toward us, and I'd stand there like I was going to take the charge, with Coop standing right behind me. When the guy went up to shoot, Coop would appear out of nowhere to block it. When the play worked right, I'd pick up the ball to start the fast break.

On almost any other team, James Worthy would have been a superstar. He was that good. But because he played for the Lakers, he was always overshadowed by Kareem and me.

I think James preferred it that way. He's a quiet person and he liked to let his game do the talking. He generally kept to himself and was never really one of the gang. Even after all these years, I can't say I know him very well.

But I certainly know how he moves. On the court he was poetry in motion, a beautiful player to watch. I can't imagine our famous fast break without him. I provided the break, but James provided the fast. There was nobody like him when it came to filling the lane in the transition game and swooping down the wing. He had breathtaking moves, brilliant footwork, great hands, and some of the best fakes I've ever seen. When I'd get him the ball, he'd just explode to the basket. James Worthy *was* Showtime.

The two of us had terrific chemistry on the court, just like I had back in college with Greg Kelser. A reporter once asked me to explain how I could always find James near the basket, even when my back was to him.

"It's easy," I blurted out. "James and I have ESPN."

I loved watching him. He had the best drop step in all of basketball, and his Statue of Liberty dunk was something to see. But James had so many amazing moves. My favorite was one I called the Dipsy-Doo-360-Clutch-Skin-and-In, where he did a complete turnaround in midair before dropping the ball into the net. Before Michael Jordan came along, James was the guy who played up high. The great thing about him was that he was one of the few players who had both the fundamentals *and* the style.

He came to the Lakers the same way I did: because of a trade involving a future draft pick. Dominique Wilkins was also available that year, but Jerry West thought Worthy would fit in better with the kind of team we were. Dominique's dunks were thrilling, but James was the ultimate team player.

He started out on the bench, but it wasn't long before he replaced Jamaal Wilkes. And during the playoffs he would raise his game another notch. If it hadn't been for James, we wouldn't have beaten Boston for the title in 1985. He was all over the floor, and he just *killed* the Celtics. In the six-game series, he scored 142 points and shot 60 percent. But the MVP award for the championship series went to Kareem. That kind of thing was always happening to James.

I was so happy for him in that series. The previous year, when the Celtics beat us, he was one of the goats. (I remember it well, because I was the other one.) We had won the first game in Boston Garden, and we were about to win the second when James made a long slow cross-court pass to Byron Scott. Every Celtic fan remembers what happened next: Gerald Henderson stole the ball, got the hoop, and sent the game into overtime. Boston won that game and went on to win the series. If it hadn't been for Worthy's bad pass, and a couple of dumb plays by me, we would have won the title.

Some people love Los Angeles from the start. Others, like me, learn to love it. But James never did. He comes from Gastonia, North Carolina, where his father is a Baptist minister. James doesn't drink, doesn't go to clubs, doesn't do commercials, and doesn't seem interested in publicity. He's never even fouled out of a game.

When you go to their modest house in Westchester, James and his wife, Angela, ask you to sign their guest register, which is a southern tradition. And in a city where most players drive fancy expensive cars, James used to ride around in an old Toyota—or on a bicycle.

Los Angeles magazine once ran a story on James Worthy. They called him, fittingly, "the invisible man." With his beard and goggles, he didn't *look* invisible. But when you talk about players who are underrated and underappreciated, this guy stands at the top of my list.

When Byron Scott came to the Lakers in 1983, most of us didn't like him. Actually, what we really didn't like was that Norm Nixon had been traded. Byron was taking Norman's place, and we took it out on the rookie.

He had a tough start. Norm had been popular with the fans, too, and it took them a while to accept the new guy. And it didn't help that Byron played poorly during his first few weeks. It was never easy for a rookie to fit in with the Lakers, but Byron took it well and kept his chin up.

As time went on, Coop and I started hanging out with him. Before long the three of us were a tight group, and we took pride in shutting down the other teams' guards. Byron was closer to Coop than to me. But Coop was married, so Byron and I, both single, often went to clubs together on the road.

When Byron was a rookie I could see that he was going to be a big part of our team, but he needed help getting adjusted to the pro game, just as I had when I was a rookie. Our opponents tried to intimidate him, playing all kinds of mind games, and I worked with him to overcome these obstacles.

Byron grew up in Inglewood, just a few miles from the Forum. As a kid, he used to sneak into the building to see the Lakers. He was the luckiest guy on earth, because very few players end up playing for their home team. But at first this was just one more source of pressure for him, because the expectations in the neighborhood were so high.

Like Norm, Byron became a big part of our bus rides. He liked to memorize comic routines of people like Eddie Murphy and Richard Pryor, and he'd perform long parts of their acts. He was really good, and he'd always have us rolling.

Shortly after Pat Riley came in, Mitch Kupchak, our new power forward, started to heat up. On November 20, in a game against San Antonio, he hit 11 field goals in 11 attempts.

Kupchak came to us as a free agent from the Washington Bullets. He had been a star at North Carolina, and had played center on the gold-medal-winning U.S. Olympic team in 1976. When he joined the team in the summer of 1981, we were all excited to have him on board. But only a month after his no-miss game, he went down with a terrible knee injury that would keep him out of action for almost two years.

With Kupchak gone, we needed another player. Fast. On Christmas Eve, the Lakers signed Bob McAdoo.

By the time he got to L.A., McAdoo had been around the block. He had started out with Buffalo back in 1972, where he won several scoring titles. He had also played for the Knicks, the Celtics, the Pistons, and the New Jersey Nets.

In his early years in the league, McAdoo was a genuine superstar. He won the MVP in 1975, and before he left Buffalo he won three consecutive scoring titles.

Riley was convinced that McAdoo could help the Lakers. But a lot of people had doubts about that. For one thing, McAdoo was well past his prime. For another, he had a reputation for making trouble and not playing hard—especially in Detroit, where Leon the Barber used to call out, "McAdoo, McAdon't, McAwill, McAwon't." The Pistons had acquired him from the Celtics in return for M. L. Carr and two draft choices. In typical Celtic fashion, one of those draft choices turned out to be Kevin McHale.

People said McAdoo was a head case. They said he was lazy and a loser. But Riley insisted on giving him a chance, and Kareem supported the idea.

I was one of the skeptics, but Riley and Kareem were right. I don't know what had happened with McAdoo on some of those other teams, but when he came to us he turned out to be the opposite of what everybody had said. He was a great character, a good player, and a tremendous amount of fun. Right from the start he understood that he wasn't going to be the main man. Just as we'd hoped, he was able to come off the bench and light up the basket. Most of all, Bob McAdoo was a winner.

He was the most competitive guy I'd ever met. He always wanted to beat you, and when he did, he wouldn't shut up about it. He loved to play HORSE with us after practice, and his outside shot was so good that just about every day he'd win ten or twenty bucks from a couple of us. Nobody could hit long shots like McAdoo.

He loved to crow about how good he was. But his style of bragging was funny and good-natured rather than annoying. And we all enjoyed teasing him, especially about some of the lousy teams he had played for. We were on the bus one day when Norm started riding him about how badly the Lakers used to beat Buffalo during Nixon's rookie year.

"That may be," said McAdoo, "but I always got mine. And I used to score forty on Kareem. Didn't I, Cap?"

Kareem just sat there at the back of the bus. He was listening, but he didn't say a word.

McAdoo was always looking for respect. There was one year back in the mid-1970s when Kareem won the MVP, although McAdoo had scored more points. McAdoo just wouldn't let it go. "Kareem," he would say, "you still keeping my MVP trophy in your house?"

But we teased him right back. "You ought to be grateful to us," I once told him on the bus when he was bragging more than usual. "Because until you came here, you had never been on national TV. You didn't even know what national TV *was*. Teams you played on had only been seen on *regional* TV. You ought to bow your head and thank us for putting you on CBS."

Doo just smiled. He knew it was true.

He and Norm Nixon used to argue constantly, but it was usually in good fun. "Doo," Norm would say, "you may have scored a lot of points, but in all your years in the NBA, you've never won a single championship."

Doo didn't like hearing that. He came back with: "Norm, you've got the easiest job in the world. All you do is throw it in to Kareem, and they double him. He kicks it back to you, and you're wide open, so of *course* you score. But if you ever leave the Lakers for another team, you'll never be heard of again. How can you compare yourself to me? I was a good player on a bad team. But if *you* were ever on a bad team, you would just disappear. I guarantee it."

Shortly after that Norm was traded to the San Diego Clippers, one of the weakest teams in the league. The next time we played there, McAdoo couldn't wait to rip into Norm. We were shooting lay-ups before the game when Bob called out, "Hold it. Everybody stop and come with me." We all followed him to the middle of the court.

Bob stood there and called out to Norm: "Mr. Big! Mr. Big!" (Norm had several nicknames. We sometimes called him Mr. Big because he was the shortest guy on the team.)

Norm was at the other end, shooting lay-ups with his new teammates. He looked over at McAdoo and waved.

"Mr. Big!" McAdoo yelled at him. "What did I tell you? I *told* you that if you ever left the Lakers you would never be heard of again! I was right, wasn't I?"

It was a very funny moment, and we couldn't believe that McAdoo would remember something like that. But when his pride was involved, Doo remembered everything.

One night in Denver, when McAdoo came into the game, the Nuggets put a guy named Bill Hanzlik on him. Hanzlik was a couple of inches shorter than Doo, and about forty pounds lighter. McAdoo was going crazy, he was so excited. "Buck!" he kept yelling. "Bring me the ball. This boy can't stop me."

He was saying this out loud in the middle of the game. I threw the ball in to him, and about four times in a row McAdoo took it to the hoop and scored. After each basket, Doo looked over at Doug Moe, the Nuggets' coach, and said, "You better get him off me and try somebody else."

Then he'd come back to the huddle and say, "Man, can you *believe* this? I led the league in scoring and they put *this* guy on me." Most players would have been thrilled to have this problem, but McAdoo was insulted.

He was a pretty good athlete, but nowhere near as good as he imagined. And he never stopped bragging. It got so bad that we had a little saying: "If you do it, Doo do it. But Doo do it better."

One morning on the bus, Norm, Coop, and I were talking about tennis. Doo wasn't even part of the conversation. But he must have been listening, because suddenly he turned around and said, "Man, I can beat *all* of you in tennis. I'm the best tennis player in the NBA."

"You're always talking," said Norm.

"That's 'cause I can do it all. You name it, I do it."

"How about baseball?" asked Norm.

"How about it?" said Doo. "I'm the best glove, plus I can hit, too."

"Swimming," said Norm.

"Ain't nobody better."

"What about track?" said Norm.

"I'll beat you," said Doo, which was crazy, because Norm was one of the fastest runners in the league.

"Tell you what," said Norm. "I'll give you a ten-yard lead in the hundred-yard dash, and I'll *still* beat you."

"You're on," said Doo. "Winner gets a million dollars in cash."

"What about bowling?" somebody asked.

Long pause.

"Well?" Coop said, finally.

"I don't bowl," Doo replied.

By now the whole bus was involved. Three or four guys called out in unison, like a chorus: *"Doo don't bowl?"*

We were still laughing when Doo said, "No. But give me a week and I'll bowl three hundred."

When the Lakers played in Cleveland, we used to stay at a Holiday Inn in Richfield, Ohio. The hotel had a game room with a Ping-Pong table, so of course Doo started telling us how great he was at the game.

On the bus back to the airport, one of the sportswriters mentioned that he had beaten McAdoo at Ping-Pong. This was great news, and we really went to town. "What? You beat Doo? No, that's *impossible*. You've gotta be lying. How could you beat the greatest Ping-Pong player of all time? Hey, Doo, why are you so quiet? This guy is saying he *beat* you. That can't be right, can it? Come on, Doo, is he telling the truth?"

It *was* true, but Doo had his reasons. Anytime Doo lost at anything, there was *always* a reason. In this case, his paddle was falling apart. And didn't anyone notice that the Ping-Pong table was a little warped on his side?

But Doo knew he had been beaten. He was so upset about losing that he vowed to get even. He practiced all year. The next season, when we returned to that same Holiday Inn, Doo arranged for a rematch, and this time he won. I wouldn't be surprised if he's still talking about it.

He loved being part of the Lakers, and we loved having him around. He ended his NBA career in Philadelphia after the Lakers let him go at the end of the 1985 season. Shortly

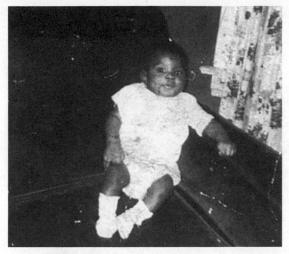

That's me at three months.

My second-grade class picture. I'm the one with the hole in his smile, last row on the right.

In the kitchen during my short-lived football career.

That's me in junior high.

Looking tough in my senior year at Everett High.

Celebrating with
Coach Fox after a big
play.

Taking it strong to the
hoop during the state
semifinals in 1976.

The Everett Vikings—state champs! I'm in the middle and Reggie Chastine is on the far left.

With Dad and Coach Fox during the recruiting crunch.

With my All-America plaque after my sopho-more year at Michigan State.

Being interviewed by Billy Packard and Bryant Gumbel during the 1979 NCAA tournament. Greg Kelser is on my left.

In action during the 1979 finals against Larry Bird and Indiana State. Some say this was the greatest college final ever.

Back at school after winning the title.

Starting the fast break—the heart and soul of Showtime.

Always look for
the open man.

In the paint with
Larry Bird.

Mixing it up with Michael Jordan.

One of the happiest days of my life: Cookie and I walking up the aisle, just married.

One of the saddest days—announcing that I have HIV, November 7, 1991.

The support I received from across the country—from fans, well-wishers, and the press—has been tremendous.

Basking in the glory of the gold after the medal ceremonies in Barcelona.

A no-look pass against Croatia.

A new life: at home with Earvin Johnson III.

after he signed with the 76ers, he came to Los Angeles with his new team. Doo was walking into the Forum when we ran into each other. We embraced, and he started crying. "You know," he said, "I never knew how good I had it until I left. When I played here, I really found out what a team was all about. Philly is okay, but it's just not the same. We don't hang out like this."

Few teams did. Doo had been around the league, so he could appreciate the difference.

Doo came down with a lot of injuries. But it was never clear to us which ones were real and which ones just happened to come along at convenient times. Like right before training camp or on the day we were playing against Detroit. We're talking here about a guy who once missed several games because—and I'm not making this up—he was suffering from "a cold in my wrist."

I've been focusing on Doo's funny side, and I love him dearly for all the laughs we had together. But there was a whole other face to this man that affected me deeply. Of all my teammates, Bob McAdoo had the strongest black consciousness. I figured this would be one of Kareem's concerns, too. But by the time I came along, Kareem was pretty quiet on the subject. Doo, on the other hand, wasn't quiet about anything.

He had been around long enough to see a lot of changes, and he used to talk to me about his experiences. He had grown up in Greensboro, North Carolina, which was still segregated when he was young. There were restaurants where he couldn't eat and water fountains where he couldn't drink. I had heard all about the old South from my parents. But hearing the same stories from one of my own teammates made it seem that much closer.

He ran into racism in college, too. Black players weren't recruited as much in his day. And some schools refused to put five blacks on the floor at one time. When McAdoo turned pro after his junior year, he was criticized in the press for not finishing his education. It bothered him that nobody raised any objections when hockey or tennis players left college early, or skipped it entirely. "Listen," he would say, "why do people go to college in the first place? Most of them go in order to get a good job. So if you have a good job waiting for you even *before* you graduate, why shouldn't you take it?"

Doo came into the NBA in 1972. As he often reminded me, the league was very different in those days. There wasn't much support from white fans, who were desperate for white superstars. There was Pistol Pete Maravich and, later on, Bill Walton. But neither of them was big enough or had enough flair. It wasn't until Larry Bird came along in 1979 that things turned around.

It was McAdoo who made me aware that white players used to be paid better than blacks. Black superstars made out fine, but there was a double standard for everybody else. And until very recently, most teams have included a couple of white players on the bench just to keep their fans happy.

McAdoo had a strong sense of history, and he helped me understand that nothing happens in a vacuum. "Things don't change by themselves," he used to say. "Each generation of black players paves the way for the next guys. People like Bill Russell and Wilt Chamberlain made things better for the Bob McAdoos and the Julius Ervings. We made it better for the Magics, just like you're going to make it better for Michael.

"Buck," he'd say, "you've got to understand that I was the Magic Johnson of my time. But nobody knew about me. Remember, we didn't have all the TV coverage and the publicity that the NBA has now.

"But the struggle isn't over yet," he would continue. "We've won this round, and a guy like you can be recognized and appreciated. Now we've got to take it to the next step. We need more blacks in coaching, in management, and in ownership. It's time to go up to the next level."

He pushed me to be a leader, to present myself well and be a role model for other black athletes. "Don't blow your money like some other guys do," he would say, although my father's influence made sure there was no danger of *that*.

"You've got a chance to change things, to do something constructive, so go for it." Blacks still hadn't made a serious breakthrough in business, but McAdoo looked forward to that day. When I bought a Pepsi distribution company, he was so proud and excited that he called to congratulate me.

In 1986, after playing for Philadelphia, McAdoo went to Italy, and he's been playing there ever since. We're still in touch, and he is still special to me.

It takes all kinds of players to form a team. I was primarily the ball handler. Kareem worked the low post like nobody else. James Worthy was a breathtaking dancer. Cooper could stop anybody. McAdoo had a great outside shot.

Kurt Rambis did none of these things. If you looked up his numbers, you might conclude that he played little or no part in the Lakers' success. But that's only because nobody has ever invented a way to measure heart and hustle.

Kurt was a power forward who averaged less than eight points a game. But we didn't need him for that. What he provided were rebounds and intimidation. Whether it was diving for loose balls, banging for rebounds, or protecting his teammates, nobody worked harder. Kurt was a guy we really loved to play with, because he was so *there*.

He was enormously popular with the Forum fans. (Even today, they still cheer him when he returns with his current team, the Phoenix Suns.) They loved his effort and his hustle, and some of them probably felt that he represented them. He adored the game. He wasn't blessed with natural gifts, never made moves that left the crowd in awe. But he played with great desire, and in his case, desire was enough.

He was the only Laker with his own cheering section. Some of our teenage fans used to show up at the Forum with horn-rimmed glasses like his and wearing jerseys with his number. They called themselves the Rambis Youth.

Shortly after Kurt's fan club was formed, a few of its members wanted to go to lunch with their hero. So Lon Rosen set up a meeting with Kurt at the Forum Club after practice. Four members of the group showed up in their Rambis Youth

T-shirts and glasses, complete with the strap around the back and the white tape on the nosepiece. But when everybody sat down, nobody had anything to say. As Lon tells the story, they all just looked at each other until Kurt finally broke the silence.

"Hi, guys," he said. "Nice glasses."

Most players think they're better than they really are. And only a few really understand or accept their limitations. Most guys want to be stars, but Kurt was never like that. He just wanted to do his job, and he was willing to bust his ass in the process.

Kurt joined the team in the fall of 1981, a few months after Houston had sent us packing in the playoffs. Moses Malone had been so powerful on the boards that the Laker management started looking for a big strong guy who could hold his own in the rebounding battles.

When Kurt was invited to training camp, he didn't expect to make the team. He did make it, but he played so little in our first few games that the crowd would greet him with a special cheer whenever the coach put him in. He didn't shoot much. But that was probably just as well: Kurt's jump shot was about the ugliest thing you've ever seen. If Worthy reminded people of a soaring eagle, Rambis was more like a rhinoceros.

He might not have played much if it hadn't been for Mitch Kupchak's injury in December. First Riley tried Jim Brewer in Mitch's place. When that didn't work out, he tried Mark Landsberger. Kurt Rambis, his third choice, got the job and kept it because of his phenomenal work ethic and his willingness to do the dirty work. Some guys need to score because they crave the recognition. Kurt can have a great game without getting a shot off all night.

Kurt was a fun guy to be around, and the two of us are still friends. So I'm sure he won't mind if I tease him a little. He had some great qualities, but he was also the cheapest guy on the face of the earth. He wore the same shoes he had been wearing since high school. And his jeans were the worst pair I'd ever seen—even worse than those old bell bottoms that we retired with Kareem. It wasn't just that Kurt was a bad dresser, although he was *incredibly* bad, unbelievably bad. I think Kurt intended to wear down these jeans until the bitter end, when all the holes were blended into one gigantic hole and there wasn't any denim left.

He dressed like an aging hippie. During his first year on the team he actually wore sandals. For five years he wore the same shirt to every home game. When he came to practice, his uniform would be dirty. We had to wash our own stuff, but Kurt was so bad at it that the colors would fade on him.

He didn't care. Most days he didn't even brush his hair. He came to practice looking like he'd just crawled out of bed.

It's amazing that Kurt and Pat Riley were able to survive on the same team for all those years. Riley was the best dresser in the league. He believed the Lakers should look like the professionals and the winners we were. But Kurt looked so bad that Riley finally put his foot down and insisted on a dress code for road trips. From then on, we all had to travel in a jacket and a nice shirt. Kurt found himself a corduroy jacket with patches on the elbows. I bet he's still wearing it.

But his dressing habits were only the tip of the cheapness iceberg. When a few of us went to the hotel coffee shop for breakfast or lunch, somebody would usually pick up the check. Or if we split it, most guys would throw down a five or a ten. But not Kurt. He's the one who always said, "Just a second. You had coffee and I didn't." Sometimes he'd actually work it out with a calculator so he wouldn't have to pay a nickel too much. And God forbid the tip should be more than 10 percent. Sometimes he'd rip the check from the waitress's hands. Or he'd call her over and say, "Excuse me—what's the tax rate in this town?" And he'd leave the exact change, to the penny.

If anything was free, you could be sure Kurt knew about it. Kurt would take home soaps and shampoos from every hotel we stayed at. And not just from his own bathroom, either. A lot of guys did *that*. Kurt would go into other guys' rooms and take the soap and shampoo from *their* bathrooms. We're talking about a man who once brought home a bath mat from a Radisson hotel because it had a big *R* on it.

In our locker room at the Forum there was a cooler full of beer, juice, and soft drinks. After every game, Kurt would fill up his gym bag and take them home. When you went to his house, everything he served looked kind of familiar. But what I didn't know at the time, and learned only later, was that Kurt would do the same thing *on the road*. He'd take soft drinks from the visitors' dressing room, bring them back to the hotel, and lug them all the way home to California.

Every player in the NBA receives a per diem allowance in the form of a check. We got about forty bucks a day when Kurt was with the team, although nobody ever made that money last for three meals a day on the road. Except Kurt. He knew all the fast-food joints in every city. He was the only guy in the league who actually turned a profit on meal money.

He used to drive an old Mercury Lynx, which was far too small for a guy his size. But it was cheap. And instead of going to the barber, he had his hair cut by one of the secretaries in the Forum. But not very often.

A lot of cheap guys are mean and unpleasant, but Kurt was open and generous. He was never cheap with his time, and like many of the Lakers, he did a lot of charity work. In addition, he and his wife, Linda, were always helping out kids in trouble.

Before she married Kurt, Linda Zafrani worked for Jerry Buss, promoting volleyball and tennis matches at the Forum. She and I were friends. One day she mentioned that she was interested in meeting this new player named Kurt. While I was trying to think of some way to introduce them, Linda asked Steve Chase, one of her co-workers, to find out whether Kurt was single.

Steve went down to the locker room after practice. He found Kurt in the Jacuzzi.

"Are you married or engaged?" Steve asked him.

But the motor was on and the water was running. Kurt

couldn't hear him very well. He thought Steve had asked him, "Are you married or *gay*?"

Uh-oh, Kurt thought, it's starting. Kurt comes from a small town, and somebody had told him that Los Angeles had a big gay population. Now he figured that Steve was hitting on him. Sitting there naked in the Jacuzzi, Kurt felt just a little vulnerable.

"No!" he shouted back. "I'm *not*!"

Eventually they cleared it up. The next day, Kurt asked me if I knew Linda. I encouraged him to meet her, but he was reluctant; he saw her as part of management, and somehow he had the idea that if they were seen together, he could get fired.

When we finally got *that* straightened out, the two of them started going out. They hit it off right away. A couple of years later, they got married in Las Vegas during the All-Star break.

People who were there told me that Kurt came to the ceremony in a nice suit. They said it almost matched his rubber tie.

CHAPTER 12

MR. INTENSITY

There are a lot of good coaches in the NBA, but Pat Riley is in a class by himself. He was our coach for nine seasons, and during those years we made it to the Finals seven times and won four championships. But despite all of that, a lot of people refused to give him the respect he deserved.

Things didn't really change until the 1992 playoffs, when Riley's New York Knicks beat Detroit in the first round and then gave Chicago a seven-game scare. That's when the rest of the country finally woke up to what fans in L.A. had known for years: Pat Riley is the best.

During the 1980s we used to hear all kinds of nonsense about him. That he was just lucky. That he was all flash and showmanship. That he didn't work very hard. That the Lakers had so much talent we didn't even *need* a coach. That Riley's job was easy, because all he had to do was throw out the ball and say, "Okay, guys, go to work."

Wrong! The Lakers were successful because Coach Riley was able to draw the best effort out of each player. Everything we had to give, he was able to get.

Maybe it's because most of the national media is centered in New York, but during those years people said similar things about the Lakers. That we were too flashy. Too self-centered. Too Hollywood. That we weren't rough enough or tough enough. That we would wilt under pressure. That we lacked depth. That we had Showtime, but not character.

In other words, that we weren't the gritty Boston Celtics. The Celtics were everyone's definition of greatness.

The Celtics *were* great, but the Lakers won five titles during the 1980s, while the Celtics won three. Both teams had talent to spare, and the Celtics had the best front line in the history of basketball.

But we had Pat Riley.

He was born to be a coach. People noticed his good looks, his elegant suits, his custom shirts, and his slicked-back hair, but that was surface stuff. Beneath it all was a fiery, hard-working, intense coach who wanted you to be the same way. He took losses hard. He even took *wins* hard if you didn't play up to his standards—or your own.

The public never saw the long hours of preparation and the exhausting three-hour practices. I don't care how much talent you have, a team doesn't go to the Finals seven years out of nine without incredibly hard work and brilliant coaching.

Riley grew up in Schenectady, New York, where his father was a minor league baseball manager. Pat was a football star in high school, and he must have been pretty good, because Bear Bryant wanted him to come to Alabama as their quarterback. But, choosing basketball instead, Riley went to play for Adolph Rupp at Kentucky. After college he was drafted by San Diego and later played for the Lakers and Phoenix. It wasn't a great career, but he was good enough to play in the NBA for eight years.

The man who became our coach in the fall of 1981 was a different Pat Riley than the one everybody knows today. The Hollywood image and the Italian shoes came later, after he had gained some confidence. But right from the start he brought a different feeling to the team. He saw the Lakers as a family, and he did everything he could to make us see ourselves that way, too. Before he came along, we were a group of good players. Pat Riley made us a team.

He came in right after the Westhead upheaval, and he wanted to make sure that nothing like that ever happened again. Riley's first rule was that we couldn't talk about each other, or about him, in the media. "I don't ask much of you guys," he said. "But nobody on this team will ever chastise anyone else in the press. Don't embarrass me, and I won't embarrass you. Every family has problems, and I'm sure we'll have our share. But when problems come up, we'll keep them to ourselves and solve them together."

Under Riley, team parties were no longer optional. We were expected to show up, and everybody did. But we also *wanted* to be there, because we were having such a good time together.

Teamwork was one key to our success under Pat Riley. Another was the way we practiced.

When you watch NBA basketball on television, the level of play is often so good that it looks easy. You might think that the players are getting their rebounds and making their shots without much effort. But the fans never see how hard these same players work in practice. They didn't see Larry Bird shooting hundreds of three-pointers. They don't see Michael Jordan leaping to the hoop and practicing his outside shot again and again. Talent is never enough. With a few exceptions, the best players are also the hardest workers.

Every coach *says* that practices are the key to winning. Pat Riley really believed it. He wanted our practice games to be twice as hard as real games. When the fourth quarter rolled around, or we got to playoff time, he wanted the Lakers to be fully prepared and confident. And most of the time we were.

If we were playing that night, the morning practice would be light. Otherwise we began our daily routine at 9:30 A.M. We'd start by working individually or in pairs on whatever part of our game needed help or improvement. That could be anything from rebounding to foul shots to passing. At 10:00 we'd gather around Riley for a five-minute talk about how we were doing. He would outline that day's agenda. Each practice had a specific goal, and every minute was planned. "Focus" was one of Riley's favorite words. He always knew where he wanted to take us.

Then came twenty minutes of stretching, followed by

drills. Usually we'd work on our transition game and on conditioning, with an emphasis on running. We'd finish with a tough scrimmage. Riley always worked us into a state of fatigue, because a lot of games in the NBA are decided when both teams are running on empty. It's not enough to hit a jump shot when you're fresh. Anyone can do that. The challenge is to be able to make that same shot when you're exhausted.

I always enjoyed myself in practice. But that doesn't mean I screwed around. Nobody did. "Basketball is a business," Riley would say. "If you want to have fun, go to the YMCA."

I showed up to work, and I gave 125 percent. Under Riley, we all monitored each other. If anyone started slacking off, the rest of us would be on his case immediately.

Although the Lakers were known as a finesse team, our practice games were surprisingly physical. There was plenty of banging and bruising. With no officials to call fouls, the level of contact grew more intense as the practice went on. Riley wanted us to get used to playing on the road, where the referees often allowed the home team to rough you up a little. He reminded me of my father on the playground back in Lansing, teaching me to ignore the fouls and keep playing. Frequently our practices were so rigorous that the actual games came as a relief. One reason for Showtime was that we found it easier to run *past* a defender than run into him. When your body is already hurting from practice, there's a big incentive to avoid contact.

But the real key to Showtime was good defense. All through the Riley years, the Lakers had a reputation for concentrating only on offense. That's ridiculous. The only way you can score, *especially* if you depend on the fast break, is by stopping your opponent. We happened to be a great defensive team, but our fast break was so powerful and dramatic that most people couldn't see beyond that. The reason it was so effective was that we constantly forced other teams to make bad shots. Bad shots lead to rebounds, and rebounds allow you to run. Without tough defense, your fast break can't get started.

A friend and former teammate of Bob McAdoo's who once came to a Laker practice was stunned by how tough it was. When we were finally done, he said, "With all that money on the floor, I can't believe how hard you guys are playing." He was shocked that our management was willing to accept the risk of injuries in order to keep us at the top of our game. Most teams wanted you to hold back in practice and save your best efforts and energy for the game. But Riley didn't buy that.

In our practice games, it was usually the starters against the bench players. But the bench guys knew all our moves, and they were used to defending us. They were also playing for their jobs, so their intensity was sky-high and the games were usually close. Sometimes Riley would announce that the losing team had to run extra wind sprints. Talk about motivation!

After practice, most guys went home to take a nap. But as professionals, we welcomed the opportunity to work that hard. If you couldn't put up with Riley's intensity—and a few players couldn't—you didn't last very long with the Lakers.

To Riley, practices were almost sacred. Once, after a fan fell over a railing and injured himself at the Forum, Kareem, James, and I were subpoenaed to appear at a court hearing. We hadn't even witnessed the accident, but we had to show up. When we told Riley we'd have to miss the next day's practice to be in court, Riley announced that practice would begin at 7:00 A.M. so everybody could be there.

It helped a lot that every practice had a purpose. If we were preparing to play a great passing team like Denver, Riley would set up drills where the bench players would execute a running offense without taking a shot. That way we'd get used to playing a full twenty-four seconds of good defense.

He was always trying to anticipate game situations. "You have to rely on instinct," he would remind us. "If you stop to think, it's too late. You have to *know* whether it's your shot, or what the right move is." And the only way you knew was because the same situation had already come up in practice. "The key to success doesn't lie in talent," he would say. "Success comes from learning how to do something right, and then doing it right every time."

We were a great running team, but Riley thought our fast break could be even faster. So he brought in a running coach, an Olympic sprinter named Henry Hines. Henry showed us how to use our arms more effectively, among other things. Just as Riley intended, our transition game went up another notch.

Although I loved our tough practices, Kareem hated them, and he wasn't the only one. Riley knew he was asking a lot. And part of his skill as a leader was in knowing when to loosen up.

Sometimes, on mornings when he could see we were tired, he would start practice by lining everybody up at half court. Each player would be given one shot. If anybody made a basket, practice would be canceled. We had some good outside shooters, and every now and then one of us would get lucky.

The first time Riley tried this, we couldn't believe he was serious. Then Byron Scott threw up a jumper that was straight as an arrow. While the ball was still in flight, everybody ran for the exit. By the time it dropped in, we were already in our cars.

Sometimes Riley made little deals: Hit ten foul shots in a row and you don't have to run today. In the middle of a tough practice he might start playing a little shooting game for money. He liked excitement. If the gym was too quiet, he'd say, "Hey, where's the chatter? Where are those high fives?"

Sometimes he pushed us too hard, but he usually knew how to back off. After a day when he'd run us ragged, we might get a call that the next day's practice was canceled. We felt so grateful when he did that! Or we'd be waiting for a flight in the terminal, and suddenly Riles would buy ice cream for everybody. He did things that other coaches just wouldn't think of. I had to smile when I heard that just before the 1992 playoffs began, Riley took the Knicks to see the movie *White Men Can't Jump*.

I'll always associate Showtime with Riley, because he worked so hard to make it sparkle. When the Lakers were running, we generated an excitement that no other team could give you. When the fans left the arena, they went home remembering three or four plays that were just unbelievable. Night after night, the Forum was sold out. If you missed one of our games, you really missed something.

Maybe it was James Worthy streaking down the wing, and my feeding him a no-look pass. Or Coop jumping over two guys to block a shot. Or getting the ball in to the big guy with the prettiest shot in basketball—the skyhook. Or Kurt Rambis diving onto the court to go after a loose ball and leaving a twenty-foot sweat mark on the floor, but somehow making the pass to Byron from down there, and we were off to the races again.

When we ran the break I was in another world. It was the greatest feeling I've ever known. My eyes would light up, and I'd feel crazy down to my knees. If there were two defenders back, and I had a guy on each wing, filling the lanes, I just knew it was scoring time.

My role was to get it all started. Even when I wasn't involved in the scoring, I would get the defensive rebound and make that first pass. The first thing I'd look for was who was out in front of his man. Most often it was James. But if nobody was open I would take the ball as far as I could until the defense committed and I saw an opportunity for somebody.

Sometimes that somebody was me. But there were also times when I'd just stand back and watch, feeling so proud to be part of this incredible show.

Riley was a strong leader, but he wasn't a dictator. Like most good leaders, he knew how to follow. He listened to his players, and paid attention to our ideas. He understood our emotions. If a coach hasn't played in the NBA, it can be hard for him to know what the players are feeling. But with Riley, you knew that whatever you were going through, he had already been there. He knew how it felt to be a bench player or to suffer an injury or a slump.

Under Riley's leadership, good players became better, and average players became good. He was most effective with guys who were willing to work hard, which may explain why he had so much success with Coop and me. He saw Worthy's gifts right away, and we ran plays for James that took advantage of his talents.

No matter how much you had accomplished the previous season, he always tried to push you further. That was fine with me, because I'm the same way. Every summer he'd send you a long detailed letter, letting you know what he thought of your performance last year and what he expected out of you in the coming season. He put a lot of thought into those letters, and we took them very seriously. They always ended with a reminder that you had better get in shape *before* you showed up at training camp. Guys who didn't disappeared real quick.

Among other things, Riley encouraged me to be more efficient. Instead of making the fancy pass, I learned to concentrate on making the *good* pass. In my first couple of years I was a bit of a hot dog, and sometimes my creative moves resulted in turnovers. Riley didn't mind a little showmanship, but he got me to limit the fancy stuff to certain parts of the game. I learned to select my spots. If a turnover might prove too costly, I wouldn't take the risk.

Riley pushed me to become more of a scorer, too. When I first came into the league, the scouting report said that I couldn't hit the outside jumper. But I worked on my outside shooting until I became really accurate from twenty feet out. Other teams expected me to drive to the hoop, so they'd back off and wait for me to come in. But once I got my shot down, they had to come out to guard me. Then I was free to go inside again.

Later on, he encouraged me to improve my free throws. That's more of a mental skill than a physical one. Players tend to hit most of their foul shots during the first three quarters, but miss them near the end of the game, when they're tired.

That often happened to me—especially during the 1984 Finals with Boston, when I missed several big ones down the stretch.

I've always been pretty good from the line, and during my first five seasons I averaged 78.8 percent. But I knew there was room for improvement, and I decided to work harder. Larry Bird was hitting in the 90 percent range, so that became my goal.

I started shooting free throws before practice, and especially after practice, when I was wiped. It didn't take long to see a difference. I didn't make any physical adjustments. It's all about practice and attitude. If you have the knack, and most guys do by the time they get to the NBA, you can hit a free throw with your eyes closed.

When I'm shooting a free throw, I always believe that my shot will go in. You have to concentrate—but not too hard. If you think too much when you're at the line, it's all over.

During my next seven seasons I averaged 87.5 percent at the line, which was a big improvement. With about half a dozen games left in the 1988–89 season, I was running a close second to Jack Sikma of Milwaukee, who was hitting about 90 percent. (Larry Bird was injured that year.) Then Jack got hurt and missed the last few games. That put more pressure on me. But by then I had plenty of confidence. During the last week of the season, I hit something like 32 free throws in a row. Then I missed one, but I was able to come back and hit all the rest.

I finished that season with a free-throw percentage of 91.1 percent, which was tops in the NBA. Jack Sikma was second with 90.5 percent. Bird had led the league three different times, but he had never led it with over 91 percent. I guess Larry was watching me as closely as I was watching him, because—wouldn't you know it—the following year he came back to lead the league with an incredible 93 percent. I finished second with 91.7 percent—my best ever.

In Riley's first year as coach, he asked Kareem to come over to his house. "You're not working hard enough on defense,"

Riley told him, and then he showed Kareem a tape of his defensive lapses.

"That's interesting," Kareem said. "But the next time we meet, I'd like you to show me something more objective."

So although Riley believed that the mental component of the game was critical, he started to put a lot of effort into keeping detailed statistics. Every team keeps stats on their players, but Riley went beyond the usual categories. In addition to achievement, he started keeping track of *effort*. He knew how often you were diving for loose balls, or how many rebounds you fought for—even if you didn't get them. He wanted to know that you were working. The numbers didn't lie, and Riley could point to a flaw in your game that you weren't even aware of.

The NBA had its own rating system that measured just about everything you could think of—shooting, free throws, rebounds, assists, blocks, steals, and probably one or two other things I wasn't even aware of. The only two guys who consistently scored above 700 were Larry Bird and me. (This was before Michael Jordan became a real power in the league.) Riley would always throw those numbers at me, and every time I slipped a little, he'd let me know.

Unlike some coaches, Riley wasn't a big screamer. If you were doing something wrong, he'd rather show you than yell at you. He wouldn't holler during a game. But he could be very tough on us when the team was alone.

"Buck," he might say, "I keep reading that you're a great player. But you're playing below your capacity. Look at you! Your rebounds are down, your assists are down, and you're not getting the job done." Then he'd start in on the next guy, and go right down the line. He didn't hesitate to get right in your face and let you know what you were doing wrong.

When he was finished, we'd go out and practice like hell.

Sometimes he got mad after a victory. "Don't be feeling good about yourselves just because you won," he'd say. "Those guys aren't very good, but *you* guys were lousy." Because we had talent, and a good work ethic, he expected us to be excellent every night.

Once, in the fall of 1987, when we blew a game, he exploded, "You call yourselves winners? You're nothing. *Nothing!*" He would get us so upset that by the time the next game came around, we were ready to *kill* our opponent. We'd want to beat them by 40 points, just to show Riley. Sometimes the Lakers lost. That's inevitable. But we didn't often lose two games in a row.

The most memorable team meeting we had with Riley came during the 1985 Finals against Boston. The Celtics had beaten us the previous year, and we spent that whole summer and most of the next season thinking about nothing but revenge.

We were all juiced up when we met Boston in the Finals again, because this was going to be our year. But the Celtics brought us down to earth real quick. The first game of the series, on Memorial Day, was a total ass-whipping. They outrebounded us, outhustled us, and outplayed us from start to finish. They finished with 148 points, a record for a championship game. We were 34 points behind them. That game became known as the Memorial Day Massacre.

Well, you didn't have to be a genius to know that Tuesday's practice would be a little rough.

When we got there, Riley sat us down in front of the VCR. All he said was "Watch this." The room was totally quiet as we viewed the previous day's humiliation in Boston Garden. We had all played badly, but Kareem had had one of the worst games of his career. Robert Parish had just run circles around him.

As the tape ran, Riley started in on Cap. Every time Parish outran him, Riley put the tape into reverse and played it again. "What's wrong, Cap? Getting old? Can't play no more? Just *look* at that. Robert's running right by you!"

Kareem normally sat in the back, but he knew what was coming that morning, and he also knew he deserved it. He sat right in front of the screen, and he took in every word Riley said. When Riley was finally done, Cap said, "It's true. But it won't happen again."

Kareem got the worst of it, but we all had to sit through

that tape. Riley got us so fired up that we were actually fighting each other in practice. Kareem was elbowing Mitch, and Coop was hurting me even more than usual. For the next two days we had to deal with the embarrassment of that first game. When Game Two came along, we were ready.

That afternoon, as we left the hotel to go over to Boston Garden, Kareem asked Riley if his father could ride with us on the team bus. Nobody was ever allowed to do that, but Riley knew this was a special situation, that Kareem had to find a way to redeem himself. As he looked at the two of them sitting there, father and son, Riles thought about his own father. And when we got to the locker room, he decided to tell us about Lee Riley.

The last time Pat Riley had seen his dad was in 1970, when Pat got married. And in the locker room, just before Game Two began, he told us what his father had said to him that day: "Remember what I told you, son, when you were younger. Somewhere, someplace, sometime, you're going to have to plant your feet, make a stand, and kick some ass."

He didn't have to say any more. We knew that this was that time and that place. It wasn't easy, but we went out and beat the Celtics in Boston Garden. And a tall bald guy with goggles led the way with 30 points, 17 rebounds, eight assists, and three blocked shots.

Riley wrote a book called *Show Time*, which began with these words: "There are two possible states of being in the NBA. Winning and misery." Nobody wanted to win more than Riley. And there's nobody he wanted to beat more than the Celtics.

Riles had been part of the old Lakers, who used to get steamrolled by Boston year after year. He just hated the Celtics, and he always assumed the worst. When we practiced in Boston Garden, he suspected the cleaning crew was spying on us. Once, when the Celtics left us a container of drinking water, he made the trainer, Gary Vitti, wash it out and refill it. You never knew. Maybe Red Auerbach was trying to poison us.

He often told us inspirational stories from his childhood,

or about Adolph Rupp, his college coach. But he usually saved the best ones for our games against Boston and Philadelphia. Whenever we needed a boost, he'd come up with the right anecdote. He was a master storyteller. You could easily imagine listening to him on a cold night with the fire going.

He planned all his pregame speeches, writing them out in advance with a blue felt-tipped pen on a blue card. He was continually reading books, looking for quotes that might motivate us. And he loved inspirational one-liners like "No rebounds, no rings."

WHAT IS HUSTLE? he once wrote on the blackboard before a game. HUSTLE = HARD WORK? NO! HUSTLE IS A TALENT.

Or he'd say, "What do you get when you squeeze an orange? Orange juice. Put anything under pressure and you'll bring out what's inside."

This was the sort of thing he liked to say when playoff time came around. That's when money and pride were on the line, and when even the casual fans started tuning in. And that's when Pat Riley was at his most intense. "Tell your friends and family to leave you alone," he'd say. "Tell them you're unavailable for the next few weeks. You've got to give these games your complete concentration. If you want to win that diamond ring, you have to make sacrifices." There was no music in the locker room at playoff time. He even unplugged the phone in the training room.

He tried to eliminate everything that might disturb our focus. He was especially wary of what he called "peripheral opponents"—which meant anyone who would divert your energy and your concentration away from basketball. This included friends who wanted tickets, agents who came to you with endorsements, and especially the media, who wanted interviews.

Another peripheral opponent was the referees—but only if we allowed them to be. Riley didn't want to see any of us arguing with an official, because that was a distraction. When a team starts complaining about the calls, it's usually a sign that they've lost their concentration and their desire to win.

But Riley may have gone too far when he included wives and girlfriends in his definition of peripheral opponents. During the playoffs, he refused to allow them to travel with the team. He got a number of complaints on that one, but he stuck to it. As he saw it, we were on a mission that required our total attention. He would say, "No wives—and no excess baggage." "Excess baggage" was his term for girlfriends.

The players' wives normally got along well with Riley, although Wanda Cooper and Anita Scott were upset about his playoff policy. Their husbands wanted them to come along, and they showed up at some of the games anyway. They couldn't travel with the team or stay at our hotel, but even Riley couldn't stop them from attending the games. He always knew they were there, because the team's complimentary seats were all in the same section.

Wives would occasionally come along on road trips during the regular season. That was all right, as long as you told Riley in advance. But usually we traveled too fast for a pleasure trip. Three cities in four days is not most people's idea of fun, which is one reason the playoffs were so attractive— it was the chance to stay in the same city for three or four days. For the women, it was an opportunity not just to go to the games, but to visit friends, shop, or take a little vacation that wasn't possible during the regular season.

Wanda Cooper used to sneak into some of the cities we went to. But she'd always register at a different hotel than the one we stayed at, and Michael would ask the ball boy to get her a different seat, so Riley wouldn't know. Late at night, Michael would sometimes leave our hotel and take a cab over to visit his wife. He'd be back before dawn, and Riley had no idea.

"Do you realize how exciting that made our marriage?" Wanda used to say. "It was great. I felt like a secret agent. Michael and I had been married for ten years, and there I was sneaking around after him."

Maybe it was to compensate for his policy on wives, but Riley always took especially good care of us during the playoffs. When we spent a week in Detroit in 1988, and again in

1989, the Lakers took over the entire top floor of the Guest Quarters Hotel in Troy, Michigan. There was a huge suite when you got off the elevator, which Riley set up as a rec room with a big-screen TV, pool table, and video games.

He had the hotel put a VCR in every room so you could watch game tapes. You could also order up movies from a local video store. That way, you wouldn't be so tempted to leave the hotel. There was a security desk beside the elevator so that nobody would bother us. And he actually had an assistant go out and buy colored towels for all the bathrooms—so the place would feel less like a hotel and more like home.

Right after the 1987 playoffs against Boston, Riley did something that astounded the entire sports world. About five minutes after we had defeated the Celtics in their own arena, and while the champagne was still flowing in the visitors' locker room, a reporter asked him the inevitable question: "Can you guys do it again next year?"

Any NBA coach can answer that one in his sleep. "Well, John," he'll say, "it was a long, hard battle to get here, and now we're going to enjoy ourselves and relax for a few days. But when next season rolls around, I promise you'll see a team that is just as competitive as the one you saw out here tonight."

In other words, get off my back and give us some time to celebrate.

But when Pat Riley was asked, "Can you repeat?" he replied, "I guarantee it."

Some of us figured Pat had been drinking too much champagne. But he told us later that he had made up that line a week in advance. He was just waiting for somebody to ask the question so he could give that answer. His only regret is that he now thinks he should have said it even *before* the champagne. "People would have crucified me," he says, "but that's the attitude it takes."

"I guarantee we're gonna repeat." He said that again and again, until every fan had heard it and every reporter had written it. He told us that it was because he wanted us to think about another title all through the summer so we'd be ready to go in the fall.

Our reaction was, Oh, no! Give us a break. Just let us go on vacation. We've worked so hard this year!

We weren't exactly mad at him, because it's hard to be angry when you've just won the title. But we wondered: What's *with* this guy? Why does he have to start talking about next season *now*?

This was our fourth title in eight years, but none of them had been easy. We knew how hard it was just to win *once*. Many great players have never been on a team that won a title. Quite a few have never even played in a championship series. And this guy was guaranteeing another one? Without even asking us?

But if Riley wanted us to start thinking about another title, he did the right thing. Everywhere I went that summer, people all had the same question: Pat Riley said you guys are going to repeat. Is he right?

How are you supposed to answer a question like that? The only thing you can do is agree with the coach. "Yep, we're gonna do it again."

But it's not an easy promise to keep. Repeat titles had become rare in the NBA. When Riley made his statement in 1987, no team had won two consecutive titles since the Celtics had done it eighteen years earlier. Early in the 1960s the Celtics actually won *eight* consecutive titles, which is hard to imagine. Four of those eight had come against the Lakers, which is why it was so great to finally beat them in 1985.

Why is it so hard for a team to win back-to-back titles? Mostly because every other team is gearing up just for you. In my early years in the league, all we really cared about was beating the Celtics. And every time we won a title, all the Celtics cared about was beating us. Everybody wants to win, and the road to victory cuts right through the defending champs.

The season after you win the title, every game you play becomes an ordeal. For you it's just another game. But for your opponents, this is the big one, the one they've been looking forward to for weeks. That's especially true when you're on the road. Every game you play is the other team's big opportunity to knock off the champs in front of the home crowd.

And if you're visiting an Eastern Conference team, it's the one time all year they'll see you on their home court. They've been waiting all season for this one, and the players and the fans are sky-high. They're saving their best effort just for you. If they can beat you, they don't mind too much if they lose their next three games. And that used to happen: A team would beat the Lakers and then go into a losing streak. Once the big game was over, they simply let down.

Being the defending champs can wear you down. But it can also give you an edge. When everybody's playing their best against you, it keeps you sharp. And when you get to the playoffs, there are no surprises; you've already seen these teams at the top of their game.

A few weeks after Riley issued his guarantee, he sent us all a letter in which he explained why a repeat title was so important:

Next year is not about winning another championship or having one more ring or developing bigger reputations. It's about leaving footprints.

After four championships in eight years, we have arrived at a point in this team's history where there is just one thing left for us to accomplish. That is to become a team for the ages and eras, the greatest basketball team ever. We do not merely want to be considered the best of the best. It is time to separate ourselves from the pack and become the only ones who do what we do. Unique. That is the essence of Showtime.

The future is now, fellas.

When we met together for training camp, he repeated it. "A piece of history," he kept saying. "This goes beyond winning and losing."

It may sound grandiose, but his words motivated us. We already knew we were the best team in the league. And looking back now, I think we were probably the best Laker team ever. Our starting five was always dangerous. And with Coop, Rambis, and Mychal Thompson on the bench, we were deep, too. And now we had a bigger goal to shoot for.

In training camp that year, everybody came in focused and ready to play. We didn't have to start from scratch. We were mentally alert and completely ready. When the season started, there were games when we were frothing at the mouth, just waiting to play. There was one stretch of five days without a game when we were practicing so hard that Riley had to cut practices short so we wouldn't kill each other.

We did repeat that year, but it was the hardest championship of all. After finishing the season with a record of 62-20, and beating San Antonio in the best-of-five miniseries, it took 21 more playoff games to go the distance: Utah, Dallas, and finally Detroit each took us to the seven-game limit before we finally made good on Riley's guarantee.

When we got to the locker room after that last game, Kareem pushed a towel in Riley's mouth. But one guarantee was enough—even for Riley. There was talk of a "three-peat," but no guarantees.

His plan had worked. All season long we kept our eye on that prize, and in the end we were able to get it. There were no regrets. You recover from the pressure and the fatigue, but the pride and the memories stay with you forever.

One reason we were willing to work so hard for Pat Riley was that he himself was an incredible worker. There were times when you looked at him and knew that he hadn't slept for days. He was always on. Barely a moment went by when he wasn't thinking about basketball or planning for the next game.

But as tired as he was, he always looked good. He's a handsome man, and he was very particular about his clothes.

And yes, about his hair, too. He was always checking in the mirror to make sure that every strand was in place.

In addition to all our practices, he spent hours by himself, preparing videotapes for the team. Riley had a gift for video, and he had his own editing studio at home.

He'd prepare special tapes for each of our opponents. One tape might concentrate on their offensive plays, another on their defense. He even had his assistants prepare individual tapes about each player on the other team. He gave these out to the guys on our team who would be guarding them.

Captain Video also made us watch ourselves. When we weren't playing well, he'd run a "lowlights" tape, which consisted of our worst plays and mistakes. If we weren't rebounding, and other teams were killing us on the boards, he made us watch half an hour of that. If we were turning the ball over, we'd have to see forty or fifty consecutive turnovers. He'd make us watch really bad plays four or five times. "How could you do that?" he'd ask. "That guy wasn't even open."

When a practice began in the locker room, we knew it was tape time. The only question was who the victim would be. He might show half an hour of your bad plays, with everybody watching you screw up fifty or a hundred times. Riley could have done this privately, but he treated almost every problem as a team problem.

He also used more positive tapes to motivate us. He loved putting together videos of our most beautiful plays, complete with exciting background music. In the locker room before the sixth game of the 1987 championship series, when we were leading Boston three games to two, Riley didn't say a word. He just put in a tape showing some of our best plays in the series, including dunks, blocked shots, great passes, and good defense.

The message was obvious: This is what you guys have done against the Celtics—now just go out there and do it one more time. It worked.

There are limits to how much intensity a team can endure, and eventually Pat Riley burned himself out. As the years went on, he just pushed and pushed. But after a certain point he was no longer effective. No coach can last forever with the same team. Eventually the players stop responding to his motivational techniques, because they've heard them and seen them for too long. Riles became more distant from the guys, and more controlling. He started getting involved in small details like who should sit where on the team plane, or when the band should play at the Forum.

Some of the players grew apart from him. Two or three started to really dislike him. It got to be wearing on everyone, and the Lakers weren't having much fun anymore.

Very few coaches have lasted so long with one team, or have done so well. No other coach has won 73.3 percent of his games—which is an astounding record. And no other coach except Red Auerbach has won over 100 playoff victories, either.

In 1989–90, Riley's final season, we finished first, with a record of 63-19. But when we lost to Phoenix in the second round of the playoffs, it was clear that something had changed. Detroit went on to win a second straight championship.

Riles had always said that if he ever felt he couldn't motivate us any longer, he'd walk. And after the 1990 season he kept his word.

Before the announcement, he came to my house to tell me in person. We sat out on the patio, just after it rained. He was crying when he told me, and I cried, too. It was the right decision, but I hadn't expected it and I certainly wasn't prepared for it. It was hard for me to imagine the Lakers without him. And it was even harder to imagine Riley as anything but a coach.

Riley stayed in Los Angeles, and started working for NBC Sports as a basketball analyst. I saw him a few times that following year, but it felt a little strange when he interviewed me on NBC. During our first interview he kept calling me Buck, but somebody must have whispered in his earpiece, because he suddenly switched to Earvin. Earvin may have sounded right on television, but it didn't sound right to me.

We had been Buck and Riles for too long, and we always will be.

I was thrilled for him when he went to the Knicks a year later. This was the perfect job for the man, and the perfect man for the job. There were only two places in the country where Pat Riley could be Pat Riley, and the Los Angeles years were over. He saw himself as a star, and he couldn't resist coaching in New York. People already think of him as a great coach, but he'll be even greater if he can be the guy who restores greatness to the Knicks.

His first year in New York was a terrific success. He got the Knicks to believe in themselves and to play together as a team. But Riles is smart enough to know that there's a long way from a winning season to a championship. It takes time to assemble a great team and to bring in all the right pieces.

It's a big challenge, but Pat Riley thrives on challenges. And make no mistake—someday the Knicks will win it all. Because Pat Riley won't rest until they do.

CHAPTER 13

THE CELTICS

No other team would get me fired up the way Boston did in the 1980s. When we played the Celtics, I was as emotionally high as I could possibly be. The basketball was just that good, and so was the competition. We played them only twice during the regular season, once in the Boston Garden, and once in the Forum, but there was so much excitement in those two games that they were the highlights of the year.

Although there have been other great rivalries in sports, I don't think there's ever been a rivalry like this one, especially for the fans. No matter which team you liked, and no matter who won, you knew you were going to see great basketball: the best shooting, the best passing, the best defense, the best fast break, the best of everything.

And the three championship series during the mid-1980s were even better. People still come up to me to say how great those games were. They watched the games, they taped them, and they definitely remember them.

It wasn't just the fans who felt that way. Imagine how the players felt in that atmosphere of energy and excitement. If you could bottle it up, it would be worth millions. All you'd have to do is unscrew the top and it would make you crazy.

Every time we got on that plane to fly to Boston, we knew we were going for business. And we loved coming into Logan Airport during playoff time and feeling the respect of the people. You could sense that the whole city was getting ready, that the entire place was about to shut down so the fans could concentrate on the games.

It wasn't just Boston, either; all of New England stood behind the Celtics. Los Angeles is more diverse. We have plenty of Laker fans, but we also have Knick and Celtic fans—there are so many people who moved to California from other places and still feel loyal to their former teams.

New England is much more unified. When you get to Boston, you get the feeling that everybody has lived there for nine hundred years. And that they've cheered for the Celtics for at least half of that time. Wherever we went in Boston, even just to pick up a sandwich or lining up to see a movie, the fans were talking about the Celtics.

And what a team they had! Their big three—Bird, Parish, and McHale—were all in their prime during the mid-1980s. We're talking about the best front line in the history of basketball.

Larry Bird was a special case, and you'll hear more about him shortly. For now I'll talk about Parish and McHale.

It's hard to believe, but Robert Parish kept getting better every year. He came into the league in 1976, and played four years for Golden State. But he didn't really shine until he was traded to the Celtics in 1980. When Kareem retired from the game in 1989, Parish became the oldest player in the NBA.

In all the years I've known Robert, I've never seen him change his expression. I always thought Kareem was stone-faced, but Parish makes Kareem look like my friend Arsenio. The Boston fans call him The Chief because Cedric Maxwell, his former teammate, thought Parish looked like the silent Indian chief in the movie *One Flew Over the Cuckoo's Nest.*

When the Lakers played the Celtics, Parish would be matched up with Cap. The two of them would really do battle. Kareem used to dominate most centers, but Robert gave him a tough time, especially when he was hitting that beautiful rainbow jumper. Kareem respected him, and I'm sure the feeling was mutual. They fought hard, but they were also friends. After the game, the two of them would sometimes go out to dinner. That wasn't too surprising, because big men often hang together.

Robert always gave us trouble, especially in the transition game. He ran the floor very fast, especially for a man his size. He'd get down there early and camp out until Larry threw him the ball. Like James Worthy, he does his work quietly. But year after year, he's been one of the top centers in the league.

Kevin McHale is one of the greatest post men in the history of the game. Matchups are everything in basketball, and even Larry could be stopped—occasionally. But no team has ever figured out a way to shut down McHale. The only guy I've seen who could stop him was his old Minnesota teammate Mychal Thompson. It was Mychal, by the way, who gave McHale the nickname Herman Munster.

Everybody notices those great shoulders and long arms. But what really sets McHale apart is his incredible footwork. He and James Worthy have the best footwork in the league. I love to watch the way they pivot, drop-step, cross over, duck under, and dance all around the basket without traveling. Just when you think you've stopped McHale with a double team, he steps around you. Suddenly, somehow, he's worked himself free. He's also a great shooter, especially with that deadly fall-away jumper.

I first met Kevin when he was a freshman at Minnesota and his school was trying to recruit me. I like him a lot: He's friendly, funny, and a great family man. Most big men are introverts, like Kareem, Parish, and Ewing. They're so affected by their height that they tend to withdraw a little from other people. But McHale has a gregarious, outgoing personality.

Of all the Celtics, I was closest to Dennis Johnson. He lived in Los Angeles, and the two of us were friends. Dennis always guarded me, and there was nobody better. He's big and strong, but he's also quick. That's an unusual combination, and I couldn't get around him very easily.

You had to be careful when you put the ball on the floor, because Dennis had among the quickest hands in the game.

He could steal the ball away before you even knew you'd lost it. I scored my points against him, but he made me work hard for every one of them.

D.J. and I respected each other, and we had some terrific battles. There's an unwritten rule in the NBA that if you knock a guy down, you don't help him up off the floor—you let his teammates take care of that. But when Dennis and I knocked each other down, we always stayed around to pick up the pieces.

Although I respected him as a competitor, I didn't know Danny Ainge very well. He often struck me as a brat. He wanted things to go his way, and he was always the first to complain to the officials when they didn't.

I think he got spoiled playing for the Celtics. After he was traded to Sacramento, I fouled him a couple of times in a game and nobody blew a whistle. When he started moaning to the refs, I went over to him and said, "Hey, Danny, you gotta remember something. You're not wearing the green-and-white anymore, so you won't be getting those calls." He laughed because he knew I was right.

There's no question that the Celtics and the Lakers were treated well by the officials. Successful teams, like successful players, get their share of calls. When a player has been around for a few years, and he's good, the referees get to know his moves and his abilities. If Larry Bird missed a lay-up, and somebody was guarding him closely, that guy was often presumed guilty.

It wasn't only their lineup that made the Celtics great. It was also their pride and their outstanding history. No team had ever dominated in any professional sport the way the Celtics had during the 1960s—not even the New York Yankees or the Green Bay Packers or the Montreal Canadiens. And no other professional team has ever won eight consecutive championships.

When you played the Celtics, you weren't just playing against Bird, Parish, McHale, Dennis Johnson, and all their teammates. You were also playing against those legendary

Celtic teams, Bob Cousy, Bill Russell, Tommy Heinsohn, Dave Cowens, and John Havlicek. You've grown up hearing about these guys, and suddenly you look up and now you're a part of that same rivalry. And they weren't just ghosts, either. Some of these guys used to show up at our games, which made it even more exciting.

Celtic fans plugged right into that history. As soon as we landed at the airport, they would start reminding us about all the times the Celtics had beaten the Lakers. As he drove us to our hotel, the bus driver would be making comments like "Good luck, guys. You'll need it." He even had a little leprechaun hanging from the rearview mirror.

The first time I ever saw Boston Garden I was shocked at how old and dirty it was. And the visitors' locker room was so small that you could barely get the whole team in there, let alone our equipment. There were only two working showers. I was a rookie, and I remember thinking that every single arena where Michigan State had played had better facilities than this dump.

But when we got out on the floor that night, it was clear that Boston Garden was a great arena for basketball. The lighting was perfect, and the backdrop behind the basket nice and dark. It was a shooter's court, and I could see why Larry was lighting up the place.

And the fans were terrific. Boston and New York crowds were the most knowledgeable in the league. They really appreciated good plays—even from the visiting team. We had to earn their respect, but when we finally did, they were incredibly generous.

Kareem used to say that playing in Boston was like singing opera in Milan. These people had *standards*.

But you had to watch out for that parquet floor, with all those loose bolts and dead spots. I've played on *driveways* that were smoother than that.

I don't ask much from a floor. All I ask is that the ball go up and down when I bounce it. In Boston it goes down just fine. But sometimes it just stays there.

You're dribbling up the court and suddenly it's, Hey,

where's the ball? The dead spots are in the corners, so you've got to be extra careful in there. The Celtics were always ready when that happened. If you weren't paying attention, they'd chase you into the corner and steal the ball.

Larry Bird and I had been in the league for five years before our teams met in a championship series. And in 1984, when it finally happened, the hype was enormous. This was the matchup that everybody wanted—the press, the fans, CBS, and especially the players.

It had been fifteen years since the Lakers and Celtics had met in the Finals. There had been a total of seven championship series between our two teams. And in all that time, the Lakers had never won.

Both teams were strong in 1984, but in different ways. Boston played a more physical game, while we relied on the fast break. These were real differences, but they got exaggerated by the media, who tried to describe this battle by using every possible contrast: not only Bird vs. Magic, but East vs. West, Worktime vs. Showtime, and blood, sweat, and tears vs. glitter and gold.

Pat Riley used to get angry at the way this rivalry was portrayed. The Celtics were always described as "hardworking" and "tough," while the Lakers were pictured as all glitz and flash. Riley was our taskmaster, so he *knew* how hard we worked. He was insulted by the idea that the Laker show was all smoke and mirrors. To him, this kind of talk was just one more peripheral opponent, especially when it came up again in 1985 and 1987.

"It's not just the Celtics we're playing," he said. "It's those same damn ideas that just won't go away."

We knew that no team worked harder than we did. But it was also true that the Celtics, and Eastern teams in general, were more inclined to bump and grind. The officials weren't so quick to blow the whistle in the Eastern Conference, so these teams got used to a rougher style of play.

When the Celtics and the Lakers met for the Finals, the officials must have decided that the games would be played Eastern Conference style. We weren't prepared for that, and we had never been bumped and bruised so badly. During the regular season, most of our opponents would retreat after they took a shot to protect themselves against our fast break. But the Celtics gambled on a different approach. They knew we couldn't break without the ball, so Bird, Parish, and McHale were all right in there, crashing the boards. Where other opponents would spring back, the Celtics ran alongside us, bumping us the whole way up the court.

We started off strong in the 1984 Finals. In the first game, at Boston Garden, we were up by as many as 18 during the first quarter. The Celtics eventually made a game of it, but we still beat them easily with our running game, 115–109.

We should have won the next one as well. With fifteen seconds left in the last quarter, we were ahead by two. McHale had a chance to tie it, but he handed us a gift when he went to the line and missed two free throws. Game over? Almost. All we had to do was inbound the ball and wait to be fouled.

I threw it in to James Worthy. And this is where James threw that famous cross-court pass to Byron. Except that Byron never got it. Next thing we knew, Johnny Most, the Celtics' radio announcer, was screaming: "Henderson stole the ball! Henderson stole the ball!"

It was a crusher. You're on the biggest high you can have, and suddenly all the air whooshes out.

Henderson went in for a lay-up that tied the game. But it still wasn't over. We had the ball with thirteen seconds left, which again gave us an excellent chance to win. All we had to do was run down the clock and put the ball in the basket right before the buzzer. If we did that, we'd be flying back to Los Angeles with a 2–0 lead in the series. With the next two games at home, we could even sweep them. And if the Celtics managed to win one at the Forum, we'd still be up 3–1.

We set up the same play we always used in this situation: I would get the ball in to Kareem, and he would do the rest. But it wasn't hard for the Celtics to figure that one out, and they were all over him. I couldn't find an opening. With

Dennis Johnson hanging on to me, I lost track of the clock. I was still looking for Kareem when the buzzer went off to end the fourth quarter.

The Celtics went on to win in overtime, 124–121.

We won Game Three, which was Showtime at its best. But the Celtics came back in Game Four, whose ending was all too similar to Game Two, the final score 129–125 in overtime. We were up by five with under a minute to go, but the Celtics came back to tie it up. I had the ball with sixteen seconds left. With the Game Two disaster still ringing in my head, I was especially careful. Kareem had fouled out, so Riley called for a two-man play for James and me. I would either pass it to him or take it to the hoop myself.

But I was *too* careful. When I finally passed it in to James, Robert Parish knocked the ball away. Once again we went into overtime. The game was tied at 123 with thirty-five seconds left when I went to the free-throw line. Two shots—and I missed them both. Bird scored, we threw away another pass, and the series was tied, 2–2.

Boston really did a number on us in that game. The Celtics had been giving us the choke sign during the overtime period, and the pressure got to us. This was also the game where Kevin McHale tackled Kurt Rambis and sent him crashing to the floor. Kurt had a clear path to the basket, and this was one of the most blatant and violent fouls we had ever seen. Both benches cleared and we almost had a big fight on our hands.

McHale's move took us out of our game. I can see today that it was the turning point of the series. From then on, some of us probably held back just a little when we went in for a lay-up. I don't mean this as an excuse, because we should have been tough enough to win anyway. We were certainly *good* enough to win. But when the Celtics intimidated us with their physical game, we just rolled over.

Cedric Maxwell put it best after the game. Before McHale fouled Rambis, he said, the Lakers were just running across the street whenever we felt like it. Now we were taking the time to stop at the corner, push the button, wait for the light, and look both ways. That's not exactly a formula for an effective fast break.

Game Five was back in Boston. When we came in, the city was in the middle of a terrible heat wave. That shouldn't have been a problem, except that the Garden was built back in 1928, before air-conditioning. I'm pretty sure that windows had been invented, but you'd never know it. At game time, the temperature outside was 97 degrees. Inside it was hotter. The crowd showed up in T-shirts and shorts.

The Celtics have always been known for harassing their opponents off the court. And sometimes their fans help them out. They'd come into our hotel at night, knocking on doors, setting off fire alarms, and making it difficult to get any sleep. That never mattered too much, because you couldn't sleep anyway when you were playing Boston.

But this was the first time in history that the Celtics had been able to monkey around with the weather. Everybody knew that Red Auerbach had ordered up this heat wave. But to this day, nobody has ever figured out how he did it.

The Celtics had to cope with the same weather, of course. But when you're playing in your own building, you have a big psychological advantage. They had been in this situation before. Living in Los Angeles, we were used to air-conditioning.

The heat was particularly hard on Kareem, who had to use an oxygen mask on the bench. When a reporter asked him to describe how it felt, Kareem put it beautifully: "I suggest that you go to a local steam bath, do a hundred push-ups with all your clothes on, then try to run back and forth for forty-eight minutes. It was like we were running in mud."

We did what we could. We brought huge fans and dehumidifiers into the locker room and sat there with wet towels on our heads. But it wasn't enough. Larry Bird took over the game and shot 15 for 20 from the floor. The Celtics beat us easily.

We tied up the series in Game Six back at the Forum, where James Worthy gave Cedric Maxwell a pretty good shove, right into the basket support. There was a lot of bad blood after the McHale-Rambis incident, and it was only a matter of time before one of the Celtics got floored. It was a close game, but we held on to win.

Now came the seventh game back in Boston. Their fans were so riled up for this one that we needed a police escort to drive from the hotel to Boston Garden. When we finally got there, M. L. Carr came out in goggles to mock Kareem.

The Celtics were up by as many as 14 points. But in the fourth quarter, we mounted a comeback. With just over a minute to play, we had cut their lead to three. I had the ball when I was met with a beautiful sight: James Worthy open at the basket. I was about to pass it in to James when Cedric Maxwell knocked the ball right out of my hands. Dennis Johnson grabbed it, got fouled, and hit both free throws.

We had come close, but not close enough. The Celtics won the seventh game and the title.

For years afterward, when I closed my eyes I could still see James Worthy open under the basket.

It was an ugly scene when we left Boston Garden that night. Even though their team had won the series, the Celtic fans were mad at us. Several hundred people surrounded the bus, and some of them threw rocks and bottles. It got pretty hairy when they started rocking our bus. We all ducked down with our hands over our heads in case they smashed the windows. The police got us out of there fast.

I'm sure we were all thinking the same thing: I'd hate to see what these people would be like if we *won*. What were they so upset about? I still don't know. We were the ones who had thrown away the title!

I didn't sleep at all that night. My friends Isiah Thomas and Mark Aguirre had come to Boston for the game, and the three of us stayed up in my hotel room until sunrise. We talked about music, cars, women; we talked about practically everything except basketball.

Actually, Mark and Isiah did most of the talking, because I was somewhere lost in space. I love to play in pressure situations, but this time I had let my teammates down. And this time the better team didn't win. The Celtics were able to change the flow in Game Four, and we lost because of a few stupid mistakes.

And most of them were mine.

Back in Los Angeles, I went home to my apartment and didn't go outside for three days. The press was nasty. Every day for weeks there was a different article on why we had lost. Our fans took it hard. They were sick of getting beaten by the Celtics and tired of hearing how great the Boston franchise was. After fifteen years, we'd finally had a great team and a chance to redeem everything that had happened in the past.

And we'd blown it.

I understood their anger, because we should have won. But when it was all over, I sat back and thought, Man, did we just lose one of the great playoff series of all time, or what? Basketball didn't get much better than this, but all you read about was how bad I was.

The truth was a little more complicated. I had played some good games in that series. I'd averaged 18 points a game and even set a record for the most assists in a playoff series—95. But in the fourth quarter, when the game was on the line, I'd screwed up. In three big clutch situations I hadn't come through. My new nickname in the press was Tragic Johnson. And some people were calling us the L.A. Fakers.

That summer I got truly depressed. Funk in the pits, I called it. It took me about a month to get over the worst of it. But it *still* bothers me that we lost. We should have beaten them four straight. It's the one championship we should have had but didn't get.

For me, this was even more painful than the Westhead affair. At least then I knew I had done nothing wrong. I could also work out my frustration on the court. After the 1984

Finals, there wasn't much I could do except wait for next season.

Some mistakes are so serious that when you make them once, you just know they won't happen again. My blunders in that series were mental—letting the clock run down, letting D.J. steal the ball, and missing those two key throws in overtime. And we all learned that no matter what the other team does, you've got to stay strong and keep on playing your game. You can't let your opponents get you off track.

They had done it not only physically, but verbally, too. M. L. Carr taunted us at the free-throw line by saying things like "You don't have the heart to make both of these." Cedric Maxwell gave us the choke sign. Larry talked a lot of trash during that series, and so did Kevin. "I remember when you were a freshman," Kevin said to me in the middle of a game. That's not exactly nasty, but I allowed his comment to do just what he must have intended: interrupt my concentration.

The problem wasn't that the Celtics said these things. Boston played hard, but they didn't play dirty. They weren't like Detroit in the late 1980s. McHale's foul on Rambis was totally out of character, and I know he didn't really intend to hurt anyone. The problem was that we let these things affect us and throw us off course.

But now that was history, and there was nothing we could do about it. Next year, we had to be sure to get to the Finals again. We would learn from our mistakes. And we would beat Boston.

We were a team on a mission. As soon as training camp began in the fall we started preparing for the Celtics by playing a more physical game. Riley even put in a no-lay-up rule: Anyone who came down the middle for a lay-up would get bumped and banged—even in practice. It took a few weeks, but after a while the officials got used to our more aggressive game, and we established a more physical style of play in the Western Conference. This added dimension made our fast break even more dangerous. We were now creating more misses. More misses led to more rebounds, which led to more fast breaks.

All season long we secretly rooted for the Celtics to win most of their games, just so we could meet them in the Finals. They were the only team we wanted. We had already won two championships, and winning a third just wasn't enough; it had to be a win over Boston.

Just as we had hoped, we met the Celtics in the Finals again. We came to Boston hungry for revenge, but the Celtics were unstoppable in the first game—the notorious Memorial Day Massacre. We couldn't get anything going that day. Boston could have beaten us with blindfolds on. Scott Wedman hit all 11 of his shots, and Danny Ainge scored 15 in the first quarter alone.

We were stunned. To get to the Finals we had sliced through other teams like a knife through butter. In the three playoff series leading up to the Finals, we had lost a total of only two games. And now this, one of the worst defeats in Laker history.

After Riley's dramatic locker-room speech about his father, we came out breathing fire and won that second game. We didn't dominate, but we played smart, and it was the kind of game that Boston usually wins on their home court. Kareem was his old self, running the floor, grabbing the rebounds, and tossing in skyhooks. When the clock ran out we ran off the floor happy and excited. The job wasn't over, but at least we were back on track.

That year the Finals followed a 2-3-2 format, which made for a little less traveling. After the split in Boston, we took two out of three at the Forum, so when we flew back East, we had a 3–2 lead.

In theory, we had two chances to win one game. But in practice, we knew we had to beat Boston right away. If Boston won Game Six, they would also win Game Seven.

By now the Celtics were tired, and we kept running at them. McHale had a big game, but it wasn't enough. The sweetest sound I ever heard was the silence in Boston Garden after we took a commanding lead in Game Six of the 1985

Finals. There were times when it had been so noisy in that building that we couldn't even hear Pat Riley talking in the huddle. But as Game Six started winding down, the whole place fell into a spooky silence.

The fans were stunned. They didn't really believe that such a thing was possible. Never before in Celtic history had Boston lost a championship series on their home court.

And now the same crowd that had been so nasty a year before actually started applauding us. We had finally won their respect, and maybe they were embarrassed about their earlier behavior. In any case, these people knew a winner when they saw one. If somebody had to beat their Celtics, they seemed to be saying, the Lakers deserved that honor.

After the game, Coop and I stayed in the showers a long time. "Coop," I told him, "I thought winning the NCAA was great. And I thought it was great when we beat Philadelphia in 1980. But this—this is the *ultimate*."

We were totally exhausted, but we had finally done it.

Kareem said later that our victory over Boston in 1985 was the highlight of his career. That goes for me, too.

What a great series it was! The level of play was even better than it had been a year earlier, and the atmosphere was much more positive. Maybe it was because Larry and I had finally become friends the previous summer. Or maybe it was because the Lakers had become a more physical team. Whatever the reason, there were no cheap shots and no unnecessary roughness. There was just great basketball.

By now the Celtics and the Lakers were almost mirror images of each other: Larry and I the same size, playing similar roles; Kareem and Parish, the big centers, each with his own unique and devastating shot; Kurt Rambis and Kevin McHale, the two blue-collar guys; Byron Scott and Danny Ainge, the streaky outside shooters; Dennis Johnson and Michael Cooper, the defensive specialists who could also score;

and M. L. Carr and Larry Spriggs, the towel wavers on the bench.

When we won the title, we were invited to the White House. We flew to Washington for a ceremony in the Rose Garden, and then it was back to the airport to continue on to Los Angeles. When we landed, thousands of fans were there to greet us and thank us. We had won our revenge, and finally, after all those years, the Laker fans could enjoy the victory they had long been dreaming about.

Two years later, in 1987, the Lakers and the Celtics met in the Finals for the third and last time during the 1980s. We had gone through Denver, Golden State, and Seattle with only a single loss. The Celtics had a rougher time—they swept the Bulls, but Milwaukee and Detroit each took them to seven games.

The Lakers had a team brunch on the day of the final Boston-Detroit game, and we all watched it together on a large-screen TV. Detroit was leading in the fourth period, but then Bird and Ainge took over the game, and Boston pulled through. It was a little strange; we were all cheering for them.

Although we went to six games in the Finals, it wasn't that close. The Celtics were good, but looking back on it, I don't think *any* team could have beaten the 1987 Lakers. We were fast. We could shoot. We could rebound. We could go inside. Hit the three-pointer—everything. Normally you have to play around some weakness, some flaw. But this team had it all.

We crushed Boston in the first game at the Forum, even though Bird hit 11 in a row during one stretch. And we blew them out again two days later when Coop hit six of seven three-point shots.

When the series moved to Boston, the Celtics won a game when Greg Kite, their reserve center, was able to shut down Kareem and dominate on the boards. This was the first time I can ever remember a player become the hero of a game without scoring a single point.

Game Four is the one I'll always remember, because that's when I hit the biggest basket of my life.

In the fourth quarter, with twenty-nine seconds left, the Lakers are down by one.

Coop sets a pick on D.J. I dribble up the right side and hit Kareem for a nice alley-oop. Now it's the Lakers by one.

Bird comes right back and hits a three. It's Boston by two with twelve seconds left.

We get the ball to Kareem. He puts up a hook shot. He misses, but McHale fouls him. Seven seconds left.

Kareem makes the first shot. Boston by one.

The second foul shot hits the rim. McHale gets the rebound. He loses the ball out of bounds.

Five seconds left, Boston by one. Laker ball.

The play is designed for me to go inside to Kareem, if I can hit him. Otherwise I'll shoot. Back in 1984 I blew those two games in this exact same situation, right here in Boston Garden. That was three years ago, but you better believe I'm thinking about it now.

Cooper inbounds the ball. I catch it on the left side. McHale switches over to guard me. I fake toward the baseline and come across the middle. I know I can get past Kevin. Parish is on Kareem pretty tight, so I can't risk a pass. Suddenly Bird and Parish come toward me. Now I'm facing their entire front line.

There's only one thing to do in this situation, and that's the hook shot. I put it up a little higher than usual, because Parish is right on top of me. It feels good on the release, and it goes in—right over the entire Celtics' front line. What a feeling!

When the ball drops through the net, all you can hear is a dozen guys screaming their heads off. The rest of Boston Garden is silent.

But it's not over yet. We're up by one, with two seconds left. Bird is on the floor. He throws up a prayer at the buzzer, and for a moment or two it looks pretty good. We're all holding our breath.

"Don't go in!" Wes Matthews yells from the bench. Bird is standing right in front of him, shooting from the corner. The ball listens to Wes. Bird's shot hits the ring and clangs off.

"You expect to lose on a skyhook," Bird says later. "You just don't expect it to be from Magic."

CHAPTER 14

LARRY BIRD

During my career in the NBA, I've gone up against hundreds, maybe even thousands of players. Many were good. A few were very good. A tiny handful even deserved to be called great. But there was nobody greater than Larry Bird.

Michael Jordan can do incredible things, including moves I've never seen before. There's nobody like him. But Larry was the only player I ever feared. I felt confident that the Lakers could beat any team in the league, and we usually did. But when we played the Celtics, no lead was safe as long as Bird was on the floor. That's why our championship victories over Boston in 1985 and 1987 were the most gratifying of all. When you beat Larry Bird, you knew you had beaten the best.

Larry and I came into the NBA at the same time, just after that final game of our college careers in 1979. And ever since then we've been linked in people's minds—"inextricably linked" is how the writers usually put it—although we played on opposite ends of the country. But it's true. There has always been a special bond between us, even during the years when neither of us wanted to admit it.

It took us a long time to become friends. Since we'd play each other only twice during the regular season, during our first five years in the league, most of our contact came through intermediaries—usually reporters, who kept asking us about the other guy.

If Larry scored 35 points the night before, they wanted to know why I hadn't done the same. If I dished off 15 assists, they came running to Larry. "Who's better?" they wanted to know. "You or Larry?" "You or Magic?" "Magic or Bird?" That question was asked again and again in the nation's sports pages and on countless radio talk shows. Maybe the fans enjoyed this debate, but it certainly didn't do much for our relationship.

It wasn't long before the press started reporting that we didn't like each other. They said Magic was too flashy for Bird, that Bird was too gloomy for Magic. After a while, we both started to believe it. If you're constantly being compared to somebody, and you hear often enough that you don't like each other, and you've never even had a conversation with the guy, eventually you start to resent him.

Every time the Lakers played against the Celtics, the game was hyped as a grudge match, especially by CBS. It was always "The Magic Man versus the Bird Man," as if we were still back in college. Before long, Larry and I started playing the roles that people expected of us. Before the game, we didn't say a word to each other, didn't even shake hands. We just gave each other a look that said, Yeah, okay, I know who you are, so let's get on with it.

All this changed in the summer of 1984, after our big matchup in the Finals, when we filmed two commercials together. The first one was in Los Angeles for the oil company Amoco. Then I flew out to his house in French Lick, Indiana, to shoot a spot for Converse. When you shoot a commercial you spend most of your time just standing around waiting. And while we stood around, Larry and I started talking.

As it turned out, we had plenty to talk about. We started with basketball, of course. Then we got into salaries—we had a lot of fun with that one. In 1979, when we came into the league, the NBA wasn't very glamorous. TV ratings were falling, arenas were half empty, and the average player made less than $150,000.

Five years later, attendance had soared. TV ratings were

way up—especially during the 1984 Finals. The average salary for an NBA player was now well over half a million dollars. And while I'm sure there were other explanations as well, everybody knew that one of the main reasons for the dramatic increase in salaries was the presence of Larry Bird and Magic Johnson.

Larry and I weren't exactly being underpaid. But we weren't making as much as we deserved, either. Soon we were laughing and gossiping about all the players in the NBA who, in our opinion, were both overrated and overpaid. As we sat there in Larry's living room in Indiana and compared notes, I knew that this was a guy I could talk to and laugh with.

It didn't take us long to realize that all of the supposed hostility between us had no real substance. It was a creation of the press, and nothing more. It had been going on for five years, but it took us only about an hour to see that there was nothing to it.

But the most important thing we learned about each other that summer had nothing to do with basketball or money. We discovered, as we should have known all along, that deep down we had a lot in common. It's true that on the surface we seem incredibly different. Even beyond race, people associate me with Hollywood. And they often think of Larry as a hick.

The truth is that we're both a couple of small-town boys. We're still close to our families, our teachers, our former coaches, and the people we grew up with. It's no accident that Larry went back to French Lick every summer, while I returned to Lansing. We knew where we came from, and where we ultimately belonged.

Becoming friends with Larry Bird meant a lot to me. It's not just that I respect him so much, although I do. There's also a part of me that wants to get to know the great players of our time. It's not enough to play against them or watch them on film. Years from now, I want to sit down with my kids and pop in a videotape of Michael Jordan's dunks, Julius

Erving's moves, or Larry Bird's passes. And I'm glad that I'll be able to say, "See that guy? I know him."

After our meeting at Larry's house, everything was different between us. We were still rivals, of course. But now there was a warmth that made our competition much more fun. One time I was out with an injury when the Celtics came to the Forum. Before the game started, Larry walked over to our bench to say hello. "Magic, you're not playing? Then I'm gonna put on a show for you. I want you to sit back and enjoy the Larry Bird show."

Larry had an amazing afternoon, with something like 36 points, 20 rebounds, and 15 assists. And every time he scored, he looked over at me and smiled. I just shook my head. What a strange feeling it was: My team was getting blown out, and this guy was doing it in my honor! After the game I congratulated him on what he had accomplished. But we both knew that I couldn't wait to return the favor in Boston Garden. And before long, I did.

As the years went on, we sent each other funny notes and gag gifts, especially when one of us was injured and needed a lift. When I started a T-shirt company and sent Larry a few samples, he wrote back a thank-you note. "Thanks for the shirts," it said. "P.S. Get a job."

And when I started putting on an annual exhibition game in Los Angeles to raise money for the United Negro College Fund, Larry was the first guy I called. The Celtics didn't normally let him participate in charity games. But Larry wanted to play in this one, and he convinced Red Auerbach to allow it. We were on the same team that night, and we had a ball.

Sometimes it felt like the two of us were the only members of an exclusive club. Julius Erving had retired, and Kareem was on his way out. Michael Jordan was clearly the man of the future, but in his early years in the league he wasn't ready to join us. To be in this club you needed more than talent; you also had to be a winner.

Neither of us was ever satisfied with his own game. Take Larry's magnificent season in 1983–84. Not only did the

Celtics beat us for the world championship, but Larry was voted the league MVP. At that moment he was undeniably the best basketball player in the world. So what did he do when he won that trophy? Did he sit back and relax? No way! He stashed it away in a drawer and spent the entire summer back in French Lick, making himself even better. He lifted weights all morning, and practiced his shooting every afternoon. What a great competitor!

The amazing thing about Larry is that he achieved his success without some of the natural talents that other players take for granted. My own physical gifts are limited, but compared to this guy I'm one of the Flying Wallenda Brothers. White men can't jump? He was living proof. Some white men don't move too quickly, either. A lot of players run faster, and yet Larry always seemed to beat them up the court. Maybe that's because he knew exactly where he was going and what he intended to do once he got there.

His physical shortcomings only added to my respect for him, because he never allowed them to stand in his way. Larry Bird was a testament to the importance of fundamentals. He learned to do it all, whether it was passing, rebounding, driving to the basket, or outside shooting.

And, like me, he did it the old-fashioned way. He worked and worked, and then he worked some more. I don't think I've ever seen a more dedicated athlete. To most players, basketball is a job. To Larry, it was life.

He understood the game at a higher level than most other players. Neither of us was brilliant as a one-on-one defender. But when it came to *team* defense, we were as good as they come. A team defensive player sees the whole picture. He understands the other team's plays. He relies on instinct and intuition. He reads the floor and anticipates what's going to happen. That's why the two of us came up with so many steals. We had point-guard instincts in big-man bodies.

Sure, Larry was technically a forward. But in his heart he was a point guard. He was the guy who directed most of the plays, and the ball usually went through him before anything happened. He was the only player I knew who could control the game without taking a shot. More than any guy I've seen, he made everybody around him play better.

Including me. Although Larry and I rarely played on the same court, he was always the yardstick I measured myself against. I was continually looking over my shoulder at him, just as he was doing with me. Every morning I would open the sports pages to see what Larry had done the night before. Did he get a triple-double? If so, I had to work harder.

During the summer, when I was working on my outside shooting, I might go for an hour and get tired. I'd be about to stop, but then I'd think, No, wait, I bet Larry is still out there practicing. And that would motivate me to shoot for another hour.

In 1987, after eight years in the pros, I finally won the MVP award. Larry had already won it three times, but who's counting? We were like two successful executives in the same big corporation who were competing against each other every step of the way. Three times there was a job open at the highest level, and three times he was able to advance over me. And now, at long last, I had beaten him out.

That's why the MVP meant so much. As a team player, I had accomplished everything there was to accomplish, but as an individual, something was still missing. Winning had always been my ultimate goal, and the same was true for Larry. But I would have been disappointed if he had left the league with three MVPs and I with none.

When I picture Larry Bird on the court, I always see him being guarded closely by my teammate Michael Cooper. Michael would continually come up with ways to shut Bird down, and Larry would always come back with some new trick. Coop was the best in the league at stopping Bird, which meant that he was successful about half the time. Coop used to watch hours of film in order to become familiar with every move in Bird's repertoire. He was obsessed with Bird, even taking videotapes of Larry on his vacations. And I've heard

Larry say that when he practiced by himself in the summer, he imagined that Cooper was guarding him.

Cooper and Bird were also two of the best trash talkers in the league, and all through the games they'd yap at each other. It was always fun to listen to them, especially when they made each other laugh. If Coop blocked Bird's shot, Larry would say, "Okay, you stopped that one, but you won't get *this* one." *Swish!* Or Bird would hit a jump shot and then turn to Cooper. "You can't guard me," he'd say. "There's no *way* you can stop me." And Cooper would say, "You've been lucky, baby, but you won't hit the next one." And he wouldn't.

In one game during the 1984 Finals, Cooper made two great defensive plays in a row on Bird. Next time down the court, Bird said, "Coop, I'm going to wear you out on this one." Bird got the ball from Dennis Johnson, and when he went up to make the shot, Cooper went up with him. Coop *knew* he had it blocked, but Bird fooled him: Instead of shooting the ball, he threw a supernatural pass to Robert Parish that seemed to loop right around not only Cooper, but Kareem, too. I thought Coop was going to faint right there on the court. When Parish dunked the ball, Bird looked over at Coop and smiled. He didn't have to say a word.

When we played Boston again in the Finals the following year, Bird and Cooper were back at it. It used to drive Michael crazy when Larry would tell him exactly what he was planning to do. "I'm gonna take your skinny butt down low," Bird said in Game One of the series. Three seconds later, Bird posted up and jumped right in Cooper's face. *Swish.*

It took two years, but Coop evened the score when, during the second game of the 1987 Finals, he set a playoff record by hitting six three-point shots against the Celtics. On the first one, Larry had left him open. When Coop hit the second one, Larry said, "Luck." When number three went in, Coop said, "Luck, huh? You better come out and fucking guard me." After number four, Coop said, "Hey, Larry, better get on me 'cause I'm wearing your ass out."

When he hit number five, Coop said just one word: "Face"—which is NBA slang for "In your face." But when he hit the last one, Cooper kept silent. There was nothing more to be said.

Black fans were always aware of Bird, even in the beginning, when they pretended not to notice him. At first, many blacks didn't think he was all that good. It was hard for them to accept that this guy could really play, that he could do almost everything the best black players could do. Some of these fans resented him. They thought he was nothing more than a media creation, a white star produced to satisfy the white public. Actually, Bird did everything possible to stay away from the media. I was the one they kept interviewing, because I enjoyed the attention. He never did.

Sooner or later, the black fans came around. They might not have liked Larry Bird, but they had to respect him.

He was like no white player they had ever seen. It wasn't only his talent that they noticed; it was also his attitude. When you were on the court with him, he gave off the aura that you couldn't touch him. The fact that he talked trash was even more surprising. That's playground stuff, and blacks weren't used to hearing it from whites. It used to bother some black players. They wondered, Is he talking that stuff to *me*? But he backed it up night after night, and that's what counts.

If Larry could have done a 360 dunk and laughed at you, he would have. But he couldn't. So instead he'd hit a three-pointer and laugh at you.

Larry Bird could walk onto a playground in any black neighborhood and fit right in. I always figured he grew up playing with blacks, but I couldn't imagine how that could have happened in a small town in Indiana. I learned only recently that there was a big resort hotel in French Lick, and that the black employees used to play basketball every afternoon during their break. When Larry was in seventh grade, he used to run right over there after school. He was only a kid, but they always let him play.

The filmmaker Spike Lee has been taking digs at Larry for years. But I've always thought that this was just an act. Spike may not admit it, but if he didn't respect Larry, he wouldn't be doing that. Besides, New York fans are well aware of the Celtics, because they're the one team the Knicks could never beat.

Detroit used to have a similar problem. Back in 1987, when the Celtics beat the Pistons in the Eastern Conference Finals, Dennis Rodman was asked about Bird. Now Larry had just scored 37 points in the seventh game of that series, and the Celtics had won by three points to advance to the Finals. Rodman must have been incredibly frustrated to have come so close. He was putting down Bird, and when a reporter asked him why Larry had won the MVP three times, Rodman said it was because he was white. The reporters took the quote to Isiah Thomas, and Isiah agreed with Rodman.

We were getting ready to play the Celtics in the Finals, but the only thing the press wanted to talk about was Isiah's comment about Larry. People wanted to know how I felt. I've always been a Larry Bird fan, and I wasn't going to change my opinion because Isiah had said something stupid. On the other hand, Isiah was my friend. And I, too, had said some stupid things in my career, especially when I was pressured and frustrated. I thought Larry handled the whole thing beautifully when he said, "I knew right off the bat that those remarks didn't come from Isiah's heart. They came from his mouth."

Early in 1991, during the All-Star weekend, *Sports Illustrated* decided to shoot a cover photograph of the starting five players who would represent the United States in the 1992 Olympics. The team hadn't been picked yet, but the magazine had its own candidates in mind: Michael Jordan, Charles Barkley, Karl Malone, Patrick Ewing, and me. There's nothing wrong with that list, but where was Larry? Unless he was included, I didn't want to be in that photograph. I just couldn't imagine an Olympic team without him.

That's our decision, not yours, said the magazine's editors. Besides, Larry hasn't decided if he wants to play.

When I called Larry, he confirmed that he hadn't made up his mind. He wondered if he was too old for the Olympic team, and thought that maybe his spot should go to somebody younger. But several of us kept working on him, and in the end he came around. After we spoke, I went ahead and posed with the other four guys.

It meant the world to me that he showed up at my "retirement" ceremony at the Forum. We were playing the Celtics that day, but Larry's back was killing him, and he wasn't traveling at all during that period. He had missed the All-Star Game a week earlier, and yet he insisted on making the long trip from Boston.

Naturally, he got to the Forum early, well before the rest of the team. We had a few minutes to talk, and he told me how much he was enjoying the baby boy that he and his wife had adopted. He wasn't able to play basketball, but he had found something else that was even more satisfying. To a guy who was a couple of hours away from retirement, and who had a baby of his own on the way, those words sounded pretty good.

Later, during the actual ceremony, Larry spoke to the crowd about all the battles between our two teams, and the mutual respect between the Celtics and the Lakers.

When Larry was introduced, I was thrilled when the Forum crowd gave him a standing ovation. They cheered him so loudly that he told the fans, "Hey, *I'm* not the one retiring here." But I think our fans were saying good-bye to both of us at the same time. They might have hated the Celtics, but they respected the individual players. And there was nobody they respected more than Larry. Whenever he came to town, the boos would turn to oohs.

I had always imagined that the two of us would retire together—at the exact same moment. It's the seventh game of the Finals, the Lakers against the Celtics. There's one minute left in the game, and the score is tied.

And then, suddenly, it's time to leave. Larry and I just shake hands, walk off the court, and disappear.

But even that wouldn't be the end of it. When we were old, we'd sit down together every summer and play checkers.

And I'd whip his ass.

CHAPTER 15

ISIAH AND MICHAEL

Sometimes an NBA championship series contains a single defining moment that people remember for years. In 1984, it was Kevin McHale tackling Kurt Rambis. In 1987, it was my junior, junior skyhook that won Game Four against the Celtics. The following year, against the Detroit Pistons, the Lakers made good on Pat Riley's guarantee of a repeat victory. We were the only team in *any* professional sport to win back-to-back championships during the 1980s. It was a bruising, difficult, seven-game series. But what people remember most clearly from those two weeks is a controversial play that actually happened before the games began. They remember the kiss.

Before the start of each game, Isiah Thomas and I greeted each other with a kiss. The two of us are close friends, and this was our way of saying hello. I hug and kiss my dad every time I see him. I do the same with my brothers and my close friends. So do a lot of men—especially in other countries.

But some people had never seen American men kissing each other. Especially on national TV. And especially athletes. And I guess it made them uncomfortable. Of course, anytime you show affection for another man, people are going to whisper. The press jumped all over us. Some people in the media thought it was funny; others thought our behavior was inappropriate.

Some of our teammates didn't like it, either. I'd go over

to shake a guy's hand before a game, and he'd say, "Just don't kiss me like you do Isiah." Some of the guys on both sides thought we should be showing a little more hostility toward our opponents. And I know that Coop didn't approve. To him, it was like kissing the enemy before the battle. He felt better about it when he decided that my kissing Isiah was like giving a cigarette to a condemned man before you lead him to the firing squad. But Isiah and I didn't really care what people thought. Everybody who knew us understood what was going on.

I had met Isiah years ago through Mark Aguirre, who played for Dallas and then Detroit. Mark went to DePaul, and I met him in 1979 when he played in the Final Four against Bird and Indiana State. He and Isiah knew each other from Chicago, where they both grew up.

For years, the three of us hung out together, mostly during the off-season. One time, early on, we all took our future wives to Maui for a week. And every summer the six of us used to spend a day at Cedar Point, a big amusement park in Ohio. We'd meet in Detroit and rent a bus to Cedar Point, just for the chance to be kids again.

I didn't want to go near the roller coaster, but Mark, Isiah, and the women teased me into it. My legs are so long that I had trouble getting into my seat, and I somehow threw off the timing on the whole machine. The roller coaster came to a complete stop just before Cookie and I got to the top. I've never said so many prayers. When we finally got off, the manager came over and said, "I hope you don't mind, but we'd appreciate it if you didn't ride this again." Hey, no problem!

We'd spend most of the day playing carnival games, like the baseball toss, or tossing rings over milk bottles. The three of us won so many stuffed animals that we had to hire a police officer and a cart to follow us around the park. Other people would stop playing to gather around and watch us. First you'd win a small animal. If you kept on winning, they'd give you bigger and bigger ones. When that happened, the attendant would ring the bell, and call out, "We have another chooooooicccce winner!'' to attract other customers. We just loved it. Sometimes we stayed too long, and they'd ask us to move on. When it was time to leave, we'd take all the stuffed animals and give them away to kids at the park or to a charity.

We haven't done anything like that for a few years now, and I regret it. I miss hanging out with Mark and Isiah, and just being ourselves. When you get successful, you become so busy with your own agenda and your various businesses that it's a lot harder to see your old friends.

Both Mark and Isiah grew up in such tough circumstances that I sometimes wonder how they survived. Isiah was hassled by gangs who wanted him to join. One time his mother had to stand at the door with a shotgun to keep them away. There was plenty of crime in their neighborhood, and Isiah could easily have gone down that road. But he didn't—in part because his mother sent him to a good private school in the suburbs.

He was the youngest of nine kids. His father left when Isiah was three. The family was so poor they didn't have enough beds for all the kids. They used to eat ''wish'' sandwiches—two slices of stale bread, and they wished they had something to put in between.

Mark came from a similar world, with poverty and violence all around. His neighborhood was so bad that when he was in high school he wouldn't even allow college recruiters to come to his house.

My own upbringing, of course, was very different. And unlike my two friends, I still had my father. But all three of us had known tragedies in our teenage years. With me it was the loss of Reggie Chastine and then Terry Furlow. With Isiah it was a brother who became a drug addict and his teammate Landon Turner, who was paralyzed in a car accident a few months after Indiana won the NCAA title.

My friendship with Isiah was based on a lot of good conversation. He is a real student of the game, and we've had some long, serious discussions about exactly what it takes to be a winner. Ever since he came into the league, he'd been fixated on being a champion. Over the years, I told him most of my secrets, and I think I helped him learn a lot—especially about leadership.

Every champion team needs a leader, and everybody on the team has to follow the main man. He's got to stay on his teammates, making sure they keep their edge on the court. But what happens off the court is just as important. The talent takes care of itself, or you wouldn't have gotten this far, but the guys also have to get their rest. If they saw me, the biggest bachelor, going to bed early in the playoffs, that sent a message. Riley couldn't monitor everybody by himself, so I used to talk to the guys individually. Sometimes I yelled at them. That's the sort of thing I would talk to Isiah about.

Isiah and Mark were there for me when I was so down after Boston beat us in 1984. Three years later Isiah had a similar experience. In the 1987 Eastern Conference Finals against Boston, he made a bad pass with five seconds left in Game Five. Bird picked it off, and the Celtics won, taking a 3-2 lead in the series. As soon as the game was over, I called Isiah in his hotel. I knew what he was going through, and how much he had to be hurting. I warned him to expect a lot of criticism. People would be looking back to that play again and again, and he had to be prepared for the backlash. It was tough on him, but he knew that if anyone could understand how he was feeling, I could; I had been there. That wound up being the key game of the series, and the Celtics went on to win it. That was also the year that Rodman and Isiah made their comments about Larry Bird being overrated.

For a few years, Isiah and I went to New York every summer, where one of the few ways we could talk outside without people bothering us was to ride through Central Park in a horse-drawn carriage. With some friends I go out dancing or partying, but Isiah and I usually stay in and talk. Sometimes we'd hop on a plane for some other city at the last minute. His wife, Lynn, lived in Atlanta before they got married, and once we went down there to visit her.

When I lived in Bel Air, I had a room in my house set aside for him—I called it the Isiah Room. Other visitors could stay there, too, but it was special for him. Sometimes Mark came along, and there were nights when the three of us played HORSE all night on the indoor court in my house. We were having so much fun that we lost track of the time. Next thing we knew, the sun was coming up.

But the fact that Isiah played for Detroit, and that Mark joined the team in 1988, didn't mean I liked playing the Pistons. I love competing against my friends, so that wasn't it. It was the way the Pistons played that I didn't care for. Some teams are physical, and there's a place for that in the NBA. But the Pistons go beyond that. As Rick Mahorn once said—and he should know—a physical game for the Pistons is when everyone is bleeding from the mouth.

During the 1988 Finals against the Lakers, these guys were more than physical. They were vicious. The Bad Boys, they called themselves. Somebody else called this series Beauty vs. the Beast. Detroit tried to intimidate us with their style of play. As Boston had done in 1984, they tried to take us out of our game. But they played a lot nastier than the Celtics ever did. They'd foul you, and they'd hit you one more time after that. They'd even stand over you to make sure you knew who had done it. Like a boxer whose opponent was already on his knees, they liked to give you one more elbow to your head.

Bill Laimbeer was the worst. Or, as Tony Kornheiser once referred to him in *The Washington Post*, Bill "Would It Be Terribly Inconvenient if I Jammed My Fist into Your Kidney on This Possession" Laimbeer. He's limited in talent, and playing rough is how he survives in the league. Some people call him a dirty player. To me, he's more of a cheap-shot artist. Fouling is one thing, but Laimbeer will try to punish you at the end of the foul. He'll smack a guy on the head or push him all the way down so he'll hit the floor harder.

And yet off the court he seems to be a nice guy. And you can't deny that he's been an effective starter for Detroit. He's big, and he takes up a lot of room. If you sag down in to guard him, he can hit the three-pointer. Most big guys can't do that. He's also a good defensive rebounder. But most players hate him. He is definitely the most unpopular guy in the league.

Although I don't like the Pistons' style of basketball, Chuck Daly deserves a lot of credit for having made it work. We beat them in 1988, but in 1989 the Pistons came back and beat us. They repeated the following year, against Portland. They didn't have that much talent, but Daly was brilliant in using the skills they had. And they certainly played tough on defense. The Pistons aren't the nicest players you'll ever meet. But they got the job done, and I've got to respect them as winners.

When we went to Detroit during the 1988 Finals, I was so tense that I didn't even see my family. I asked them not to come to the hotel, and they understood; I was there for business, and I had to be focused. Sometimes I got moody and tense during the playoffs, and I didn't want them to see me like that. They would have thought something was wrong.

But that was just the intensity of our team during playoff time, and especially in 1988, when we were trying to repeat. We all realized that this might be our last and best shot at another title. We didn't know how long Kareem would stay around, but it was clear that he wouldn't be playing much longer. Riley's guarantee put the goal right in front of us, and it was time to go to work.

We didn't start well. We were exhausted from two tough seven-game series, and Detroit stunned us in the first game at the Forum when Adrian Dantley hit 14 of 16 from the floor. They intimidated us, and we didn't stand up to them. When that first game was over, we knew we had to be more physical. It was like Boston in 1984. But this time it took us only one game to figure that out.

Just before Game Two, I came down with a severe case of the flu. I had the chills real bad. I was also running to the bathroom every five minutes. I was just miserable, but insisted on playing. I was exhausted after about two minutes on the floor. At halftime they had to give me an I.V. for fluids. For the first time in my career, I had to pick my spots, when to play and when to rest. There was no choice. If we lost the first two games at home, we could kiss that series good-bye. I *really* wanted us to win, and I managed to score 23 points. Riley called it a "hope" game—you just hope you get through it. And somehow, we did—well enough to beat them, too, 108–96.

Then it was on to Detroit, where we beat them pretty good in Game Three. The Pistons came back to take Game Four. I remember that one very clearly, because Isiah and I got into a fight. The Pistons must have decided to get physical with me, because every time I went to the hoop, I got hammered. Detroit was up by a big margin in the fourth quarter. I drove to the basket and two of the Pistons hit me real hard. I'd had enough of this rough stuff. Okay, I said to myself. The next guy who goes to the hoop, I'm gonna take him out.

Well, the next guy happened to be Isiah. I caught him in his rib cage with my elbow and knocked him down. When he got up, he threw the ball at me and started pushing me. Our teammates had to separate us. "You see what I've been getting," I told him. "Well, now I'm giving it back."

The series was tied now, two apiece. And everybody was waiting to see what would happen with Isiah and me before the next game. One writer said that watching us fight was like watching Wally belting the Beaver. Were we still friends? Would we still kiss each other? The two of us talked about it, and we both felt the same way. This was basketball. It was not personal. When you're going for a championship, there's no room for friends. When I hit him, he had to retaliate.

But we could still greet each other in our usual way. The kiss was just our form of a handshake.

Detroit won Game Five, which gave them a 3–2 lead. It was a good thing we were headed back to the Forum.

Isiah was absolutely incredible in Game Six. He scored 43 points, including 25 in the third quarter, a Finals record. And he did that with a sprained ankle. With a minute left in the fourth quarter, the Pistons were up 102–99. If they could just hold on for another sixty seconds, the title would be theirs.

But a minute is a long time in the NBA. Byron caught a pass from James and hit a fourteen-foot jumper. That brought us to within one. When Isiah missed from the baseline, James got the rebound and called time out. We got the ball to Kareem. Laimbeer fouled him—not very hard, especially by Laimbeer's standards. Kareem wasn't even injured, and he hit both free throws. With fourteen seconds left, we were up by one, 103–102.

Dumars came down for the Pistons and put up a shot with eight seconds left. It hit the rim. Rodman lost the rebound. Byron picked it up. Rodman hit him hard with an intentional foul. Byron was so mad he missed both shots. But Detroit couldn't score, and we held on, tying the series at 3–3.

Game Seven looked like a sure Lakers blowout—especially with Isiah on crutches. But just as I expected, he forced himself to play. We were ahead by 15 in the fourth period, but Detroit just wouldn't give up. Riley kept warning us that the game wasn't over. "Stop the celebrating," he said. "Keep pushing. Be prepared."

The Pistons kept narrowing our lead. From 15 points it fell to 10. With four and a half minutes left, it was down to six. And Kareem and I were both playing with five fouls.

With only nineteen seconds remaining, the Lakers were up by five. But Detroit had the ball and it wasn't over yet. Dumars hit. Lakers by three. Sixteen seconds left. James was fouled. He made one. Lakers by four. Only six seconds left. Then Laimbeer hit a three-pointer. Lakers by one. I found A. C. Green, who threw it in. Lakers by three, 108–105. With one second left, Isiah got the ball at midcourt. He and I collided. No foul either way. He couldn't get off a shot.

Detroit had staged a magnificent comeback, and we were lucky the game ended when it did. It wasn't the most glorious win in our history, but we had finally achieved the most difficult goal of all: a repeat.

Until then, no team in NBA history had ever won three consecutive seven-game series. And no playoff series had ever been played so late. The season finally ended on June 21. It was the longest day of the year—in more ways than one.

The next year we played Detroit again. Before we got to the Finals, we won 11 playoff games in a row. It was starting to look like we would win our third consecutive title. "Three-peat," as Byron termed it.

But then our luck ran out. Just before the Finals started, Byron came down with a torn hamstring. There was no time to adjust to playing without him, and we lost the first game, 109–97. Then, in Game Two, what happened to Byron happened to me: torn hamstring. I almost wished I had gotten hurt earlier in the season instead of getting that far. I'll never forget the sad expression on my teammates' faces when I got injured. They were looking at me, still hoping I was okay. But there was nothing any of us could do. I tried to play in Game Three, but just couldn't cut it. Although James scored 40 in that one, it wasn't enough.

Our guys played great. But without our starting backcourt, we couldn't beat Detroit. They swept the series.

I don't like to blame injuries, but I still wonder about that series. Nobody can deny that the Lakers were on an incredible roll. We were hot, and everybody knew it. We hadn't lost a single game since the playoffs began. When we came into an opponent's airport, and their fans started talking about the home team, that just made us swell up even more. I remember thinking, Okay, when we come back here Sunday, I'll be looking for that same guy. I want to see what he's going to say *then*.

If it hadn't been for a couple of hamstrings, things might have been different. But you never know. Detroit played some good basketball, and maybe they would have won anyway. If we couldn't win, however, I'm glad Isiah's team did. He had waited a long time for this moment, and he had come so close the previous year. Now, finally, he was in the winner's circle.

In 1990, the Pistons did it again when they beat Portland in five games. A year later, however, they were swept by

Chicago in the Eastern Conference Finals. That was a bitter series that ended on a sour note. Before the last game was even over, several of the Pistons walked right by the Chicago bench and off the floor without stopping to congratulate the winners.

That was an embarrassment, not only to themselves, but to the fans and the game of basketball. It was bad sportsmanship, and there was no excuse for it. The Pistons wanted respect, but they didn't give it. For the previous three years, they had beaten Chicago in the playoffs. And each time, the Bulls had been gracious in defeat. Detroit wasn't. They were disrespecting their opponent, and no player likes that.

Isiah behaved badly, and I told him that. He's a great player, and he's certainly good enough to have been chosen for the 1992 Olympic team. But when he walked off the court, I believe that sealed it for him. The incident was in the papers for weeks, and the fans will never forget it. That was plain ugly. And wrong.

There's a lot of bad blood between the Pistons and the Bulls, and especially between Isiah and Michael Jordan. As far as I know, the problem between them started at the 1985 All-Star Game in Indianapolis. Jordan had a bad game, getting only nine shots. Some people, including Michael himself, were convinced that Isiah had kept the ball away from him to teach him a lesson. It's possible. The previous day, in the slam-dunk contest, Michael had shown up in a Nike sweatsuit and gold chains instead of his uniform. Some guys thought he was bragging about his many endorsements.

Michael was mad at Isiah, and at me, too. According to one article, Isiah and I had conspired to deny Michael the ball. But that's ridiculous. I wasn't even on Michael's team. I was playing for the West. We were *supposed* to deny him the ball. But I was also a friend of Isiah's. And back then, Isiah and I had the same agent. Maybe that gave people ideas.

For a year or two, everyplace I went I was asked about Michael. It was a little like my early years with Bird, when we didn't know each other and the press made us out to be enemies. Finally, before a game between our two teams, we sat down and talked. "The media would love for us to be fighting each other," I told him. "But I don't want that to happen. And I think it would be a shame if we left this game without knowing each other."

Since then, I've come to know him well. He's one of the first people I talked to when I got the news about HIV. And I believe I helped persuade him to play on the 1992 Olympic team. At first he was reluctant, but could you possibly imagine an American basketball team without Michael Jordan? It's crazy.

I've read stories that say I'm jealous of all his endorsements. Fortunately, I'm not the jealous type. And when you're making the kind of money I'm making, you have no business being jealous of anybody. If you are, you've got the wrong priorities.

But I certainly would have enjoyed being in Michael's position. ProServ did a tremendous job for him, and I take my hat off to them. Earlier on, I had tried to talk Converse into doing for me what Nike did later for Michael. No, they said, a Magic Johnson shoe would never sell. Why not? I asked. Because nobody would buy a shoe with a player's name on it.

Oh, really?

Eventually, Converse did put out a Magic Johnson shoe. But by then it was a few years too late.

Michael Jordan might be the most popular athlete ever. But I wonder if people realize how tough a burden that must be. Everybody wants a piece of him, and people expect him to represent the game of basketball. For years, Dr. J. was the ambassador. When he stepped down, I knew it was my turn. And now Michael knows that he's the man.

Larry Bird and I were two of the smartest players you'll ever see. But Michael can do things on the court that we could barely imagine. He's just incredible. Even if he has a bad game and goes 1 for 10, which is rare, that one shot might be the most amazing move you've ever seen. In terms of the excitement he creates, Michael Jordan is the greatest player who ever laced up a pair of sneakers.

There aren't many guys I'd pay to watch, but he's at the top of my list. Everybody knows about his offensive abilities, and there's not much I can add to that except to say that the players enjoy watching him just as much as the fans do. But Michael is even better than most fans realize. In addition to everything he can do with the ball, he's also a great defensive player.

And I've got to admire the way he's adjusted his own game to make his team a winner. For a while, the Bulls consisted of Michael and eleven other guys. He was great to watch, but Chicago wasn't winning. Michael always wanted to win, and he realized that the Bulls could never win a title unless he became less dominating. A lot of players *say* they want to win, but they find it impossible to see beyond their own stats. They're into the "I" syndrome instead of the "we." Michael understood that one player can't win in the NBA, no matter how great he is; five guys can always shut down one. But if that one guy is a *team* player, and he has a partner like Scottie Pippen to work with, that's another story.

A few years back, the idea came up for a one-on-one match between Michael Jordan and me. It would be shown on pay TV, and a lot of the money would be given to charity. But not all of it. Michael and I both play in a sport where each team has a salary cap, and we thought it would be fun if for just one night, we could make as much as the market would allow. Both of us were excited about it, and our agents, Lon Rosen and David Falk, started discussing how it might work.

But the NBA has a clause in its collective bargaining agreement that says any sporting event involving a player has to be approved by both the league and the player's team. My contract had a "love of the game clause," which would have allowed me to participate in the one-on-one. Michael's contract was a little more limiting, and there would have been problems.

Then Lon came up with an interesting twist: Michael and

I would both retire from basketball, play our game, and then come back again. We kicked it around for a while, but we decided against it. The last thing we wanted was a fight with the NBA.

Then the players' association came out against the whole idea of Michael and me playing each other. The head of the players' association was Isiah Thomas. Michael's response was that this was personal on Isiah's part, and that if Isiah was playing, nobody would be interested.

In the end, we decided not to go ahead. But I still think it would have been an amazing event. We would have staged it shortly after the playoffs. The format would be two fifteen-minute halves, using the half-court. It would have been a huge moneymaker, not only for ourselves, but for several good causes.

When our match was still under discussion, *USA Today* listed Michael as an 8–5 favorite. That suited me fine, because I enjoy being the underdog; it always makes me work harder.

We still talk about it. Whenever I see him, he says, "I could have beat you."

"No way," I reply. "I would have won."

"You can't stop me."

"Maybe not, but you can't stop me, either."

Maybe we're both right. If that's true, the last guy with the ball would win.

CHAPTER 16

WOMEN AND ME

This chapter will probably be the most widely read part of this book, for several different reasons. Some people may still be wondering if I got HIV from a homosexual encounter. Others will want to know what it was like to be with a number of women. Some may be hoping that I'll get down and dirty. (I won't.) And still others may be looking for me to apologize.

The truth is, I wouldn't be writing this chapter at all if I hadn't contracted HIV somewhere along the way. That's why I have a responsibility to deal with this subject, although I'd be a lot happier not to. This is my private life we're talking about.

I'm not writing about the women in my life in order to brag; I'm no Wilt Chamberlain. But I have to acknowledge that the virus in my body, which came from a casual encounter, has created tremendous curiosity about the role sex has played in my life. So I owe it to the reader to be candid. At the same time, I owe it to the women I've known, and also to Cookie and to myself, to be discreet. So there are no names here, no numbers, no graphic descriptions.

And no apologies. In the age of AIDS, unprotected sex is reckless. I know that now, of course. But the truth is, I knew it then, too. I just didn't pay attention. As often as I had heard about the importance of being careful, I never took it seriously. I couldn't believe that anything like this could happen to me.

Let me deal with the gay issue first, because people keep asking about it. I can understand the doubts of those who still wonder if I'm gay. For one thing, only a small percentage of Americans who have HIV or AIDS are men who got the virus from having unprotected sex with women. For another, in spite of everything I've said, a lot of people—and especially athletes—still *want* to believe that I got the virus through a homosexual encounter. Because if I did, that would let *them* off the hook. If they, too, have been promiscuous with the opposite sex, especially if it happened with any of the same women that I was with, it would be a big relief to know that Magic Johnson contracted HIV because he was gay or bisexual.

But I'm not. And it didn't happen that way. And it didn't happen through sharing a needle, because I've never done drugs.

I've already said it, but I'll say it again: I have never had a homosexual experience. I'm not gay or bisexual. If I were, I would say so. It's not my style to hide or deny something like that.

But given the history of AIDS, I guess it was understandable that there were rumors and speculation about my sexual orientation. I know that after my announcement, several major newspapers even put teams of reporters on the story. In fact, the rumors had started even before I found out I was HIV positive. Some people wondered why Isiah Thomas and I used to kiss each other before every playoff game. Others noticed that I often appeared at benefits and other social events around town without a date.

Kissing Isiah was about our friendship, not our sexuality. And the reason I didn't date much in public was out of respect for Cookie. She knew I saw other women. But that didn't mean I had to throw it in her face.

I'm now starting to understand just how naïve and insensitive I used to be on this whole topic. The day after I announced I had HIV, I appeared on Arsenio Hall's show. When I said that I wasn't gay, the audience broke into applause. It was a strange moment, and I felt a little awkward when it happened. And yet it didn't really occur to me that gay viewers would be offended by that applause. Today, of course, I understand their outrage. But I had to be sensitized on this whole topic, and I'm still working on it.

A few months later, I did an interview with *The Advocate*, a gay weekly magazine. During our conversation, the interviewer asked me an interesting question about my appearance on Arsenio:

"How do you think the crowd would have reacted if you had said you were gay?"

"I don't know," I replied.

"Do you think you would have gotten the same applause?"

"I'm sure not."

Growing up in Lansing, I didn't know any gay people except for one guy in our neighborhood who had been in jail.

"He's funny," people would say. "He's done guys."

I wasn't even sure what that meant. But I didn't want to admit it, so I just nodded. Later, when I moved to Los Angeles, I became a little more aware of gay people and the gay community. But until this happened to me, I was never really comfortable with gay people. Like many heterosexual men, I was always afraid that a gay man might come on to me. How would I react? Would I get angry?

But since my announcement, I've sat down and talked with a number of gay people, both individually and in groups. And especially people with HIV. The bond is there; I'm in the trenches with them and I'm fighting beside them. But until I contracted HIV, I didn't really understand their struggles or their gripes. Or what gay-bashing was all about. These days, when I go out and speak, I tell people that no matter how somebody got this virus, we've got to open our arms up to everybody who has it—and not just to me, because I'm heterosexual.

* * *

Where do we draw the line on the private relationships between men and women? The answer is, that line keeps changing. Is it really wrong for an unmarried man to have consenting sex with an unmarried woman? With many women? That's what some of the criticism has been about. Well, then, how much is too much? As long as nobody gets hurt, what's wrong with sex between unmarried adults?

From what I've seen, men and women feel very differently about these questions. And yes, there is definitely a double standard when it comes to sex and promiscuity. After my announcement, Martina Navratilova said that if a female athlete had contracted HIV after having many sexual encounters, she would have been treated far worse than I was. People would call her a slut, and she'd probably lose her endorsements right away. I'm sure that Martina was right about that.

People make all kinds of choices in their lives. Some drink. Some smoke. Some eat too much. That wasn't me. My pleasure was being with women.

All of this happened during my long, on-again, off-again relationship with Cookie, which she'll describe a little later. Some people can't understand how I could love one woman and be with others. But there was a part of me that was always with Cookie. Maybe that was Earvin, and the other part of me was Magic.

In any case, I was a single guy in my twenties. I had a job that took a lot out of me, both at home and on the road. And aside from hanging out with my teammates, one of my favorite ways to relax was being with women.

And I guess the feeling was mutual. The longer I played in the NBA, the more women seemed to be attracted to me. They say power is an aphrodisiac. Maybe so, but it's not the only one. So is success, and fame, and wealth, and winning.

My name played a part in it, too. All through my career there have been jokes and puns about it. Let's face it: "Magic" is a romantic, sexy name. When Fred Stabley first called me that back in high school, neither of us ever imagined some of the places it would lead.

But as much as I loved women, I loved basketball more.

I played hard and practiced hard. I told all the women I knew that they'd have to take a backseat to basketball. Only one woman really understood that and accepted it. And that was Cookie.

All through my years in the NBA, I felt that I couldn't get married until I retired from the game. Basketball used up everything that I had—emotionally, physically, and mentally. I wanted to be the best. I wanted to win. It wasn't enough to be playing in the NBA or to be making a lot of money. I wanted to win the championship every year, and I wouldn't settle for anything less. And I just didn't see how I could be that way and also be a good husband. Maybe other guys could, but not me.

Eventually, I wised up and married Cookie. As things turned out, less than two months after we were married, I thought my basketball days were over.

Until then, women were a big part of my life. But they weren't the only part. When I wasn't playing or practicing, or taking a nap, I had plenty of other things to keep me busy. I often went out with the boys—to movies, dinners, concerts, discos, and clubs. I was active in half a dozen businesses, and busy with all sorts of charities. I ran basketball camps for both kids and adults. I visited my family and my friends back in Michigan. I spent time with Cookie. I spent time alone.

And yes, I also fooled around. After Norm Nixon was traded, I became the team leader in that department. But until my announcement, most people didn't know that about me. I was discreet, and I kept it quiet. My teammates knew, of course. Coop knew the most, because he and I were so close. The other guys all had a pretty good idea, because we all stayed on the same floor of the hotel. But what I did, most of them were doing, too. Nobody ever said the Lakers were boy scouts.

There's an old joke in the NBA, and it's probably told in other sports as well. Question: What's the hardest thing about going on the road? Answer: Trying not to smile when you kiss your wife good-bye.

But nobody should be shocked by this information. Men on the road have always looked for diversion, whether they're athletes or traveling salesmen. It's natural, and it's been going on forever.

When you play in the NBA, there are women waiting to meet you in every city along the way. That's especially true with a high-prestige team like the Lakers. During the 1980s, the Lakers were seen as the sexiest and most glamorous team of them all. Los Angeles was glamorous. Winning was glamorous. Our fast break was sexy. And being the best team in the league made us seem *very* sexy.

Just about every time the bus brought us back to our hotel after a game, there would be forty or fifty women waiting in the lobby to meet us. Most of them were beautiful, and a few were just unbelievable. Almost all of these women were in great physical shape. Many of them spent as much time in the gym as we did.

Some were secretaries. Some were lawyers. Quite a few were actresses or models. Others were teachers, editors, accountants, or entrepreneurs. There were bimbos, too, but not that many. Most of these women were college-educated professionals. Some were black, some white, Hispanic, or Asian. Some of these women were very open about what they were doing, and some were more discreet. A few would even brag about all the players they had slept with. For others, all this was part of a very secret life.

Most of them were in their mid-twenties. Every now and then you'd come across a teenager, but if you were smart you stayed away from her. These kids were simply too young—not only legally, but emotionally, too.

Usually, the women waiting for us in hotel lobbies would pretend to be interested in autographs. But autographs were just a socially acceptable way of meeting the players. Even so, I rarely saw a player bring a woman up to his room right away. You never knew who was watching, and nobody wanted to be too obvious.

But you might sign that autograph and write down your

room number beside your signature. Or you might write your name and whisper, "Call me," or "See you in an hour."

When I got up to my room, there would always be a stack of phone messages. Dolores called, she's waiting in the lobby. Arlene called, she's wearing a red dress. Marian called, she's by the elevator.

Often, before I even checked into the hotel there would be a dozen or more calls from women I had never met. New York was the busiest. An operator at the Grand Hyatt once told me that I held the record for phone calls. In all the years she had worked there, she had never taken so many messages for a guest.

Sometimes I wouldn't even pick up the phone. Or I might ask the operator to hold all calls. But women kept calling, and some of them got through.

"Hello, Magic. This is Cheryl. Did you get my message?"

"But I don't *know* you."

"That's all right. I'll be at the game tonight, section forty-two. I'll be wearing a black sweater."

Or, "Hello, Magic. I'm just calling to ask where the Lakers are going after the game."

Sometimes the women who called were more direct. "Hello, Magic? I'm downstairs in the lobby. How would you like me to come up and satisfy you?"

This sort of thing happened constantly—especially in the larger cities. New York, Atlanta, Chicago, and Houston were hot towns. In the smaller cities and most of the South, the women were generally less aggressive.

Every large city had certain restaurants and night spots where the players would hang out. Most guys didn't enjoy staying in a small hotel room, especially after a game, so often a whole bunch of us would go out dancing. In Los Angeles it was Carlos & Charlie's, a restaurant-disco on Sunset Boulevard. In New York, the China Club was popular.

With so much competition, women who wanted to meet us were always looking for an edge. Some would send us cookies and cakes. Some would send flowers. You'd see big bunches of roses in the visitors' locker room of just about every NBA arena. At the Forum, some of the married guys would take these flowers home to their wives.

We also received a huge amount of fan mail. Every day, hundreds of perfumed letters arrived at the Forum. Some of the mail got pretty explicit, and it wasn't just letters, either. Sometimes women would send along photographs of themselves—usually out of uniform. And even videotapes, just to make sure you got the idea. Others sent their underwear. There was nothing subtle about it.

On the road, women who wanted to meet you would sometimes bribe hotel employees to find out what room you were in, or what floor the Lakers were staying on. I never allowed a woman into my room who just showed up and knocked on the door. But I can't say I wasn't tempted. In some hotels you could open your door at just about any time of day or night and find a beautiful woman standing there in the hall, hoping to be invited in.

There were times, especially in the first few years, when I brought a woman I had just met in the lobby up to my room. But that always made me nervous, because you'd hear stories. . . .

One guy on our team met a woman in the hotel lobby. She asked for an autograph, she was beautiful, and she made it clear that she was available. They spent the night together. Early the next morning, she left. When he woke up, he noticed that his wallet was missing. Except that this particular woman hadn't even bothered to remove the wallet from the guy's pants. *She'd taken the pants, too.* He had to borrow a pair of slacks for the bus ride to the airport.

You were definitely taking a chance when you brought a strange woman up to your room. That's because a few of them really *were* strange. Two players on our team had the experience of entertaining women who turned out to be slightly different from what these guys had expected. For one thing, the women weren't as beautiful as they had seemed at first glance. For another, it eventually became clear that they weren't women at all—they were men in drag. The guys were pretty upset, but they didn't keep it a secret. They told the rest of us, and we teased them about it for weeks.

At one point we were warned about a pair of groupies who had a scam going around the league. They would meet a player in the lobby or the bar of the hotel, and offer themselves as a kind of two-for-one special. When they got up to your room, they'd ask you to order drinks from room service. While one girl distracted you, the other would slip a sleeping pill into your glass. Before long you'd fall asleep, and then they'd rob you. And these two gals certainly did their homework. They usually showed up at the beginning of a long road trip, when everybody had plenty of cash.

It didn't happen very often, but every now and then you'd hear of a guy who paid for female companionship. A lot of people have heard that one of my teammates was arrested in Houston for trying to do business with an escort agency. Unfortunately for him, the agency had recently been taken over by the police.

A couple of years earlier, I was alone in my hotel room one night when I heard a woman crying out in the hall. Coop must have heard her, too, because we both opened our doors at the same time. We saw a young lady in tears—and not much else. When she stopped crying, she told us she was a hooker. She had been with one of our teammates. They'd had some kind of argument, and he'd thrown her out of his room without paying.

Could we do her a favor? she asked.

"Sure—what do you need?"

"Will you come down with me to my pimp's car and tell him what happened?"

Coop and I just looked at each other. It sounded like a great way to get ourselves killed! Just then a door opened, and the young lady's clothes came flying out into the hall.

Coop and I ended up consoling her as she got dressed. But there was no *way* we were going down to meet that pimp.

I never paid anyone for sex, and as far as I know, the two incidents I've just mentioned were unusual. You get to know your teammates pretty well when you travel together, but I guess you don't know everything.

I could never understand how a player could sleep with a woman on the day of a game. Some guys did, but I couldn't imagine doing that. I might spend the afternoon with a woman, but I would never have sex until the game was over.

Some people have the impression that ballplayers fool around everywhere they go. That they have somebody waiting for them in every city they visit. That they spend every free moment in bed. In my entire career, I've only known one or two guys like that.

One of my teammates really did have a woman in every city. We were playing in Cleveland, although the Coliseum is nowhere near the city—it's way out in the country, halfway to Akron. There was a terrible blizzard, and it took us forever to reach the hotel. When the bus finally pulled in, it looked like we were at the North Pole. We figured the whole state of Ohio had been shut down. But no sooner did we get off the bus than two women, all bundled up like Eskimos, came blowing in from the snow to visit this guy.

But that was rare. With most guys, basketball came first. That was certainly the case with me. I knew when to fool around with women and when not to. If I had a day off, no problem. After a game? Sure—unless we had another game the next night. In that case, forget it. I needed my rest.

There were players who stayed out all night, but I could never do that, either. Maybe in baseball you can get away with it. The game is different, and the players get to stay in the same city for three or four days. But basketball is strenuous, and the travel schedule is brutal.

Every person is different, of course. Some of the married players didn't fool around at all. Or if they did, they were so discreet that nobody knew about it. There were also a few players in the league who abstained for religious reasons.

Some guys would expect any woman they slept with to spend the night. Some women were happy to. Others wouldn't even consider it.

I myself never spent the night with a woman. It just didn't

feel right. Often, after we slept together, she'd want to stay. That's why I always explained in advance that I preferred to sleep alone, and that no matter what happened between us, I would be asking her to leave when it was over. That way it was her choice.

There were women who refused to go to bed with you unless they could also wake up with you. I can understand how they felt. For some of these women, it was a question of respect. But I would rather get turned down—and sometimes I did—than run into a misunderstanding later on.

Some guys liked women who were petite. Others liked them tall, or dark, or blond, or busty. For me, none of that mattered. What attracted me was a woman's sex appeal, the way she carried herself. I liked a woman who could make me laugh, who was self-assured, who could walk in and command a room.

I also liked women who could carry on a conversation. It sounds funny, but sometimes you'd meet a perfectly nice woman who just couldn't talk. No matter how beautiful she might be, I hated to be with anyone who just giggled. That's because being with a woman on the road is not just about sex. It's also about conversation and relaxing, and not being lonely. It's impossible to enjoy yourself with somebody if you can't communicate with her. If a woman had nothing to say, I'd find some excuse to end it quickly.

But most women talked easily. And if they didn't talk much, they'd ask questions. How does it feel to be famous? What's Kareem really like? Tell me about Arsenio.

Sometimes the questions were very explicit. Not about sex, but money. How much was I being paid? How much was So-and-so making? The more you told some women, the more turned on they would be. Most of the women in this group already had a good idea of our salaries, because they read the papers and paid attention to things like that. I sometimes felt that it wasn't so much me, but my paycheck that got them excited. They just couldn't resist the idea of going to bed with a guy who was making millions of dollars.

I also met women who were a delight to be with and became my friends. Even so, I never let myself get emotionally involved with somebody I met on the road. Sometimes you'd see a rookie do that. Every couple of years a new guy on the team would fall in love with a woman in another city. But these things would always end badly. We tried to protect our younger teammates, but a few guys got hurt anyway.

For example, a rookie might meet a young lady and fall for her. He'd be over at her place and notice that she was getting phone calls from other players. He'd feel betrayed, even though we had warned him that this would happen. Didn't she like him? Sure she did. But maybe she just wasn't interested in a relationship with one guy.

What it boiled down to was that many of these women were doing to men exactly what men have been doing to women all these years. They were treating us like sex objects. What they wanted was a conquest. And for some of them, most of the thrill was in the chase.

For others, the thrill was in fulfilling a particular fantasy. Sometimes it was simply having sex with a man who was famous or wealthy. Often, at least in my experience, the woman's fantasy involved having sex with you in some unusual place. On the roof of a hotel. On a beach. In an airplane. One woman wanted to try it in a hotel elevator. I went along for the ride.

Another woman I was friendly with asked me to come to her office. She had always dreamed of having sex right there on her desk while her colleagues were sitting in a board meeting in the very next room. We got away with it, but that one was definitely the scariest.

I enjoyed making women's fantasies come true, but you have to draw the line somewhere. One woman wanted to take me into a little phone booth at the back of a restaurant. That might be all right for a jockey, but a basketball player has certain limitations.

I had my own fantasies, too. Like many men, I had always wondered what it would be like to be with more than one woman at a time. There were times when I was able to arrange such an evening with two women. Or more. Usually I brought together women from different cities in order to protect my privacy—and theirs. Half the fun was in setting up these encounters, and in the secrecy.

Some people classify all of these women as groupies, but it's more complicated than that. To me, a groupie was somebody who more or less collected athletes, who was interested in meeting lots of them. There's a story about one famous player who met a gorgeous woman. She invited him home, and he was happy to accept. In return for her hospitality, she asked him to bring along a pair of autographed sneakers. When she opened her closet door to put them in, this guy practically fainted. There must have been about a hundred pairs of shoes lined up in there, arranged alphabetically by team.

In my early years in the league I often went off with groupies—or freaks, as they were called in the NBA. "Freaks in the house" meant there were women waiting in the hotel lobby. If your teammate went off with somebody, you'd say that So-and-so was "on" tonight. Or that he was "chosen."

After I was in the league for a while, I graduated to a more sophisticated group of women. Usually I met them through other people. I had many women friends, including some I never slept with. But they would often introduce me to *their* friends.

When it came to fine women, Los Angeles was tops. Every team enjoyed coming out to L.A., because even though most of them didn't fare too well when they played us in the Forum, Los Angeles had some of the most beautiful and sexiest women in the country. The players' wives knew that, too, which is why some of them made a point of coming along on their husbands' road trips to California.

As much as I enjoyed being with women, I wasn't always crazy about the bachelor's life, especially when women left messages: Why didn't you call me? Or: I heard you went out with So-and-so.

I was always straight with these women, and I treated them well. But some of them became more attached than they expected to. I can't pretend that dating lots of women was always easy, or that it was never awkward.

There were other problems, too. In 1990, I heard from a lawyer who claimed that I was the father of a two-year-old child in Maryland. Not surprisingly, the child's mother was interested in being compensated. My name even appeared on the child's birth certificate. There was only one problem: I had never even heard of this woman. But she came forward with a story about how I had visited her a number of times. I even agreed to take a blood test, but when I did, the lawyer claimed that the blood wasn't really mine—even though he was right there when the blood was taken! I actually had to take a *second* blood test before this ridiculous story finally disappeared. But not before a distorted version of it appeared in the *National Enquirer*.

I know *how* I got HIV. That's clear. But I don't know who gave it to me. I called a number of women before I made the announcement, so they could get tested. I also called women after the announcement. They knew about it by then, of course, but I still felt some responsibility toward them. Of the women I have talked to, nobody has tested positive—at least not yet. Thank God for that.

When I was with other women, I always told them about Cookie. Most of them already knew about her. I made it clear to everyone that I wasn't looking for a girlfriend. Some women took me at my word. I think that others saw Cookie as a challenge. And a few even told me: "I'm going to spoil you so much that you're going to forget about her."

But nobody ever succeeded.

Cookie and I were married on September 14, 1991, shortly before the season began. I had only one request: that the wedding should start on time, at six o'clock on the nose. Cookie has a habit of running late, so I told her to come to the church at three o'clock, if she needed to. "The ceremony is starting at six," I said. "If you're not there on time, I'll be gone."

I was at the altar at five minutes to six. The music started, and there she was. To see her walking down the aisle with her father, looking so beautiful in that dress—it was just breathtaking. It was the happiest day of my life, and the best thing that had ever happened to me. I knew all over again that I had made the right choice.

And then, just a few weeks later, I got the bad news. I'll talk about that shortly. But first, I'd like Cookie to tell you what some of this was like from her perspective.

When you're talking about Earvin and women, the first thing you have to understand is that Los Angeles is a big part of the story. If Earvin Johnson had been drafted by Cleveland, Detroit, Milwaukee, or even New York, we would have been married a long time ago. But L.A. is totally different. It's the land of stars, the land of fantasy. And this guy was smack in the middle of it.

He was only twenty when he moved here and started meeting all of these beautiful people. And many of them really *are* beautiful. In all my life, I've never seen so many stunning women out to catch somebody. The plastic surgery, the gorgeous clothes, you see it all.

After basketball, Earvin's two favorite things are movies and pop music. So L.A. was an enormous turn-on for him. Every time there was a movie premiere, they'd invite him to come. The MTV awards? Get Magic Johnson. People like Michael Jackson were actually calling the house. Whenever he went out, he was Magic, with everybody pulling and tugging at him.

I didn't really understand it at first. I never knew how much celebrities cared about him until I moved out here and actually saw them fighting for the chance to say hello to him. We were at Mortons one night, and Julia Roberts got up from her table to say hello. Julia Roberts! Even Earvin was stunned.

It's almost like Earvin can split himself into two people. There's the Hollywood world, which he deals with all the time. He enjoys it, but he doesn't take it too seriously. That's the world of Magic, and he's perfect for it.

But nobody knows Earvin the way I do. People saw only the public side, and they thought, There's no way he could care for her. But I knew the Hollywood scene wasn't really him. He never changed his basic personality. As long as I've known him, he's been down to earth and real lovable.

The Forum is like Fantasy Land. It's all so out in the open. You see businessmen there from other cities with bimbos on their arm. You'll see a guy in a dark suit and white shirt, and beside him is a woman in an incredibly short skirt. The first time I went, I watched as a girl in a bright orange dress, tight and low-cut with her boobs hanging out, strolled and strutted all the way around the court. It was incredible. Men actually wrote numbers on pieces of paper and held them up, like judges in the Olympics. She walked all the way over to where Jack Nicholson was sitting. She bent over and said something to him, and then walked back to the guy who brought her and gave him a hug. You would never see that anywhere else.

I've watched it happen so many times. Men come out here on business, and they know that Los Angeles is Play Town. They pick up a young chick to be with. It happens in other places, too, but not so publicly. Back East, if a man is with a sleazy-looking woman, he does it behind closed doors. But out here they flaunt it.

Showtime wasn't just on the court. Part of the show was all those gorgeous women walking around the Forum, on display. And the players noticed. Definitely. They'd be at the free-throw line, and on the bench, and they'd look, too. They'd start thinking, Well, I guess this is mine for the taking. And they were right. I'm amazed they were able to be so discreet about it.

No wonder Earvin took so long to get married. He didn't want to let go of that world. What man would? Look at Hugh Hefner, with the big mansion and the parties where who knows what goes on. Could a man like that exist in any other city? Only in L.A.

When Earvin said he loved me, I knew he meant it, even when he was with other women. After I graduated from Michigan State, I spent eight years working in Toledo. I didn't expect Earvin to be a saint when I wasn't around. I had to face reality, and not live in a fantasy world like some women do. A lot of wives and girlfriends sit around and say, "Oh, my man would *never* do that." But most of them are kidding themselves.

Earvin and I didn't talk about any of this, although he did tell me right away about Andre. He said that Melissa was carrying his child, and that he was going to help take care of the baby. I first met Andre when he was three, at Earvin's parents' house in Lansing. When I saw this little kid come through the door, looking like a clone of Earvin, my heart went, *Whoa.* It was one thing to know Earvin had a son, but to see him, looking so much like his dad— that was amazing. I fell in love with Andre right away, and we've been close ever since. When he comes to visit us, I'm more like his buddy than his second mom. But when I need to discipline him, I do.

I didn't have a problem with Andre's birth because it happened during a period when Earvin and I had broken up, and because I knew that Earvin and Melissa didn't have much of a relationship. If Earvin and I had been together, and this had happened, it would have been a lot harder.

During these years I knew about Earvin's personal life in general terms. But I didn't know the details, and I didn't want to know. And never once did any of this get thrown in my face. I've had friends who went somewhere with their boyfriends, and some other woman would be there. I never ran into anything like that. If Earvin went to some big event, a benefit or an awards ceremony, he never brought a date. That was out of respect for me. I never knew who he was with, or when. But I always assumed there were others.

Whenever I came to town, I was his girlfriend, and everybody knew it. The Laker wives always treated me well. As soon as I moved to Los Angeles they let me in.

Maybe they felt sorry for me. Or maybe they wanted to encourage Earvin to get moving.

For years, my friends told me, "Forget this guy. He'll never marry you. He's this big star, and he's into the Hollywood scene." And there were times when I wondered how long I should wait around. But usually I'd tell my friends, "You can't live my life for me."

Everybody thought I was nuts to be so patient, especially after he broke two engagements. At first, my mom said, "You can't wait forever for this guy." But she didn't really know Earvin. When she saw how I felt about him, she said, "Well, if you really love him, maybe you have to let him sow his wild oats and hope that he'll come back."

When Earvin and I finally got married, my friends came up to me at the wedding and said, "Cookie, I'm glad I was wrong about him." *They* were glad? Imagine how *I* felt!

The first time Earvin and I got engaged was in 1985, around the time Isiah got married. Everything was fine until Earvin went back to L.A. Then he called me and said he wasn't sleeping, and he just couldn't go through with it.

He was so scared. He cared so much about basketball, and he was afraid that if he got married he wouldn't be able to play well. He was so intense about it, and about not having anyone around before a game. He had his own rituals to prepare for games—watching tapes, listening to music, and most of all, being by himself. He just didn't want anyone around at those times.

It was even worse during the playoffs. He'd get moody and uptight before a game. He thought he couldn't be married and still play ball with that same intensity. If I was around, he was afraid of being rude to me during those times.

So basketball was a big part of it. I think the other part was not wanting to give up life in the fast lane. Like many men, he thought that if he was married, he'd become dull, he'd be stuck.

When he broke that first engagement, he couldn't even give me a reason beyond "I'm scared. I just can't do it."

I see now that this *was* the reason. But back then I was furious. I said, "Forget it. That's it. We can't just be friends, and we can't keep going on like this. I'm getting older and I want a future. If you don't see a future with me, tell me now."

We broke up that January, and went a whole year without any communication between us. I started seeing other guys, but it wasn't the same. And by 1987 we were seeing each other again—we couldn't stay completely apart for more than a year.

In 1989 I finally decided to force the issue. I didn't want to be forty and not be married. I was thirty at the time, and I had known Earvin for eleven years.

We had an important talk on the telephone. I said, "The only way we have any chance of making this work is if I move out there and you get used to having me around." (Actually, we both had to get used to that.) I told him that after I moved to Los Angeles, he might decide that he didn't want this arrangement. But we'd never know unless we tried.

He wasn't sure. He said, "Let me think about it."

He thought about it. Finally he said, "Okay, let's try it."

I moved out in October 1989. I found a job with a sportswear company and got my own apartment right outside Beverly Hills. Earvin and I had been apart for so long that I couldn't just move in with him. If we were going to make this thing work, first we'd have to get used to living in the same city. And I also wanted to preserve my independence.

He was living in a huge house in Bel Air. It had everything—including an indoor basketball court. But a few weeks after I moved to Los Angeles, he bought another house in Beverly Hills. I could never have moved into the

Bel Air house; it would have seemed like an invasion. He and Lon had already chosen the new house. I helped decorate it and make all the major decisions.

In February 1990, about four months after I moved to Los Angeles, we became engaged again. We were getting along fine, and I guess he felt we were ready. Now that we were living in the same city, he was feeling a lot of pressure to get married. Not from me—I knew better—but from our friends and our families.

Then the same thing happened all over again. He got scared and just couldn't go through with it.

This time I didn't leave him. I could see he was afraid. It wasn't about another woman. If it was, I would have left; I had been through way too much to be dealing with that. Instead of fighting another woman, I was fighting his fear of what being married would be like. His friends had told him that as soon as they got married, things had started going downhill.

The wedding was set for Labor Day weekend. He broke the engagement in April. He was feeling a lot of pressure on the team. Kareem had retired the previous year, and Earvin was now the leader. They were going into the playoffs, and he just couldn't handle basketball and me together. There was no room for me.

It was hard. There was a lot of crying on both sides. But I believed in him, and I held on. Deep down I knew he loved me. I knew this wasn't a lie.

This time we didn't actually break up. We postponed the wedding date, calling a truce. We would just be ourselves again. I decided not to mention it again for a while. His attitude was: If you can leave me alone about when we'll get married, I'll be okay.

But I was still very upset that it had happened again. The whole thing was so public, and so humiliating. I said, "Okay, I won't pressure you about a date. But let me keep this ring on my finger. You've got to leave me with something. If I take this ring off, it's all over."

We fought about that, too, but he agreed to it. Finally

we decided to forget all the pressure, to just relax and enjoy being together. When we did that, everything was okay again. We became closer, and spent more time together. I still hadn't moved in with him, but I was spending more time at his house than ever before.

The following spring, in 1991, he asked me to come with him for the playoffs. I knew that was big. It was his way of saying, I'm not afraid—and the whole world can know. Pat Riley had never wanted wives or girlfriends to make the trip. He felt the players would lose their concentration if we were around. He wanted the Lakers to eat, sleep, and drink basketball, with no distractions. The wives and girlfriends were allowed to come to the championship games on the road—but only if we stayed in a separate hotel. We weren't allowed to see the guys, except for dinner.

But Riley was gone now, and the new coach, Mike Dunleavy, had a very different attitude. Jerry Buss was even paying for all the wives and girlfriends to go. He invited us to fly on the team charter, and they let us stay in the same room with our men. After all those years of Pat Riley, we couldn't believe it. When the Lakers lost to Chicago in the Finals, we half expected that we would be blamed. But nobody said a word.

I had gone to some of the earlier playoff games with Earvin. Then, when the Lakers got to the Finals against Chicago, he said, "I want you to come on this trip. I want you to share this with me. I don't know when we'll be this close again to winning it all."

This was a breakthrough. This was new. A big-time signal. I didn't ask, and I didn't expect. I knew how intense this was.

But it was also a tough decision for me. If I went with him, I'd have to quit my job. I was working downtown as a sportswear buyer for a buying office, similar to what I had been doing in Ohio. This was market week, the most important and busiest time in our industry. I had already taken off two Fridays to travel with him to earlier playoff games against Golden State and Portland. But this was different. If I went to Chicago, I wouldn't be able to return to my job.

I felt terrible about leaving work. This was a small company, teetering on the edge. They really needed me. If I let them down now, it would be awful. I had to make a decision. I said to myself, Look, I've missed every one of his five NBA championships. I missed the Final Four in college. This may be my only chance to be there with him, and I'm not going to miss it.

I didn't sleep all night. I called Earvin that morning and told him I'd be coming.

The Lakers lost to Chicago in five games. Right after that, Earvin and I went to Maui. This was the first time he ever talked to me about how he felt about losing. In the past, he had shut me out. This was another breakthrough, another sign that we were getting closer.

When we got back from Maui, he said, "I can do it. We can get married." He had said that during the playoffs, too, but I didn't take it seriously. We talked about eloping, but Earvin really wanted a wedding. He said our families deserved that much, and he was right. But given what had happened in the past, I was nervous. And imagine how I felt when a newspaper in Michigan ran a story with a headline that read MAGIC ENGAGED YET AGAIN.

At the end of July, he went to St. Thomas in the Caribbean. He called me from there and said he wanted to get married at the end of the summer. I was still scared to make definite plans. When he got back, we talked about it again and set a date.

The wedding was in Lansing. We arranged it so quickly that we had to invite our guests by phone—there wasn't time for invitations. People had to decide then and there if they were coming.

The wedding was hard to plan because I was also helping Earvin prepare for the opening of his new sports-apparel store a week before we got married. His sisters Pearl and Kim were my wedding coordinators. Kim had helped me the previous year when we were setting up *that* wedding. We had picked out the florist and the cake maker, and now we called everybody to see if they were still available on short notice.

I still had my wedding dress from the year before—a long white gown with lots of sequins. The bodice was antique lace with sequins and beading, and the skirt was very full and made of tulle. There was a small train, too. The headpiece was a rhinestone tiara with a long veil. It was gorgeous.

Together with my mom and my sister, I had flown to New York to visit the showroom of Paula Barcelona. I knew her dresses from my days as a bridal buyer back in Ohio.

Earvin didn't see me in the dress until just before I walked down the aisle with my father. He was standing up there with the best man, Dale Beard, his old friend from Lansing, and rocking back and forth on his heels. When he saw me in that dress he stopped rocking—and a huge grin spread over his face.

We were married in the Union Missionary Baptist Church in Lansing. It was a traditional ceremony. Earvin wore a double-breasted white jacket and black pants. He looked sensational.

He had warned me that if I was a minute late, he would leave. And I'm always late. But I wasn't going to be late that day. I got to the church about three hours early, and I kept waiting to hear that Earvin had arrived. And even when they said he was in the church, I still wasn't sure. I was still wondering if he'd change his mind, so I sent somebody to look for him, to make sure he was really there.

He was so funny during the ceremony. He was in a great mood, and he kept whispering funny things into my ear, like mentioning all my old boyfriends and asking if they were in the church. And I'm going, "You're crazy. You're just *crazy.*" It was all I could do to keep a straight face.

The reception was at the Kellogg Center at Michigan

State. A lot of people waited outside the church, hoping to see celebrities. The day before, the papers printed a list of stars who were supposedly going to be there. Most of them weren't even invited. Isiah was one of the groomsmen, along with Mark Aguirre. Earvin's brothers were the ushers. Greg Kelser and Bob Chapman were there from Earvin's Michigan State team, and his old friend Darwin Payton. We both have a lot of family members and friends. It was a big wedding, about three hundred people.

When Earvin and I walked out of the church together to go over to the reception, hundreds of people started screaming and blowing their horns. It was like being back at a basketball game. But the whole thing was wonderful, and the weather was beautiful. I felt like God was saying, "Girl, you went through so much with this man that I'll give you a great wedding."

PART THREE

Now

CHAPTER 17

BAD NEWS

Friday, October 25, 1991

The phone call came at 2:15 P.M. The Lakers had just checked into our hotel in Salt Lake City. That night, we were to play a preseason exhibition game against the Utah Jazz. Dr. Michael Mellman, the team physician, was on the line from Los Angeles.

"Earvin," he said, "I'd like you to fly back here and see me right away."

"Why?"

"I've just learned that you failed your insurance physical."

As part of a complicated deal, my latest contract with the Lakers had included a low-interest loan. Because of it, I had taken a routine life-insurance physical a few weeks earlier. It was so simple that I barely remembered it. During my annual Laker checkup, somebody from the insurance company had come in to take a blood test.

"Can't this wait until tomorrow?" I said. "We just got here." He must have known we had a game that night.

"It really can't."

I didn't ask any questions. Whatever this was about, something in Mickey's voice told me we'd have to discuss it in person.

I dialed Lon at his office. "Mickey just called," I told

273

him. "He wants me to come right back. Do you know anything about this?"

"Yeah, he called me, too," said Lon. "But he wouldn't say what this was about. He needs to talk to you first. Do you want me to get him on the phone?"

"Sure."

Lon put me on hold as he set up a conference call. As I sat on the bed, listening to that dumb "hold" music, I wondered what the hell this could be. And why couldn't it wait?

Mickey came on the line. "Does it really have to be today?" Lon asked him. "There's a game tonight. Can't he come back tomorrow?"

Mickey was grim. "Lon, it's my medical opinion that Earvin should come back immediately."

"Okay. Earvin, is there anything you want to ask Mickey?"

Nothing that he would answer on the phone. "No," I said. Mickey signed off.

"I'll book you a seat on the next flight out," Lon said. "Stay right there. I'll call you back."

Five minutes later: "It's all set," Lon said. "There's a prepaid ticket waiting for you at Delta. It leaves at four twenty-eight and gets in at five-fifteen. Don't worry about checking out. Just leave the hotel and take a cab to the airport. I'll pick you up, usual spot."

It wasn't until I was on the plane that I had a chance to really think about this. For the past five days, ever since we'd returned from a week of exhibition games over in Paris, I had been feeling run-down. Then, just after we returned, there had been back-to-back games at the Forum. But Mickey had mentioned the insurance physical. That had been about a month ago. So what could it be? High blood pressure? My father had that. Cancer? I hoped not. AIDS? Not likely. Didn't you have to be gay to get that? Or a drug user?

Whatever it was, I had to pay attention. You don't get called back from Utah for a pulled hamstring.

The flight was on time. When I got out to the curb, Lon was sitting in his car, waiting for me. We made small talk on the way to Mickey's office, which is near the airport. Both of us were worried, though neither of us admitted it.

We got there at 5:40. The waiting room was empty. As we waited for Mickey, I picked up a copy of *Ebony* magazine. Michael Jordan was on the cover, with his wife, Juanita. It was a terrific photograph—the two of them looked great. "You know," I said, "it would be nice if Cookie and I could be on the cover like that."

Just then the door opened, and Mickey came out. "Come on in, Earvin," he said. I got up. I had assumed Lon would be joining us, but he didn't move. "Get up," I told him. "You're going to hear this anyway, so you might as well come in with me."

Mickey led us into his office. He pointed to an empty chair, and cleared some papers from a second chair so Lon could sit down, too.

Mickey sat facing me. He's about seven years older than I am, and he'd looked after me for most of my career with the Lakers. He had always talked straight to me. We weren't just doctor and patient—we were friends, too. Mickey had watched me grow up. We had shared a lot of laughs together, and a few championship trophies.

But today he looked drawn and pale. I could see by his eyes that this was difficult for him. Whatever it was, the news was going to be bad. Maybe very bad.

He turned toward the desk and opened a Federal Express envelope. Inside it was a smaller envelope.

He looked straight at me. "Earvin, I have the test results from your life-insurance physical. It says here that you tested positive to HIV, the virus that causes AIDS." He went on to explain exactly what that meant.

Lon and I looked at each other without speaking. Then Mickey explained the test results, and what they showed.

I didn't want to believe him. But this was Mickey talking, and I could see that he didn't want to believe it, either. Inside, I knew, he was crying for me.

I was in shock, too stunned to react.

"These tests are rarely wrong," he said. "But just in case, I'd like to run them again. You never know."

"What about Cookie?" I asked. "She's pregnant." Mickey didn't know that. We had found out for sure only that week, and we weren't telling people yet.

"I don't know about Cookie," he replied. "We'll have to test her anyway, as soon as possible."

"And the baby?"

"If Cookie is negative, the baby will be fine."

We sat there for a long time as Mickey told us about HIV and the various treatments. A lot of what he said was just a blur to me. But one thing I remember clearly is that he mentioned other patients of his who had the virus. Some of them had been living with HIV for as long as ten years without any symptoms of AIDS. He explained that the virus reacted differently in different individuals. In some people it stayed inactive for a long, long time.

"What should I be doing about this?" I asked.

He told me about AZT, and how the medicine made it harder for the virus to multiply in your blood. He wanted me to start taking it immediately.

"What about my basketball career?" I asked him. "Is it over?"

"If we're extremely lucky, and the next results come back negative, you can go back and play. But assuming you have the virus, I don't know yet. We'll have to get all the test results and see how this has affected your immune system."

Mickey told us about Dr. David Ho, who had been a resident with him years before at Cedars-Sinai Medical Center. Dr. Ho was a leading authority on HIV and AIDS. He worked in New York, as director of the Aaron Diamond AIDS Research Center, where a team of researchers studied HIV. Dr. Ho was only thirty-nine, but he had been involved in AIDS research since 1981.

"I'm going to ask David to handle your test and Cookie's," Mickey said. "But I won't tell him who it is. I'm pretty sure we can get some additional information. Sunday morning, nine o'clock, I'd like you and Cookie to come over here.

We'll draw some blood, and we'll send it right up to David in New York.''

When we left Mickey's office, I wasn't ready to go right home. I needed time to think. I had to tell Cookie, and I had to tell her today. But I also had to tell her the right way, whatever that meant. If I saw her right that minute, I might have blown it.

As we drove north toward town on the San Diego Freeway, I called her from the car. She was about to go to dinner with her friends Sharon and Nicole.

"I had to come back to see Mickey about something," I said calmly. No need to alarm her now. "Lon and I are going out to eat. I'll be home later."

We drove to Casa Monica, a little Italian restaurant in Santa Monica near Lon's house. I could see that he was hurting. I wasn't feeling much of anything yet. It hadn't really sunk in. All I could focus on was Cookie and the baby. I was praying they'd be okay.

Over dinner we talked about whether I'd have to retire. If I couldn't play basketball, what would I do for the rest of my life? I've always wanted to own a team, so that was one option. I could also imagine joining NBC as a broadcaster for NBA games.

During dinner, the waiter handed me a note from the people at the next table. They were planning an AIDS fund-raiser. Would I be available to speak?

It was spooky to get that note. And that's when the whole thing started to hit me.

When dinner was over, Lon drove me home. Now came the hard part. I was thinking about it in the car, how to break it to Cookie. How could I even begin to tell her about this? How could I soften it? What could I say? *How could I do this to her?* We had waited so long, and I had finally let her into my world. Now that we were married, I wanted everything to be perfect. Marrying Cookie was the best thing I had ever done. I should have made that move years ago.

And now, *bam!*

If I had been single when I got this news, maybe I could

have dealt with it more easily. But now there were two of us. Two of us *plus*. No doubt about it: Telling Cookie was the hardest thing I've ever had to do.

Lon drove off. We would talk again later. I walked into the house. Cookie was in the den. "How are you doing?" she said.

"Fine."

"What's wrong?"

She knew me too well.

At first I couldn't speak. I wanted to say it right, but being there with her, I realized there *was* no right way. I just had to be direct. "I've got a problem," I said. "I tested positive for HIV. I have AIDS."

Up until the actual announcement, Lon and I were both telling people I had AIDS. That's wrong, of course, but we still weren't tuned in to the difference between HIV and AIDS.

Cookie started crying. She thought I was going to die. We talked about that, and a lot of other things. One thing she never asked me was how I got the virus. That wasn't important. There was nothing we could do about the past. She was only thinking of the future—mine, hers, and the baby's.

I started to tell her that I'd understand completely if she wanted to leave. *Wham!* Before I even got the words out, she slapped me hard in the face. My mother and my grandmother had always told me that black women were strong, and that night I found out what they meant. She was really mad. She couldn't believe I could even think about something like that. But I felt terrible. I had jerked her around for fourteen years. And now, this.

I'll let her tell you about that day, too.

He had left for Utah that morning. Then, around seven, he called me from Lon's car to say he was back. I knew he was feeling tired, and that he hadn't really wanted to make this trip. He wasn't sick, but he wasn't quite right, either. We were both still jet-lagged from Paris. It had been a great trip, and the people in France were incredibly excited about the Lakers. Everywhere we went, they surrounded Earvin and called out, "Ma-jeek! Ma-jeek!" But it was also exhausting. And as soon as they got back, the guys had to play back-to-back games.

When he walked into the house, he had this look on his face. My first thought was that somebody had died. Then I thought, Oh God, something's wrong with him.

"Is it really bad?"

"Yeah."

Oh, no. I had just found out I was pregnant. I'd thought so in Paris, and the home test had said yes. I'd gone to the doctor as soon as we got back. That was Monday. Four days before.

I was in the TV room when he told me. He took a deep breath and just said it. I was scared. I cried a lot. All I could think about was the baby. Were we going to lose the baby?

I couldn't believe it. We had been through so much just to get married. We'd finally taken care of that, and now everything seemed so much easier. His fear had gone away. Earvin had realized that marriage wasn't what he'd expected. It was a piece of cake, being married, just like I'd always told him. And that showed me that fear *was* the problem—just like he'd always said. Because as soon as we got married, it was gone.

Earvin told me he'd understand if I wanted to leave. I couldn't believe it. I smacked him lightly on the face. "Are you crazy?" I said. "Why do you think I married you? *I married you because I love you!*"

My first thought was, What can we do to fight this thing? We've got to get into our faith and figure out how to fight this. God plays an important part in my life. I believe He can bring about miracles. I think the Lord's going to heal him.

It certainly crosses my mind that he could die, but I don't worry about it. I just hold on to my faith, and I put those thoughts out of my mind.

Everywhere we go, people come up and say, "We love

you, we're praying for you." The first time Earvin told me he wanted to go public about this, I was terrified. I thought, My God, no. They'll hate us. They won't even let us into restaurants. We can deal with this ourselves. Our love is strong. But when the whole world knows, what are people going to do with us? I was so afraid.

I didn't get mad. How can I blame him? It wasn't intentional. It happened. I go on day to day, and I'm fine. Usually it doesn't even cross my mind until I see a news story or an interview with him. Every interview, that's all people are asking. Nobody wants to know anything else. All they ask is, "When did you find out? How did you know?"

I didn't know what to expect. But I never imagined it would be such a big story.

Saturday, October 26

First thing in the morning I called Lon. "I hope you've got some food there," I said. "Because Cookie and I are coming right over for breakfast."

The Rosens, Lon and Laurie, live about twenty minutes from us. Lon and I were friends long before we started doing business together. We met during my rookie year, when he was an intern in the Lakers' PR department. One of his jobs was setting up press interviews and dealing with the media, so we got to know each other pretty well. We're the same age, and Lon really loves sports. Our two schools, Michigan State and USC, were great football rivals, which gave us plenty to argue about.

Lon was still a college student when he started working for the Lakers. But that organization knows talent when they see it. Before he even graduated, they made him director of promotions for the Forum. Over the years, the two of us started doing small business deals together—speaking engagements, endorsements, that sort of thing. In 1986, when I decided to change my representation, I asked Lon to take over as my agent. When the season ended, he left his job and started working for me.

That morning, when Cookie and I walked into their house, all four of us started crying. After breakfast, Lon and I went for a long walk on the beach. It was drizzling, and the place was deserted. We walked all morning and talked about everything—my career, my family, and some of the business deals we had done together. At the time, people thought I was crazy to go with a young agent with no experience. But we showed them. We did a lot together—basketball camps, a T-shirt company, and all those endorsements. We talked again about my dream of buying an NBA team, and about the possibility of my working for NBC.

We also talked about the baby, who was due in June. Out there on the beach, I told Lon how I hoped that our two kids would grow up together. The Rosens had wanted a baby for years, and finally, in September, their son, Brian, had been born. Okay, the timing wasn't great, because Brian decided to show up three weeks early—just one day before Cookie and I got married in Michigan. I called them from Lansing, about twenty seconds after Laurie's water broke. "Can't talk now," Lon said. "We're leaving for the hospital." The day after the wedding, we flew back to Los Angeles. The first thing we did was visit the little guy.

Sunday, October 27

Early in the morning, Cookie and I drove to Mickey's office so he could draw blood from each of us. Sunday morning is a funny time to be seeing your doctor, but Mickey wanted us to come when nobody else was around—no other patients, nurses, or assistants. This thing was a complete secret. Mickey brought the blood right to the airport and sent it to Dr. Ho in New York. He told us it would take at least a week before we got full results from these sophisticated tests. But he expected that we'd have some early information within a few days.

That afternoon, I asked Lon to meet me at the L.A. Sports Club. We got to the gym around six, and I started running up and down the court and shooting. What a relief to be there! As soon as I got on that court, I was Magic again. I was able to do what I do best. All the weight and pressure of this terrible business was off my shoulders—at least for the moment.

I was on fire that night, and I shot the lights out. After about an hour of great shooting, I turned to Lon and said, "I was born to play this game."

Monday, October 28

I couldn't keep on sitting out for no reason. But we also couldn't make any announcements until all the facts were in. After I missed a couple of exhibition games, Lon put out a statement: that I was getting over the flu, I was still a little dehydrated, and the Lakers wanted me to come back slowly. This was the first time Lon had ever lied to the press on my behalf, and it wasn't a good feeling. Later, he would apologize to the reporters.

Lon and I went back to the gym that night, and every night that week. I ran four miles on the treadmill at around eight miles an hour, followed by an hour of shooting in the gym and running up and down the court. HIV or not, I had every intention of coming back. I wanted to make sure that this brief layoff wouldn't slow me down.

Wednesday, October 30

At that point, only a tiny handful of people knew what was going on: Lon and Laurie, Cookie and me, Mickey, my parents, and the two Jerrys—Jerry Buss and Jerry West. We were afraid the story might get out before we were ready. And that night we got a real scare when a doctor who knew Lon started coming toward us in the gym. "This could be bad," Lon muttered. "This guy has been watching you for the past two nights. Maybe he's figured something out."

"You know," he said to Lon, "I've been watching Magic, and he looks pretty good to me. That must be a heck of a flu, to go on so long."

"Actually, he's over it," Lon said. "They just want him to come back slowly."

That seemed to do it. "That's good," he said. "I'm glad they're treating him right. You wouldn't want a relapse."

Or a leak.

Thursday, October 31

Mickey called in the morning to say he wanted to see Cookie and me in his office. The preliminary results had come back. The bad news was that the insurance company's blood test had been accurate. Dr. Ho's lab confirmed that I tested positive for HIV.

But the good news—no, the *great* news—was that Cookie was fine. I was so happy to hear that, so relieved!

"And the baby?"

"Also fine. As long as the mother is okay, the baby is, too. But Cookie will need to be tested again in a couple of months."

"Why?"

"It can take a while before the virus shows up in the tests. This way we'll be sure she's all right."

Mickey told us that David Ho was coming to town next Wednesday. The two of them would meet with us to go over the full results.

Friday, November 1

The Lakers were playing in Houston. It was the first time I'd ever missed the opening game of the season. The official reason for my absence was still that I was getting over the flu.

Cookie and I watched it on TV with Lon and Laurie at their house. I probably surprised them with all my yelling, but it was so hard not to be there. I couldn't help my teammates, but I still wanted to. The Rockets beat us, 126–121. Sedale Threatt started in my place, and James scored 37 points.

Sunday, November 3

Two beat reporters who had been with the team on the Texas trip called Lon at home. "What's with Earvin? How can he have the flu all this time? What's really going on here?" A few days earlier they had seen me at practice, and I looked fine. And the flu didn't usually last so long.

Lon decided to put out another statement. He said I had been to the doctor, who said I could begin "light supervised workouts." We were still trying to buy time until the announcement. But we'd know a lot more on Wednesday.

Tuesday, November 5

The Lakers were back in town for their first home game. At the morning shootaround, I did a TV interview. In the middle of it, Ron Harper of the Clippers, a friend of mine, came up behind me and said, "Hey, Earvin, when are you coming back?"

"It won't be long," I said. I hoped it was true.

I sat on the bench as the Clippers beat us, 114–109. The Clippers! That was even worse than watching the game on TV. The only good news was that Sedale Threatt finished with 25 points.

Wednesday, November 6

I finally met Dr. Ho when he and Mickey came over to the house. "You have the virus," he told me. "But so far, it hasn't affected your immune system very much. And you don't have any AIDS-related diseases. Still, it's my recommendation that you not play basketball this season. I happen to be a huge Laker fan, so I'm not saying this easily. But there's a lot we still don't know. Besides, I don't think this problem has ever come up before, of a professional athlete having the virus. It's a judgment call. And my judgment is that you don't play.

"First of all, we don't know how well you'll tolerate the medicine. Some people have side effects from AZT—headaches, diarrhea, nausea, anemia. Second, it's possible that playing could put a lot of stress on your immune system. It could also shorten your life."

"We seem to have caught it early," said Mickey. "But I agree with David. You should retire."

It wasn't that I didn't have the strength to play. But it's a very long season when you count everything—training camp, all the exhibition games, the 82-game schedule, and then the playoffs. And this year it would be even longer for a few of us, because training for the Olympics would begin in late June. I was willing to miss the season if that was necessary, but I still wanted to play on the Olympic team.

"If you were somebody else," Mickey said, "I might tell you to go ahead and play. But I know you. You have only one speed: full-steam ahead. You're so intense, and you want to win so badly that I can't see you cutting back. It's all or nothing with you. And when you play that hard every night, and you add in the stress of traveling, the late hours, and the lack of sleep, it just doesn't make sense."

About an hour into the meeting, Laurie Rosen arrived to take Cookie to the obstetrician for her eight-week checkup. The ultrasound was scheduled for that day, to make sure that the baby was okay. I'd intended to take her myself, because I wanted to be there, too, but this was starting to look like a long meeting, so I had to stay behind.

Lon and I were still talking with the doctors when Cookie and Laurie returned. Cookie called me out of the meeting to show me pictures from the ultrasound. What an amazing thing, to see the beginnings of your own baby! And how weird to look at something like this in the middle of a discussion of how to treat HIV and AIDS.

Now that the results were in and I had been advised to retire, we wanted to make the announcement as soon as possible. Wednesday was already gone. We'd use Thursday to prepare and learn more about HIV. The press conference would be Friday morning at the Forum.

During that week, Lon had been meeting and talking with several people about the impending announcement. A key member of our kitchen cabinet was Michael Ovitz, the head of Creative Artists Agency. Michael, who represents some of the biggest names in Hollywood, had, a few years earlier, taken me on as his client—the only time he had ever represented a professional athlete. He was the guy who really educated me in business, and he taught me a great deal. Now he was helping me in a very different way.

Ovitz told me that I should just be myself—straightforward, up front, and affirmative, that I should speak from the heart, without a prepared statement, and that I should answer as few questions as possible. After all, the whole point of this public announcement was to educate people about HIV and AIDS. And I was no doctor. When it came to understanding this whole situation, I was a complete beginner. So Mickey would answer questions about my health, and an AIDS expert from UCLA would be on hand to answer questions about HIV and AIDS.

That night, Jerry West and Bob Steiner, the Lakers' PR director, met with Lon at his house. Lon told them I was going to announce my retirement on Friday morning. They had only one question: How can we help?

Meanwhile, Jerry Buss called David Stern, the commissioner of the NBA. David is a good friend, and if I was about to retire, he needed to know about it. He was on his way to Utah, but as soon as he learned about Friday's press conference, he said he'd be there.

Later that night, Lon drove over to Coach Dunleavy's house. Coach had figured out that something was terribly wrong. When Lon told him the details, he was crushed. Although his whole career revolved around the success of the Lakers, the only thing he seemed to care about was my health.

This was supposed to be our day to prepare for the press conference, but it didn't work out that way. At nine-thirty in the morning, Lon got a call from a reporter at KFWB, an all-news station in Los Angeles. "We've just heard a story that Magic is going to retire tomorrow because he has AIDS. Is that true?"

"That's ridiculous," Lon said. For about a minute, he told me later, he managed to pretend that this phone call had never happened. Then he called me. "People are starting to hear about it now," he said. "We've got to announce today."

"I'm ready," I told him. "Just tell me when to be there."

Lon called the Lakers. They put out a statement at eleven o'clock saying that Magic Johnson would be holding a press conference at three o'clock at the Forum. They didn't say why.

In just a few hours, the whole world would know.

There was never any question that I would go public with it. I doubt I could have kept it quiet. Besides, I'd never lied to people, and I didn't want to start now. I've always lived straight ahead, facing up to whatever happens.

There was another reason I wanted to make this announcement. Despite all the warnings, a lot of other people were living the way I had—especially athletes and entertainers. And many blacks, too: Large parts of the black community were still in denial about AIDS, and I wanted to help my people. This had happened to me, and there wasn't too much I could do about that. But there was a great deal I could do for other people. By going public with this, I had a chance to save lives.

Suddenly there were a lot of people who had to be notified—fast. My parents already knew, of course. But I wanted to be the one to tell Andre, who was now ten and still living in Lansing with his mother. I called my father and asked him to take Andre out of school and let him know what was going on. Later on, of course, I told him myself. It's too bad Andre's grandfather had to show up in the middle of class, but I didn't want my boy to be caught by surprise. This would be hard enough for him without that additional problem.

Over the phone, Lon and I drew up a list of people who needed to know about the announcement in advance. I took care of some relatives and old friends. Lon would call some of my friends in the NBA. Shortly before the press conference, I would meet with my teammates personally at the Forum.

It was important for Lon to reach the NBA guys right away. Whatever happened, one thing was certain: As soon as I made this announcement, the press would track down these people to look for a comment. And I didn't want any of these guys to be caught off guard.

While I worked the phones, I also started thinking about the press conference. What would I wear? What would I say? How would I hold up? But I didn't get very far. Almost before I knew it, it was time for Cookie and me to leave for the Forum.

It wasn't easy, but Lon reached everybody on his list except Michael Cooper. Coop learned about it from Jerry West.

Lon tried Michael Jordan at home. Michael's housekeeper said he was at practice. When Lon called there, a PR guy said that Michael was practicing with the team and couldn't be interrupted.

"It's an emergency," Lon said.

"All I can do is give him the message," he was told. "But I can't promise he'll call you."

Michael called back within the hour. "Earvin is retiring from the NBA today," Lon said. "He has AIDS."

Michael started to cry. "No, this can't be happening!" Lon told him it was real. "Is there anything I can do?" he asked. "Anything Earvin needs? I'm here for him."

Pat Riley was at the Manhattan hotel where the Knicks

stay on game days. His line was busy, so Lon left a message. Five minutes later, Pat called him. When he heard the news, Pat couldn't speak. He hung up, then called back a minute later. "How's Earvin doing? How's Cookie? Are you sure about this?"

Nobody wanted to believe it.

"We're sure. We're announcing it this afternoon."

"In that case, I'm flying right out there," he told Lon.

"Don't do that," Lon said. "You'll never get here in time. What Earvin wants is for people to go on with their lives. The best thing you can do for him is to carry on. Besides, you have a game tonight, right?"

That night, the Knicks were playing the Orlando Magic at the Garden. Before the game started, Riley brought both teams together in one huddle for a moment of prayer. Then he asked the crowd to stand. "There's been some very bad news," he said. "In your own voice, in your own beliefs, in your own way, pray for Earvin and the one million people afflicted with an insidious disease who need our understanding." Riley recited the Lord's Prayer. Then, in a quiet voice, he said, "Let's go. Let's play."

I saw it on television. Pat is a classy man and a real friend.

Isiah Thomas wasn't home. Lon left a message with his secretary. Isiah called back from his car. "No, it's not true!" he said when Lon told him. "I can't talk now. I'm driving. I'll pull off the road and call you right back."

He drove into a gas station and called Lon from a pay phone. He was stunned. "I can't believe this," he said. "Tell me it's not true!"

Larry Bird was on his way out the door when Lon reached him at home in Boston. His first response was, "Oh my God. This can't be true."

They all wanted to know if it was okay to call me. And all of them did.

Of all the people Lon tried to contact, Arsenio Hall was the toughest to find. When Lon finally tracked him down, he took it very hard. "I won't be doing the show tonight," he said.

"You have to," Lon said, "or Earvin will kill you. He needs you to carry on with your life. That's how you can help him. By the way, he wants to come on with you tomorrow night."

"Are you kidding?" said Arsenio. "I don't even know about tonight!"

Later on, Arsenio called back from his pastor's office. "I've talked to my pastor about it," he said. "I just don't want to be disrespectful to Earvin."

Lon assured him that this wasn't a problem.

Lon called Kareem, too. "Tell me what I can do to help," he said. "And I'll be there at the Forum to support him." A few hours later, at the press conference, Kareem was right there beside me. A true friend.

After Lon spoke to Kurt Rambis in Phoenix, Kurt showed up at practice. "I have to leave," he told his coach, Cotton Fitzsimmons. "I can't tell you why. You'll just have to trust me on this one." Kurt and Linda were on the next plane to Los Angeles. They made it to the Forum in time for the press conference.

Meanwhile, the Lakers were practicing as usual at Loyola. They didn't know yet. At the end of practice, Coach Dunleavy called the whole team into the huddle. "One o'clock, I want you at the Forum. No exceptions. If you have anything planned, cancel it."

At one-thirty, an hour and a half before the press conference was to begin, I walked into the locker room to tell my teammates. Until then, I hadn't cried—not when I heard the news, or even when I told Cookie. But when I told my teammates what was going on, they were in tears. And when they embraced me, one by one, I felt that power rush through my body. And I cried with them.

The press conference was held in the back of the Forum Club. As Lon and I walked through the suite of offices to get there, he pulled me aside into a tiny room.

"Are you okay?"

"I'm fine."

"You know what you're going to say?"

"I know."

"But don't say you have AIDS."

"What?"

"I just spoke to one of the doctors. Remember, you don't have AIDS. You tested positive for HIV."

"Okay, HIV. Look, I think I'll make it through this press conference. But if I don't, I want you to get up there and take over."

But we both knew that wouldn't happen.

The last time I'd been at a press conference in that room was in 1990, when I won the MVP for the third time. Some of the same people were there then, too: David Stern, Jerry West, Jerry Buss. It was the identical setup: the same podium, the same microphones, the same blue backdrop.

But now there were more reporters and cameramen than I had ever seen before. There were so many that some of them couldn't even get in—they had to watch it on television from the next room. Meanwhile, hundreds of fans had gathered outside the building.

By now the news was out. On my way to the Forum, I had turned on the radio and heard it myself: "According to still-unconfirmed reports, Magic Johnson has AIDS and will be retiring from basketball. The Lakers have called a press conference for three o'clock today, where Johnson is scheduled to make an announcement."

As our little group walked in, a hush fell over the room. I led the way, followed by Cookie, Jerry West, Kareem, Mickey, and Lon. Practically the only thing you could hear was the clicking of automatic cameras, like little machine guns going off. Some of the reporters were live on the air. You could hear them whispering, like at a golf tournament.

I walked straight to the podium and started talking.

"Good afternoon. Because of the HIV virus that I have attained, I will have to retire from the Lakers today. I just want to make clear, first of all, that I do not have the AIDS disease. I know a lot of you want to know that. I have the HIV virus. My wife is fine. She's negative, so no problem with her.

"I plan on going on living for a long time, bugging you guys like I always have. So you'll see me around. I plan on being with the Lakers and the league, and going on with my life. I guess now I get to enjoy some of the other sides of living that I've missed because of the season and the long practices and so on. I'm going to miss playing.

"I will now become a spokesman for the HIV virus. I want people, young people, to realize that they can practice safe sex. Sometimes you're a little naïve about it and you think it could never happen to you. You only thought it could happen to other people. It *has* happened. But I'm going to deal with it. Life is going to go on for me, and I'm going to be a happy man. . . .

"Sometimes we think only gay people can get it, or it's not going to happen to me. Here I am, saying it can happen to everybody.

"Even me, Magic Johnson."

Looking back now, what I did that day was right. There were just too many questions—about my stamina, the effects of the medicine, and what the virus would do to my body. But deep down inside, I now realize, I still wanted to get back on the court as soon as I could.

CHAPTER 18

My New Job

In a way that I could never have imagined, the 1991–92 season turned out to be the most productive one I ever had. Only instead of playing basketball, I was now playing a new position in a very different game. Instead of being a point guard, I was an activist, and especially an educator. And instead of being a veteran, I was starting all over again as a rookie.

There was one more difference. Until then, I had been working for my own agenda. After the announcement, I started working for God's agenda. I believe He's got a mission for me—to help make society more aware, and to get people to care. I want to get enough funding to help the people who already have HIV and AIDS, and to prevent everyone else from getting it.

If anybody thought I could get away with just pretending to be an AIDS activist, then they didn't sit with me during my season away from basketball, listening to people with the disease talk about it. Everywhere I go, publicly or privately, people tell me that they have HIV or AIDS, or that their brother has it, or their child, or their lover. This problem is all around us, and it's a very real threat to our country.

That's why shortly after I finished my statement at the press conference, Cookie and I ducked out of the Forum through a back door. That was part of the plan, to shift the focus from me, personally, to a far more important subject—HIV and AIDS.

That night, Cookie and I had a few close friends over for an informal dinner of barbecued chicken and ribs. I was happier than I had been in days. After all, an enormous burden had just been lifted. For the previous nine days, ever since I'd been called back from Utah and heard the bad news from Mickey, I had been living a lie. Maybe it was necessary, but it wasn't me—and I didn't like it. I could live with HIV, but I couldn't live with being somebody I wasn't. It made me restless and antsy. Now that the news was finally out, I was my old self again, laughing and joking and enjoying life.

If you had been at our house that night, you never would have guessed that Cookie and I had just been involved in a huge news story. All you would have seen was a bunch of good friends hanging out together. It felt great.

Lon arrived late, because he had stayed behind at the Forum to answer questions. As soon as he walked in, the two of us went upstairs and talked for close to an hour. We had so much to go over—everything that had happened that day, as well as our game plan for the days to come. Throughout this whole period, I did everything I could to stay in control of my life. On Saturday, Cookie and I and a few friends flew to Hawaii for a week's vacation. I was happy to relax, but I still spoke to Lon several times a day.

That first night, though, we were just beginning to understand how big this story was. Until I got home from the Forum, I didn't even realize that the press conference had been broadcast live all across the country. And because of CNN, it had been seen and heard all around the world. Before long, phone calls started coming in from friends in Italy and Spain.

I hadn't imagined anything like this. As an NBA star, I was used to operating in a pretty big arena. But this was a hundred times bigger. This went well beyond sports. That night, every news show on every channel led with the story.

This was *news*—and it took me a few days to fully comprehend that.

For security reasons, the street we live on is protected by a gate. But when Lon got home that evening, there were three camera crews and a bunch of reporters waiting for him. Several tabloid reporters wouldn't leave until Lon called the police. Somebody even went through his trash, looking for God knows what. And when he finally got inside, the phone didn't stop ringing.

Rumors had already started to circulate that Cookie was pregnant. That was one detail we deliberately hadn't mentioned at the press conference. The important thing was to get people to focus on HIV and AIDS. The news of Cookie's pregnancy wasn't something we wanted to share yet. I guess we were naïve, but we still hoped to maintain a little privacy.

When Lon heard the rumors, he recommended that if anybody asked, we tell them the truth. We were both sick of hiding information, especially now that the press conference was over. That night, when a reporter called Lon to ask if Cookie was pregnant, Lon said yes. The story came out the next day.

During the next few days, Lon continued to be besieged by the media. Everybody and his sister wanted to interview me. Between Federal Express and the mail, Lon's office was flooded with requests. The paper in his fax machine had to be replaced almost every hour. There were letters, notes of encouragement, flowers, get-well cards, letters from schoolchildren, and on and on.

I had already decided to limit my interviews, because I couldn't say yes to everybody. In addition to Arsenio's show on Friday night, I had decided to talk with Roy Johnson for *Sports Illustrated* and to do a TV interview with my old friend Jim Hill at KABC.

Friday morning, Mickey and another doctor came over for further discussions with me about my treatments. There was a lot of public interest in the fact that I was taking

AZT, which was originally used only in the later stages of the illness. These days it's used as a preventive, but not everybody knew that. That may be why some people, including a few reporters, concluded that I was sicker than I actually was.

Within hours of the announcement, Lon and I started receiving calls about cures and folk remedies for AIDS. There is *no* known cure for HIV or AIDS, of course, but hundreds of people, including a few celebrities, contacted us with suggestions. One person sent me a jar of what looked like sour milk. "If you drink this," he wrote, "you'll get better." Did he really expect me to try a mysterious liquid that arrived in the mail from a total stranger? Somebody else actually advised me to drink all my blood and replace it with new blood. A lot of these "cures" were pretty bizarre. Even now, I can't go anywhere without somebody coming up and saying, "I know a friend who knows this doctor who has a cure," or words to that effect.

We heard a lot about a drug called Kemron, which was developed at a medical institute in Kenya. Some people in the black community think it has merit, but a series of careful clinical studies in a number of labs have shown no evidence of that. Besides, if this stuff is so good for blacks, why are so many of us continuing to die?

On Friday afternoon, I went for a haircut. Then it was over to the studio to tape Arsenio's show. I arrived early, and in the dressing room I did the interviews with Roy Johnson and Jim Hill. In *Sports Illustrated,* I pleaded with every athlete and entertainer who was living the bachelor life to practice safe sex, and to go out and get tested. I hope they were listening, but it's impossible to know for sure.

Going on with Arsenio was my idea. First, because he's one of my closest friends. And second, because he's got a top-rated show. I couldn't think of a better way to get out the message—that I was okay, that my life would go on, and, most important, that what happened to me didn't have to happen to anyone else. I was grateful that there was a vehicle

I could use to get the message out, especially with somebody I knew and trusted.

When the show began, Arsenio and I came out together. The studio audience was so enthusiastic and supportive—they stood and cheered and applauded, and it just didn't stop. I was genuinely moved. Finally, I began to wonder if they'd ever let me speak. There were four other guests on the show that night, including Roseanne Arnold, who was going to talk about being an incest survivor. I didn't want anybody to get cut. So I did exactly what I would have done on the basketball court: I signaled for a time-out. Then the audience started chanting my name: "Magic! Magic! Magic!" Finally they got quiet, and Arsenio got the ball rolling. Our conversation went something like this:

"You called and said you wanted to come on the show. Why?"

"I want everybody to practice safe sex. And that means using condoms and being aware of what's going on. When I talked to the doctors over the last couple of days, they told me that there were a million people out there with HIV. And many of them don't even know it. That's why I went out yesterday and publicly said I had it. I want to educate the public. We don't have to run from it. We don't have to be ashamed of it. We have to make people aware of what's happening.

"I want to educate not only the young people, but the black community as well. Because it's really spreading quickly in the black community."

Arsenio mentioned that some people might be wondering if I contracted the virus through a homosexual relationship.

"First of all, I'm far from being a homosexual." The audience applauded here, which made me feel funny. And I hope it didn't cover up what I said next: "That's the whole thing. People think it can only happen to gay people. And that's so wrong. Even I was naïve, to think it couldn't happen to me. Heterosexuals—it's coming fast. We're going to have to be prepared for it, and also practice safe sex."

Arsenio asked if at any point I had wondered, Why me?

I said yes, at first. But it hadn't taken very long for me to understand why this had happened. It wasn't a mystery.

"I'm not fearing it," I told him. "I'm not down. I'm here. I say I've got it, but I'm going to live on. You don't have to run from me, like, Here comes Magic—uh-oh! You can still give me my hugs, my high fives, my kisses. You can ask, 'You been taking your medicine? You all right? You been working out?' Because that's what I need.

"You just be you. I don't need anything else. And you don't have to feel sorry for me. Because if I die tomorrow, I've had the greatest life that anybody can want."

Later on, Arsenio asked me about the 1992 Olympic team. At that point, most people assumed that I wouldn't be able to play. He asked if I might be able to go along anyway, perhaps as a coach.

"Without a doubt," I told him. "Michael Jordan said, 'You just messed up the whole Olympic team!' All of them have been very supportive. I told Michael, 'I will *still* beat you one-on-one.' And I told Bird that I'd still beat him in checkers in five or ten years."

It was a great interview, because I was so relaxed with Arsenio. And I think you could see the affection and friendship between us. We joked around, but I was also able to make some serious points. After all, that's why I was there. "I want to let people know what time it is," I told everybody. "Please, get your thinking cap on." And then I pointed below my waist: "And put *that* cap on down there, and then everything will be all right."

Then I told Arsenio that if he ever had to miss a few days of work, I'd be more than happy to take over his show until he got back.

He just laughed. "I remember one time a point guard for the Lakers let you take over," he said. "And he never got it back!" Then we got serious again, and he gave me an important warning: "I want you to realize that as positive as you are, there's gonna be a lot of negativity out there. There are journalists—and there are *germalists*. We're gonna be with you through that. They're gonna start rumors and start talking trash.''

"They can say what they want," I replied. "I'm here. As long as you got God and your family—my parents are great, they love me; brothers and sisters, my friends, my wife—nothing else matters. That's what it's all about. What they give me, I can't buy.''

Before I left the stage, Arsenio climbed up on his chair to give me a high five.

He was right about the "germalists.'' Before long the supermarket tabloids were all over me, printing just about anything they felt like. It was especially hard on Cookie, because she wasn't used to any publicity. That part was the toughest on me, watching her suffer through it. The worst thing is to be walking through an airport and suddenly you see a tabloid rag that says, in big letters, MAGIC'S WIFE MOVES INTO MAID'S QUARTERS. We laughed about it later, but at the time it was painful. This particular story said that Cookie had renovated the maid's quarters because she didn't want to sleep with me anymore. Another story said that I'd slept with a porn star the day before my announcement. A third one said I was severely depressed. All of them were ridiculous.

But we also heard from legitimate reporters. Right after the announcement, Connie Chung had called Lon at home. She and I were old friends from when she worked in Los Angeles. "I want to interview Earvin," she said.

"I'm sorry," Lon told her, "but Earvin isn't doing any more interviews.''

"*You're* sorry?" she replied. "I'm calling you from the plane. I'm on my way out there right now!''

Early the next morning, she came straight to Lon's office. "I've got to interview him," she said again.

"He might want to do it later," Lon replied. "But not now. Do you realize how many requests I have here?''

Lon turned around and rifled through a pile of faxes. He

was looking for one request in particular, and when he found it, he showed it to Connie. It was from Maury Povich—her husband.

When I was ready to do a network television interview, I went with Connie Chung. Some people noticed that my message during our conversation was a little different from what I had said on Arsenio's show. With Arsenio, I had talked about the importance of "thinking caps"—condoms. With Connie, I stressed that the safest sex of all was no sex.

Why the change? After the announcement, a lot of people weighed in with their opinions—both publicly and in private. My teammate A. C. Green, a religious man, encouraged me to speak about the virtues of abstinence, and other people made similar statements that made sense to me. I was happy to be educated, to listen to other points of view. I was a newcomer to this whole area, and I needed help.

So I added that line about abstinence to my message, but I'm not willing to say *only* that, because it just isn't realistic. Sexual activity is up among teenagers. We can't just respond to what we *wish* was going on; we also have to deal with reality. That's why I've been putting out a two-part message ever since: that the best road to safer sex is no sex (I now say "safer" sex instead of "safe" sex because no form of sex is as safe as abstinence); and that the second-best option is to make sure that anytime you do have sex, it is as safe and responsible as possible.

Of all the people I have met and talked with since my announcement, one woman, Elizabeth Glaser, has played the most important role in educating me about HIV and AIDS. She has also helped me understand, in a more personal way, just what is going on with me. I had heard her name even before all of this happened, because Elizabeth is a well-known AIDS activist. And I was certainly aware of her husband, Paul Michael Glaser, who used to play Starsky on the TV show *Starsky and Hutch,* which I loved to watch as a kid.

Back in 1981, Elizabeth unknowingly contracted the virus through a blood transfusion when their first child, Ariel, was born. Four years later, Ariel became very sick for no apparent reason. Months later, a blood test showed that Ariel had AIDS. Only then did her doctors suspect that Elizabeth had picked up HIV during the blood transfusion, and had presumably passed it on to Ariel through her breast milk. The whole family was then tested. Elizabeth had the virus, and so did Jake, their baby son. Only Paul was not infected.

Three years later, in March 1988, Ariel Glaser died of AIDS. That prompted Elizabeth to start raising money for more research and speaking out to make our government more aware of this problem. Nobody has fought harder on behalf of people with HIV and AIDS.

Shortly after my announcement, Lon asked Elizabeth if she would meet with Cookie and me. A few days later, we went over to the Glasers' house in Santa Monica. This tiny woman, who isn't much more than five feet tall, greeted me with a tremendous hug. She introduced us to Jake, who was now seven. Elizabeth told us that Jake's teacher had discussed my announcement with the class, and that the kids had decided to make me a drawing of a quilt as a get-well gift. Jake thought that was fine. "But I think you should make one for me, too," he told his classmates. "Remember, I also have HIV."

Elizabeth Glaser keeps going and going and going. She's a model for me, and a real inspiration. She's a fighter—not only for her own life, but for the lives of many other people in our situation. When I came along, she had already been struggling for years to make people more aware of HIV and AIDS. She was thrilled that I had decided to go public with my situation and to join the struggle. "I've been carrying the baton for a long time," she told me that day. "And I've gone about as far as I can go. I can't keep up this pace. We need you to take this fight to the next level."

She told us about the Pediatric AIDS Foundation, which she had helped found after Ariel died. Her foundation is now involved in the Ariel Project, a research project aimed at blocking the transmission of HIV from infected mothers to their newborn babies. It's a very expensive undertaking, and my own foundation is helping to raise money for it.

When it comes to fighting the fight, Elizabeth has been my coach. In every AIDS-related project I've been involved with, she has been incredibly helpful. When I played in the 1992 All-Star Game, Elizabeth was there, too, for a special meeting to help educate the players' wives about HIV. Anyone who wants to learn more about this courageous woman and her fight should pick up a copy of her book, *In the Absence of Angels.*

Arsenio's show marked my own debut as an educator. A couple of days later I was invited to be an activist when President Bush asked me to join the National Commission on AIDS. Belinda Mason, a writer, and one of the commission's twelve members, had recently died of AIDS, which she had contracted several years earlier from a blood transfusion. Her death had created a vacancy on the commission, and the president asked me to fill it. When the idea first came up, I saw it as a terrific opportunity to help spread the message of safer sex—especially to young people. At the same time, I didn't want to be used as window dressing by an administration that had not done nearly enough to deal with this whole problem. But I thought it was worth a try.

The initial call came to Lon from John Sununu, the president's chief of staff. When a reporter asked Lon about it, Lon replied that I was considering the invitation. "Aren't you afraid that this is just a photo opportunity?" the reporter asked. "No," Lon replied. "Earvin Johnson won't be a photo opportunity for anybody." When Lon's remark appeared in *USA Today,* Sununu hit the roof. And that may explain why President Bush went out of his way to make me feel comfortable when he issued the following invitation:

THE WHITE HOUSE
Washington
November 13, 1991

Dear Magic:

There has been a lot of speculation about your joining the
National AIDS Commission. I know that you have been
asked to serve.

This letter is simply to say that I personally hope you will
do this. The Commission is high-level and has a wonderful
group of informed and influential members. There is genuine enthusiasm in all quarters for your undertaking this
service.

I want to add, however, that I know you are being besieged
with requests from all quarters—a tribute not only to your
achievement in life but to the way you have come forward
on this issue. But please do not feel under any pressure to
undertake this assignment if it conflicts with other things
you want to do. I do not want you to feel that you are being
used in any way. I do want you to know on a very personal
basis that I respect you, admire you, and hope that you
will be able to join the Commission. There will be times,
perhaps, when the Commission and the President are not
in total agreement. So be it! You will be a free and independent voice working with an outstanding group of leaders if you decide to accept.

We need you but, of course, my respect and admiration
will in no way be diminished by whatever you decide.

If you decide to do this, I hereby invite you to the White
House where we could make the formal announcement. I
believe that will help the education process needed nation-
wide.

In either event, Barbara and I send you our warmest best wishes and our family love and respect.

Sincerely,

George Bush

Two days later, I sent this reply:

November 15, 1991

The President
The White House
Washington, D.C.

Dear Mr. President:

Thank you for your kind letter. I am very grateful for your expression of support.

I would be honored to accept your invitation to serve on the National Commission on AIDS. I hope that my participation will help to increase the attention of the American people to the AIDS crisis, and focus their awareness on what all of us must do to fight this disease.

I appreciate your understanding that it is important for me to remain an independent voice on this issue as I work to educate the heterosexual community, African-Americans and young people to the AIDS crisis.

I hope that the Commission and your Administration will be able to work hand in hand in the fight against AIDS, and I want you to know that I will do everything that I can to make a difference.

Sincerely,

Earvin Johnson

On January 14, I attended my first meeting with the commission. I was also invited to meet with the president on that day. And I saw that as an opportunity to deliver a strong message to him. I intended to give him a letter, urging him to do more on behalf of AIDS victims and AIDS research. While I wanted to be candid and forthright, I didn't want to embarrass my host or be disrespectful to him.

Here again, Michael Ovitz and his team were very helpful. The day before our meeting, they contacted Marlin Fitzwater, the president's press secretary, and told him that I'd be carrying a letter for Mr. Bush. We didn't want the president to be blindsided, so they asked Fitzwater to recommend an appropriate time for me to give the letter to Mr. Bush. He suggested that I present it after the press had left the room. It would still be up to me to decide whether or not I wanted to tell the press about it. I decided not to. But I did share the letter with my colleagues on the AIDS commission, and the press would soon pick it up.

I spent most of January 14 at the AIDS commission meeting. I was a little nervous about joining a group of medical and other experts when I was so new to this whole area, but as soon as I got there, Dr. David Rogers, vice chair of the commission and a prominent AIDS expert, took me under his wing. I had already read the commission's reports, so I knew that this was not a rubber-stamp group. These folks were serious, and they were good, caring people. It wasn't their fault if the White House failed to act on their recommendations.

Some of the things we heard that day were very upsetting. That AIDS was the fifth leading cause of death among people aged fifteen to forty-four. That it was the *second* leading cause of death among men aged twenty-five to forty-four. (The leading cause was unintentional injuries and car accidents.) That AIDS was the leading cause of death in young men and women in New York City. That AIDS was nine times more prevalent among black women than white women, and *twenty-nine* times more prevalent among black adolescent girls than white girls. That an estimated ten million people in the world had the virus—and that this number was expected to reach *forty* million by the year 2000.

None of these facts and figures made the nightly news. Instead, the networks showed a very dramatic moment when a young AIDS activist addressed the commission and told me that I was probably going to die. His name was Derek Hodel, and at the time he was the executive director of the People with AIDS Health Group in New York. His statement *was* dramatic, and it was important, too. Only a few seconds of it made the news. But I'm going to include a big chunk of it here, because I want you to know what he said. His message was important. And as you'll see, he expressed it with great passion, and understandable anger.

This commission, the second of its kind, has conducted more hearings than I care to count, and has visited care facilities, advocacy groups, prisons, research centers. You have talked to doctors, scientists, politicians, people with AIDS. And in this time, while someone with AIDS dies every seven minutes, you have spent countless dollars and untold time preparing reports—by all accounts intelligent, forceful, landmark reports, that have been virtually ignored by a callous, meanspirited White House, led by a president who promulgates public-health policies mired in politics.

You already have the answers. You already know what you need to know. So I ask myself: Why bother?

Last November, on a day one sportscaster declared we would remember as vividly as we did the one that saw the assassination of JFK, the phones in my office began to ring. It was the media, seeking comment. And this gay white boy was forced to ask: Who is Magic Johnson?

Mr. Johnson, you must forgive me because I don't know any basketball stars. I do, however, know hundreds of people with HIV, and among them are countless young black men like yourself, some successful, some not. Although they, too, are all HIV-infected, to the best of my knowledge, the president has never called them.

Mr. Johnson, I watched as you became an AIDS hero and were added to the very short list that includes mostly children, hemophiliacs, and people who think they got it from their dentist. It includes Ryan White and Kimberly Bergalis—whom I believe someone recently called a "saint"—the so-called innocent victims of AIDS. It does not include most of the people that I know.

Mr. Johnson, I ask with utmost humility that you take great care in your newfound role. You are now one among many exclusively innocent victims of AIDS, be they gay people, drug users, or those Ms. Bergalis saw fit to imply had done something wrong.

To serve as our spokesperson, we ask you to embrace us all, gay or straight, men, women, and children, and to have the courage to speak with humanity for all those for whom you have been given a voice.

Mr. Johnson, as you changed the lives of Americans everywhere, you immeasurably changed my life. After years of fighting this disease, I saw the nation suddenly awaken to the reality that is AIDS, the reality that I as a gay man have lived with every day, the reality that has killed over 130,000 Americans just like you and me. And yet I saw that for most people, AIDS became a reality only because you upset the "us versus them" construction that had previously shielded them from fear. And they were busily, desperately trying to put it back in place.

Still, the president of our United States blames those with AIDS for refusing to change their behaviors, suggesting that AIDS is a price they must pay.

Magic Johnson, hero, AIDS anomaly, the great power you now wield to persuade, to convince, to inspire is something that I, in spite of dedicating my life to fighting this fight, will never know. I cried—again—for my brothers who desperately needed that power years ago. . . .

Tragedy permeates the AIDS epidemic, as it does this commission's work. For this noble body, a smattering of great minds in its midst, is impotent. I demand to know:

Does your responsibility extend no further than issuing reports? Can it be that your mandate, your moral imperative, permits you to identify the enemy and then abandon the fight?

You as commissioners bear great responsibility and must confront this truth. Your reports, like AIDS itself, have been ruthlessly ignored by a callous, incalculably mercenary administration for the sake of politics.

My attitude has hardened of late. I have no time for ignorance ten years later. I have no patience for those who do not wish to know. I blame inaction not on benign neglect, but on calculated, cold-blooded malice. And I equate silence with death.

I blame you for the death sentences implicit in your laissez-faire approach. It is immoral for you to have gathered such information and formulated such recommendations without screaming bloody murder until they are heard. . . .

Mr. Johnson, already you have given people with HIV great hope. By your will to live, by your will to beat this thing, your taking control of your illness and your positive attitude show great courage. Sadly, they will not be enough to keep you alive.

Mr. Johnson, what ultimately propelled me to Washington today was the opportunity to challenge you. I challenge you to call President Bush, not to listen, because we already know what he has to say, but to challenge him to provide the leadership necessary to stem the AIDS epidemic before it kills you, as I am sorry to say, it probably will. I challenge you to educate President Bush, to challenge his simplistic, moralistic thinking that blames rather than helps. I challenge you to confront the president, to push him to do more to support research into treatments for AIDS. For it is treatment, not compassion, that will keep people like you alive.

Read the commission's reports. Ask questions of those who have spent the better part of a decade fighting this fight. We'll take your call. You help us to find a new voice.

My guess is that the president will take your call, too. God knows that he won't take mine. Nor will he take the call of any gay organization, and I would wager that he won't take Dr. Osborn's, either. The choice is yours: You can demand that he provide leadership, or we can wait, we can do more fact-finding, establish more task forces, issue more reports, and pretend that we care. Send that message, Magic. We are a thousand points of light, and we are being extinguished one by one.

Right after Derek Hodel's statement, Stephen Rivers, from the Ovitz team; Vince Bryson, from the recently created Magic Johnson Foundation, which funds a variety of educational and preventive efforts concerning HIV and AIDS; and I got in the car to drive over to the White House. The three of us were so moved by Derek's testimony that it was all we could talk about. Before we knew it, we were pulling into the White House grounds—and I hadn't even started to think about what I would tell the president. But believe me, Derek Hodel's testimony that morning strengthened my resolve to make it clear to Mr. Bush that he had to do more—and also *say* more—about this whole problem.

A chill went down my spine when I actually walked into the West Wing. The door to the Oval Office opened, and Sam Skinner, the president's new chief of staff, said, "He's ready for you now." But George Bush is skillful in making you feel at ease. He really commands the room with his friendliness. The president brought in two or three of his own advisers, and we all sat down and talked.

During this brief meeting, I told the president that I thought the American public was waiting for him to show greater leadership on the issue, that he needed to come out and say he understood, that he cared, and that he'd do whatever he possibly could to help solve this growing crisis. He had mentioned AIDS only a couple of times during his presidency, and I urged him to say a lot more. He seemed to be listening.

After about fifteen minutes, the president looked at his watch. Then he took out an index card with his daily schedule typed on it. He looked up at me. "You guys got a few minutes?" he asked. " 'Cause if you do, I'd love to show you the basketball court that we have out back."

He took the three of us on a little tour of the White House sports facilities—the basketball court, the exercise room, the horseshoe pit, and the pool. When we got to the court, the president mentioned that the Chicago Bulls had been there a few months earlier after winning the championship. I winced when I heard that, because they had beaten the Lakers to get there. Mr. Bush told me he was impressed by how many three-pointers Craig Hodges had made on this court during that visit. I wasn't surprised, I said, because when it came to three-pointers, Craig was the best in the NBA.

When the tour was over, the president brought us into his private study and showed us photographs of his family and his house in Kennebunkport, which had recently been damaged by a storm. We ended up back in the Oval Office, where he gave each of us a set of presidential cuff links and a tie pin.

It was hard not to like him, but I hadn't forgotten what I was there for. Earlier, as we had stood up to go on the tour, I had reached into my pocket for the letter I had brought. "Since you wrote me such a nice letter," I said as I handed it to him, "I thought I would write you one, too."

The president had been expecting this. He grabbed it quickly and put it in his jacket pocket. "Got it," he said.

I had written the letter with the help of Elizabeth Glaser, who'd spent hours on it. As we worked on it, we tried to strike the right balance between respect and appreciation on the one hand, and the urgent need to do more on the other. This was what it said:

January 14, 1992

> The Honorable George Bush
> President of the United States
> The White House
> Washington, DC

Dear Mr. President:

I am happy to be in Washington to begin serving on the National Commission on AIDS, and I am happy to have the opportunity to accept your kind invitation to meet.

I know that we will have only a few minutes to visit, so I wanted to put down in writing some thoughts and requests that I hope you will give serious consideration to.

Every person at a point in their life faces his or her own mortality—maybe for you it was in World War II—and now I am facing mine. In the twelve months since I last met you, my life has changed.

In the last two months I have switched games, from basketball to, I guess, the biggest game of all—life and death. I have learned more about HIV/AIDS than I ever wanted to. I understand now that we are all in this fight together. That each of us has a crucial role to play. There is one person, however, who can do more than anyone else, and that is you.

I know that you will understand that, like you, I have always been a fighter *and a winner.* Therefore, I don't know any other way to approach this turn of events.

It takes a brave and honest man to say what you said in

Rome: that you know that you have not done enough to fight AIDS, and that you can do more.

In asking me to join the Commission, in fact you were asking me to join your team. You are the owner. In the NBA, no matter how good the team may be, it won't win the championship without the owner fully in the game. I don't feel you've been there until now. I have given this much thought and realize that the fight against AIDS demands a full court press. We can win this game, but not without a total commitment by everyone.

Three things must be dealt with: research, treatment and education. These are all recommendations called for in your commission report.

Education is a must, and the costs will be large. I know I can help defray these costs by making it my personal goal to educate as many people as possible about responsible sexual behavior through my access to the media. You, however, are the only one who can take on the other two:

1. Provide the missing AIDS *research money* requested by NIH for this year (1992) and the full request for 1993.
   estimated cost: $400 million in 1992
                    $500 million in 1993
2. Fully fund the Ryan White Care Bill for *treatment*.
   estimated cost: $300 million in 1992
                    $600 million in 1993
3. Allow Medicaid to pay for care of people with HIV, not just AIDS. This early intervention could save millions of lives and billions of dollars.
   estimated cost: $500 million in 1993

I am asking you to commit to these necessary funds immediately. We have to move ahead quickly. There is not a moment to lose. It's a race with the clock.

Finally, I hope that you will lend your voice and your moral leadership more fully to this fight. Let the people of this country, let the people who work in government, know that the fight against AIDS is a personal priority of yours, so that they will be inspired and motivated to get involved and re-double their efforts to stop the spread of this disease.

Mr. President, we cannot afford to lose this game. I'm a fighter and so are you. More has to be done. You know it and I know it. Let's do it together. I'll do my part—please do yours.

Thank you.

Sincerely,

Earvin Johnson, Jr.

When I returned to California, I received this reply:

THE WHITE HOUSE
Washington
January 17, 1992

Dear Magic:

It was good to see you on Tuesday; I appreciated hearing your views firsthand. This letter begins the process of re-sponding to the letter you left with me at the end of our meeting.

As we discussed, I would suggest you meet with the NIH scientists doing the research and the people running our programs to confront the AIDS challenge. The Government's response to AIDS goes far beyond me to include thousands of people who are working tirelessly. I know Secretary Sullivan would be pleased to make arrange-ments for you to visit these facilities.

You asked about my participation and made some very direct points about the resources we are devoting to AIDS. Last month I went to the Department of Health and Human Services for a briefing Secretary Sullivan organized, in which members of the National Commission on AIDS participated. Dr. Tony Fauci, who is leading our outstanding biomedical research effort, discussed the research funding issue.

He noted that we are doing an extraordinary job and that resources have risen dramatically. Are we doing enough? In Dr. Fauci's words, combating HIV is an act of discovery, and we will not be doing enough until the problem is solved.

I agree with that: we won't be done until the problem is solved. I am proud of what we have been able to accomplish thus far in meeting the AIDS challenge. You may find useful the enclosed one-page statement summarizing our strategy against AIDS.

Finally, your letter discusses moral leadership, which we talked about at some length. Rest assured I intend to do what I can to make our society one that is without prejudice against those who are infected with HIV. There *is* a role for every American to play in our response to AIDS. How we can bring each person to recognize and accept his or her role is a challenge we face together, and I look forward to working with you in that endeavor.

Sincerely,

George Bush

[handwritten:] I like your "team" analogy. Good luck, Come back.

I'm not sure whether the president got the message. But the press certainly did. The headline in *USA Today* read:

MAGIC URGES BUSH TO GET IN AIDS GAME. *The Atlanta Constitution:* MAGIC TO BUSH: GET INTO THE GAME, SPEND MORE MONEY ON AIDS CRISIS. The *Chicago Tribune:* MAGIC URGES BUSH TO SPEAK OUT ON AIDS. *New York Newsday:* MAGIC NUDGES BUSH. And *The New York Times:* MAGIC JOHNSON URGES BUSH TO LEAD AIDS BATTLE.

Sometimes the press distorts what you say, but they got this one right. *The New York Times* even ran an editorial called MAGIC AND MR. BUSH, ONE ON ONE, which was very supportive of what I was trying to do: "Mr. Johnson, the newest member of the National Commission on AIDS, gave Mr. Bush some cogent suggestions for improving AIDS treatment, prevention and research. And he was right on the mark when he criticized the President for hanging back in the battle against this deadly disease."

Months later, I realized the situation had not changed and would not. On June 25, 1992, the commission, which is a bipartisan panel, released a statement saying that the Bush administration had failed the entire nation by showing poor leadership in combating the AIDS epidemic. For the administration, it's been business as usual. But when you're trying to fight a problem of enormous proportions, business as usual isn't good enough. The United States has the largest number of HIV infections in the world, but we have no national plan to deal with the epidemic. It's a disgrace. I knew then that I would eventually have to resign.

In the spring of 1992, a few months after my trip to Washington, I became involved in two projects that were specifically aimed at educating young people about AIDS and HIV. One was *A Conversation with Magic Johnson,* a half-hour TV show that was shown on the cable channel Nickelodeon, and public-television stations across the country. The idea originated with Gerry Laybourne, the president of Nickelodeon. A few hours after my November 7 press conference, he called Linda Ellerbee, the well-known TV journalist, whom he knew from her company, Lucky Duck

Productions, which produced news and documentaries for Nickelodeon. "You know," he told her, "Magic Johnson says he wants to help educate kids. And since we're the kids' channel . . ."

The basic idea was simple. I would sit down with a group of kids between the ages of eight and fourteen, and we'd talk about some of the things kids should know to avoid getting HIV. Once the ball got rolling, our two sponsors, Nestlé and the NBA, decided to present the show without commercials. The Magic Johnson Foundation got involved, too, by making copies of the show available to schools and community groups. Public television joined the team, agreeing to broadcast the show after it appeared on Nickelodeon.

The experts Linda consulted told her that in their view, the best ages at which to reach young people with important information about sex, HIV, and AIDS was a year or two *before* they reached puberty. And we were very direct in suggesting that young people should hold off when it came to sexual activity. As Linda put it, bluntly as always, "You should postpone sex. You're still kids." At the same time, we didn't want to give out the message that all sex was dangerous—or bad.

I was clear with the kids about my own situation. "It happened because I had unprotected sex," I told them. Linda showed the kids and the viewers what a condom was, and how it worked. I repeated that the safest sex was no sex.

Another thing we wanted to do was focus attention on people—including kids—who already had HIV. Of the kids on the show with me, one boy's brother was living with AIDS, and two little girls were HIV-positive. Anyone who has seen the show will remember the sweet little girl in front who broke down and cried as we were talking. I did my best to comfort her, but my heart was breaking.

I'd been on a lot of TV shows in my life, but I'd never been involved in anything like this. This one was about saving lives, and I know that we succeeded.

* * *

The other project was a book about AIDS. A few weeks after I announced my retirement, Michael Ovitz negotiated a three-book contract with Random House on my behalf. The first one, which was published in the spring of 1992 by Times Books, a division of Random House, was a paperback for teenagers called *What You Can Do to Avoid AIDS*.

As much as Linda Ellerbee and I were able to accomplish on Nickelodeon, the subject of HIV, AIDS, and safer sex was a lot more complicated than we could present in a few minutes. The idea behind the book was that teenagers needed frank information and good advice on some basic questions: What exactly is safer sex? How exactly is HIV transmitted? How should you treat somebody who has the virus—or AIDS? What should you do if you're too embarrassed to buy a condom? How do you get tested for the virus? And where can you go for further help?

I had a lot of support in preparing the AIDS book, especially from my editor, Betsy Rapoport. From the start, we all agreed on one central point: that a book on this subject had to be direct and explicit. Instead of fancy medical terms, we would use the same words teenagers themselves used when they talked about sex. We knew that some people might be offended by the language, but we were willing to take that risk. In our view, it's not the words that are offensive—it's this disease.

So maybe I shouldn't have been surprised when two of the country's largest retail chains, Kmart and Walgreen's, refused to carry the book because of its straightforward language and illustrations. A spokesperson for Kmart called it "very graphic"—which it is. "It should be available to teenagers," she said, but not to "a three-year-old while their mother is buying a lawn mower."

Well, I don't know any three-year-olds who hang around Kmart stores looking for dirty books. Unfortunately, in many communities, the book section of Kmart is the closest thing in town to a real bookstore. On the other hand, Waldenbooks, which is owned by Kmart, does carry it.

This book was urgently needed, and Times Books and Random House helped me get it out very quickly. They priced it low, at $3.99, so just about any kid could afford it. They also published it at cost; any profits the book earns will be donated to the Magic Johnson Foundation to continue the fight against AIDS.

Here's what I told the kids right at the beginning of *What You Can Do to Avoid AIDS:*

> Many people have called me a hero because I've chosen to dedicate the rest of my life to educating people—especially teenagers—about HIV and how to protect themselves from it. But let me be clear about one thing: I'm not a hero because I got HIV. And I didn't get HIV because I was a "bad" person or a "dirty" one or someone who "deserved" it for whatever reason. No one "deserves" to get HIV. I got HIV because I had unprotected sex. I got HIV because I thought HIV could never happen to someone like me. Obviously, if I could turn the clock back, I would have acted differently. But I can't. I can only go forward. With the love and support of my family and friends, I'm going to fight this illness as best I can. And pass on to you the lessons I have learned the hard way.

This was a book of information. But sometimes having the right information isn't enough. If you're in denial, all the information in the world won't do you any good. I talked about that, too. Because when it came to denial, I was an expert. The information I needed to protect myself had been all around me. It was right there in my face—on radio and TV, in newspapers and magazines, in locker-room lectures. But I didn't pay attention. I didn't think it could happen to me. And that's the biggest problem, right there.

I also wanted kids to know that when it came to people with HIV, I was one of the lucky ones. Although a few people made negative comments after my announcement, the great majority of the public has been very responsive to me. Most people with HIV and AIDS don't get that kind of support. Many are rejected—sometimes even by their friends and their families. And they are discriminated against in all sorts of ways. Protecting yourself against HIV and AIDS is only half the battle. The other half is making sure that people who are already in this situation are treated with dignity and compassion. AIDS is not about ''us'' and ''them.'' People don't get HIV because they're ''bad,'' and they don't *not* get it because they're ''good.'' *You don't get HIV because of who you are. You get it because of what you do.*

On September 25, I sent President Bush a letter saying in part, ''I cannot in good conscience continue to serve on a commission whose important work is so utterly ignored by your administration.

''Mr. President, when we met in January, I gave you a letter in which I expressed my hope that you would become more actively involved in the fight against AIDS. No matter how good the team may be, I said, it won't win the championship without the owner fully in the game. I am disappointed that you have dropped the ball.''

CHAPTER 19

ONE GAME

When I retired from basketball on November 7, I figured that was it—at least for the season. I certainly didn't imagine that on February 9 I would be in Orlando for the All-Star Game. But when the doctors had no objection to my playing, I was thrilled.

If I really had to give up basketball—and that was by no means clear—I deserved one last game. As much as I wanted to play for the fans, I was also there for myself. I wanted to prove that I could still play this game, that I could play it as well as I had before this virus came along.

Before I left home, I put a blank tape in the VCR and programmed it to record on Sunday at 9:00 A.M., Pacific Time. Cookie was halfway through her pregnancy, and I could already imagine myself a few years in the future, sitting in the den with our son or daughter. "Let me show you something," I would say. "This is Daddy's last game, where he had a chance to say good-bye."

But there was another reason I wanted to be there and play in that game. Although I no longer played for the Lakers, I now played for another, much larger team—a team that was growing bigger by the day. And that's what made the All-Star Game so important to me. By being there, I felt that I somehow represented everyone who had HIV or AIDS. I wanted to show the world that people with HIV could still run, jump, and play basketball. And that you couldn't catch the virus from playing against us, hugging us, kissing us, or knocking us down.

On another level, I felt that I was there for people with any affliction or disability. I wanted to tell them that our lives were not over. That I was still here, and they were, too. That life was a struggle, but we had to keep going.

In many respects, this was like any other All-Star weekend. My parents were there, along with my brothers and sisters, my nephews, my son, Andre, Cookie's parents, and a few old friends from Michigan. On Friday night, we continued a tradition we had started a few years earlier during a previous All-Star weekend. The whole extended family took over a soul-food restaurant and had ourselves a big buffet dinner, with baked chicken, barbecued ribs, potato salad, collard greens, and sock-it-to-me cake, which is made with sour cream, nuts, and cinnamon. After dinner we all sat around and played cards.

I love to be with my family, but that night, my mind was on Sunday's game. Was I really prepared? I had been working out and training hard for weeks, but I hadn't played a real game in ages. A crowd makes any game feel a hundred times bigger. When it's just you and a few other guys in a pickup game, your mistakes don't matter much. But the fans react to every move you make, and you're always aware of them. If I didn't play well on Sunday, people would understand. But it was their cheers and their excitement that I wanted to hear, and not those soft moans of disappointment.

The whirlwind and commotion surrounding this game were enormous, bigger than anything I had ever experienced. Reporters were in Orlando from all over the world. Every time Cookie and I got off the elevator and walked through the hotel lobby, there was an instant mob scene. On Friday, when Cookie had flown into town with Laurie Rosen, people at the airport actually recognized her. They even asked for autographs. That was new.

That night, when we came back to the hotel from our big dinner, our car was surrounded by so many fans that we could hardly get out. People just wanted to touch me, to call out their encouragement. "We're praying for you! Good luck! Stay healthy!"

On Saturday night, Cookie and I decided we were better off staying in the hotel. We laughed and talked together, reminiscing about the good old days at Michigan State. We'd spent so many evenings talking in Cookie's cramped dorm room, and I can still picture those little bunk beds and the tiny desks. I'd known even then that I wanted to marry her, and before long I'd started shooting off my mouth about our future together. I would definitely be playing in the NBA, I told her, and then I'd be able to buy her a big house, nice clothes, and all the other things we both wanted but couldn't afford. Cookie just looked at me and smiled. He's sweet, she was thinking, but what a dreamer!

"And remember the diamonds?" I asked her when we woke up Sunday morning. In our sophomore year, just before Christmas, most of the guys on the basketball team went out together and bought diamond rings for their girlfriends. The diamonds were authentic, but very tiny. Maybe that's why the rings were only about fifty bucks each. Even so, that was a lot more than I could afford. Cookie was disappointed—she was the only girl in the group who didn't get a ring. "Listen, baby," I told her. "I'm not gonna buy you some cheap ring from a Cracker Jack box. Someday I'll buy you a *real* diamond. And when I do, you'll be able to see that thing all the way from the other side of the court."

I was a big talker in those days. But now, thirteen years later, here we were on a bright Sunday morning in Florida, sharing a fancy room-service breakfast in our luxury hotel suite at Disney World. And there, on Cookie's finger, was the same big diamond ring I had imagined buying her back when we were in college. "You see," I told her, "it worked out just like I said."

"You're right," she replied. "Everything you told me came true."

Cookie and I have had a lot of friendly times, but there was something special about that weekend. Talking and relaxing with her put me in a great mood, and it definitely helped with the nervousness I was feeling about the game. When I left her at the hotel so I could get to the arena a few hours early, she assured me that everything would be fine. "This game is just one more challenge," she said, giving me a big hug and a kiss. "Now go out there and enjoy yourself. And be sure to kick some ass!"

I always enjoy myself on the court. I had already envisioned having a great game. I even envisioned winning the MVP, although I couldn't imagine exactly how that would happen—not even in my wildest dreams, and I'm a wild dreamer.

As always, I was the first one in the locker room. I like to get there real early, because it gives me time to think about the game. My heart was beating fast, and I took some deep breaths to calm myself down. Stay relaxed, I told myself. Keep cool. If you're too eager to please, you won't play your game.

Normally there'd be only a light practice before the All-Star Game; we didn't do much more than run up and down the court a few times. But on Saturday, Don Nelson, the coach of the West team, made us scrimmage against each other. He may have done that for my sake, so I could practice against great players and build up my confidence. If that's what he had in mind, it worked. Any doubts I'd had about my ability to keep up had quickly disappeared.

Before long, the rest of the team started coming into the locker room. As soon as the chatter started, I felt at home. This was what I had missed the most in the past few months—not so much the playing, but the talk, the camaraderie, the kidding around. After twelve years in the NBA, I *knew* these guys. I had played on other All-Star teams with most of them. James Worthy was there from the Lakers, along with veterans from other teams, like Clyde Drexler, Karl Malone, Hakeem Olajuwon, Chris Mullin, and David Robinson.

I said hello to John Stockton, who at six-one was the smallest guy on the West. On the East team, Isiah was the same size as John, and so was Mark Price from Cleveland. But whatever these guys lacked in height, they more than made up in talent. And in heart, too. That's why I loved playing with them.

At Saturday's practice, my teammates had gone out of their way to make me feel welcome. Jeff Hornacek asked if the Lakers still owned my rights. If not, he said, Phoenix would be happy to sign me. "If we had you," said David Robinson, who plays for San Antonio, "we'd win it all." Several guys told me I hadn't lost a step. "You're looking good, looking good," said my old pal Clyde Drexler. He said it again during Sunday's game. The encouragement of the other All-Stars meant a great deal to me. I guess I'd needed it more than I realized.

Now I got dressed in my usual manner, starting with my jersey and my socks. Then I sat back for a moment, collecting my thoughts, before I put on my shorts and shoes. I was feeling happy and confident. I wanted to savor the moment. I'd always loved getting dressed for the All-Star Game, and running onto that great stage with all the other guys.

But today was different. As we left the locker room, I looked at myself in the mirror. There were goose bumps. As we walked toward the floor, past the reporters and the well-wishers, the tension started growing. *This is for real. In another minute I'll be out there. It's finally going to happen.*

As soon as we got to the court, I could sense that the fans were all staring at me. I could feel their eyes. And so many cameras! This game was being broadcast around the globe, from Nicaragua to Singapore, from Kazakhstan to Zimbabwe. People would be watching us in more than ninety different countries. The phrase kept ringing in my ears: "The whole world is watching."

The crowd started cheering even before I was introduced, and they continued for another two minutes after. Stay strong, I told myself. There'll be plenty of time to get emotional later.

I was able to hold my feelings in check for—oh, maybe another thirty seconds. That's when the entire East team, led by Isiah Thomas, came over to greet me. I'd had no idea that would happen. One moment I was waving to the crowd, the next I was surrounded by Michael Jordan, Charles Barkley, Patrick Ewing, and the whole gang. Their hugs and high fives meant so much to me that I almost lost it right there. It was tough to hold on. Whenever I get emotional, it takes a while to get my intensity back. And right now I needed all the intensity I could muster.

Stay strong, stay strong, I kept telling myself. But it was hard not to let go in the face of this torrent of feelings. I wonder if any athlete has ever come into a game, any game, feeling so much support, so much love, from so many people.

The game was about four seconds old when I lost the ball on a bad pass. But that was expected. This sort of thing always happened to me at the start of a big game, so I wasn't worried. Maybe it meant that most of the nervousness was out of my system. Okay, I told myself. Let's settle down here. Let's play some basketball.

At first, some of my teammates weren't keeping up with me. Maybe they weren't sure I could still play. Whatever it was, a couple of guys seemed slow and tentative. But as the game went on, they picked up the pace. Before long, we started seeing the sharp passes and the lay-ups. Dennis Rodman had already warned me that I'd have to work for my points. "I'm gonna guard you tough," he said before the game. "You're not scoring on me." When he said that, I couldn't wait to post him up. Halfway through the first quarter I hit a fifteen-foot hook shot right over him.

The point guard runs the show, so I made sure to pass out the sugar to everybody: This guy is an outside shooter, that one likes to drive to the hoop. The All-Star Game is mostly a show of great offense. For one thing, the players are so good that you couldn't stop them even if you wanted to. For another, nobody wants to risk an injury halfway through the season. If one of *these* guys went down, his team could kiss the rest of the season good-bye.

The whole game was great. But the final minutes of the fourth quarter will stay with me forever, with the one-on-one battles against Isiah Thomas and Michael Jordan, and those three three-pointers near the end.

There are times in life when you want to take a feeling and put it in a bottle, so you can take it with you forever. I had an entire season's worth of pleasure from that one quarter. My little duels with Isiah and Michael might have looked scripted, but we were writing it on the spot.

The only guy missing from that game was Larry Bird, who was out with an injured back. The All-Star Game had a perfect ending, but I did miss Larry. Someday we'll have to go out to the court behind his house and even things up.

Up in the stands, Dad was beaming. He looked happier than I'd ever seen him before. He'd had his doubts, but after seeing me play, he knew I was all right. I loved seeing the joy on his face, and I've kept that picture in my mind ever since.

What a relief this must have been for him and Mom. When I'd told my parents about the virus, there was nothing I could really say to make them understand that I was still all right. They kept hearing about AIDS, and how their son was sick. They felt so helpless and worried. I felt their pain on the phone often, especially from Dad.

Three weeks after the announcement, Cookie and I had gone to Lansing for Thanksgiving. While I was there, I worked out at the Y. There was a pickup game every day at noon, and I played a few times. My father didn't come, but he sent a friend to be his eyes, to see how I was doing.

But when Dad watched me play in the All-Star Game, he could see for himself that I was fine. We know each other so well. He knows my body language and my moves, and he watches me so carefully. And there I was, right in front of him, playing my game. That's Junior, he was thinking. That's my son, and he's all right. Cookie knows her husband, Dad knows his son. But because of the virus, nobody knew what would actually happen out there. Nobody knew how I would play.

Even I was a little surprised. I expected to have a good game, because I had worked so hard to prepare for it. When

I got to Orlando, I was *ready*. But I didn't know for sure that I'd have a great game. I was working on it all weekend, but I just couldn't come up with the right finish. I guess that final three-pointer was the ending I was looking for.

Cookie was radiant. She had watched me for years, but today she was as shocked as anyone. After the game we had a moment to ourselves in a small, curtained-off room. She must have said it five times: "I am so *proud* of you." When I hit that final three-pointer, she told me, she'd jumped to her feet. Even she hadn't expected it to go in. It was so great to see my wife light up that room, hugging me with everything she had.

Cookie had been sitting with her father, and he was even more excited than she was. He was screaming so loud during the fourth quarter that she asked him to cool it. "Please, Dad, you're embarrassing me!"

Then we went into a larger room, across from the visitors' locker room, where my family and friends were waiting for us. Andre was there, and my old friends from Lansing, and Julius Erving, and Uncle James, my mother's brother, who used to drive me around town on Sundays from one park to another so I could play basketball. If we couldn't find a game, Uncle James would call some of his friends and put one together for me.

Jim Dart was there, too, and he looked ready to cry. He gave me a couple of big hugs. And as usual, he spoke from his heart. "You know," he said, "every great warrior dies on the battlefield. Every great general goes down to the end. This is where you belong. If you're going to die, let it be on the court, doing what you love to do, what you were born to do." I've thought about those words ever since. And I'm still thinking about them today.

That night, Lon and I flew to New York for a business meeting. All during the flight, I kept flashing back to those two beaming faces: Cookie's and Dad's. How happy they'd looked, how proud.

In New York I was besieged like never before. Busboys,

maids, waiters, taxi drivers, everybody. On Monday afternoon, just before we left the city, I stopped off in a department store on Fifth Avenue to buy Cookie a leather pocketbook she had always wanted. As I was paying for it, a woman behind me asked for an autograph. "Sure," I said, while I signed the credit-card slip. "If you can wait a minute, I'll take care of it for you."

When I turned around, there wasn't just one woman standing there. There was a whole long *line* of women, stretching all the way to the door, silently waiting for autographs. I had been there only five minutes, but it looked as if somebody had put up signs: PLEASE LINE UP HERE FOR AUTOGRAPHS.

I managed to sign a few, but we had to run. "I've got a plane to catch," I called out behind me.

"We loved the game," they yelled back. "Come back soon!"

I'm used to people asking for autographs, but women in a fancy department store? That was a first. I heard later that the All-Star Game had attracted over 50 percent more viewers than ever before, including many people who had never watched a basketball game in their lives. But they had heard about this guy Magic Johnson who was playing although he had HIV, and they said, "Let's see what this is all about."

And what happened to all the people who watched that game? They got educated. They saw for themselves that a man with HIV could still play basketball, with no danger to himself or anybody else on the floor. That was the greatest good to come out of the game.

In the months that followed, I played that tape a lot. Until I actually sat down and watched it, I wasn't sure if my performance at the All-Star Game had really been as good as I remembered it. You can run for miles and lift all those weights, but until you're actually on the floor, playing against the best players in the league, there's always that doubt. And with me, the doubt had persisted even after the game. I knew I had played well physically, but after that long layoff, I wanted to be sure that my instincts were still sharp. Had I reacted quickly enough when a guy went around me? Had

I picked up right away on the rotation? Things happen quickly in the pro game, and I had been away for a long time. Would I still be good enough for the Olympic team?

I liked what I saw. I even used that tape to motivate myself to train harder for the Olympics. While my Olympic teammates were completing the regular season, I had to make sure I was keeping up with them. That tape inspired me so much that after a while I didn't even need to watch it. Just *thinking* about it was enough to send me to the gym.

But if I really had retired, there's one thing I could be sure of: that I couldn't have asked for a better ending.

CHAPTER 20

"RETIREMENT"

Only a week after the All-Star Game, with the cheers of the crowd still ringing in my ears, the Lakers retired my number. As I look back on it, I see that my retirement ceremony wasn't really about my retirement. Because in my heart, I wasn't ready to leave. And everybody knew that. In reality, the ceremony was a way for the Lakers to pay me a tribute, and for me to express my appreciation back to them.

The ceremony took place at halftime during a game against the Celtics. That was no accident. If I had to retire, I wanted to do it when the Celtics were in town. That rivalry had always meant so much to me, and to our two teams. The Laker fans arrive early for only one game, and that's Boston.

I didn't think it would be possible to match the glow of the All-Star Game. But this turned out to be a very different experience. The All-Star Game was a celebration. I played the way I wanted to play. I was still healthy, and I was still good.

The retirement ceremony was more complicated. It was bittersweet, and emotional, and not so clear. It marked an ending—unless it didn't. The bitter part was that I wasn't retiring because I wanted to. The sweetness was the outpouring of love and affection from my teammates and the fans. And all those great memories at the Forum, where I had played my heart out so many times.

The uncertainty was there because even after all the plans

had been made for this day, I was still thinking of coming back to the Lakers. It was probably too late for the 1991–92 season, but the next year was still an open question.

I definitely intended to play in the Olympics during the summer, but that was different. For one thing, it would last only a few weeks. For another, all of us on the team could share the burden equally; there wouldn't be too much stress on any one guy.

But after the Olympics? I still didn't know. When the retirement ceremony was over, Coach Dunleavy joked with the press that when the Lakers had put my jersey up on the wall, they had attached it with Velcro.

Still, I had announced my retirement, so a testimonial was inevitable. And like the All-Star Game, this one was broadcast on national television.

The night before, Arsenio took me out to dinner. The two of us had been friends for years, ever since we were both just breaking in and trying to make it in Los Angeles. When we first met, Arsenio was doing standup comedy and opening for other entertainers—mostly singers and successful comedians.

During dinner, we looked back on our careers and laughed about old times. I took that happy feeling home with me, and I was still laughing when I got into bed. But I didn't sleep too well that night. Usually I can picture an event in my mind, but I couldn't do that with the retirement ceremony. I didn't know the format, or who would be speaking first. The whole thing was too hard to imagine.

Sunday morning I woke up early. The game was scheduled for noon. I picked out my suit and tie, and drove to the Forum in my workout clothes. When I got there, I realized that I had forgotten my belt. When Arsenio showed up, he took his belt off and gave it to me.

As I had been doing for weeks, I worked out with the Lakers before the game. Then I sat with my teammates in the locker room as Coach Dunleavy went over some defensive strategies against the Celtics. The plan was to double-team Parish. They'd play everyone else, including McHale, man-to-man.

Larry Bird, who wasn't playing because of his bad back, arrived about an hour before the rest of the Celtics, and when I went out on the court to practice my shooting, guess who was already there? We started shooting together, just the two of us, alone on the court.

The Lakers' management had asked me to stay in the locker room during the first half of the game. Arsenio came in there with me, and we watched it on TV. When the first half came to an end, Lon stuck his head in. "It's time," he said.

The hardest part was knowing that I might be coming down that tunnel for the last time. And wearing a suit instead of my uniform. I had made that walk hundreds of times, but this one was so different. I remembered what it was like when Kareem had retired a couple of years before. Even so, I had no idea what my own ceremony would feel like. How do you say good-bye—especially when you don't really want to leave? Some of the people in this building had known me since I was nineteen years old. Inside, my heart was crying.

When I got out there, I saw that the lights were low. And some of the great Laker legends from the past were lined up to greet me—Wilt Chamberlain, Jerry West, Elgin Baylor, and Kareem. And my family was sitting there, too—my parents, my sister Pearl, my son, Andre, and Cookie. And there was Larry Bird, and a few of my former teammates. People were yelling, "We love you, Magic!" I knew this was it. I felt all my emotions getting ready to come out.

I was doing pretty well until Kareem spoke. When he told the crowd that I'd made him realize he was actually having *fun* out there, I just lost it. Kareem is a man who doesn't often speak his feelings—especially in public. It was very powerful, and it made me cry.

While he was speaking, I thought about our history together. I remembered how, at the beginning, he'd stayed away from me. Back then, he didn't allow anyone into his world. Five years later, he finally let me in, and before long he was sharing everything with me, telling me things he probably didn't say to anyone else. He went from being a complete stranger to being a brother. I'd asked for his advice many times over the years, and he'd asked for mine, too.

When I hugged him, I remembered the very first time I had hugged him, after his hook shot that won the first game of my career with the Lakers. He'd thought I was crazy. When I used to seek him out for a high five, I had to pull it out of him. Later, he'd hit a big hook shot and then look for me. I thought about a lot of great moments we'd had over the years. The Philadelphia series at the end of my rookie season, when we won the championship in his honor. And all the other championships, especially against Boston. And the night he set the scoring record in Las Vegas. More than anyone else, Kareem symbolized my years with the Lakers.

That afternoon, it wasn't just Kareem speaking to Earvin. It was the older brother telling the younger one how much he cared. I didn't want to hold my feelings in anymore, and I just broke. I hugged him for so long. I didn't want to let him go.

And of course Larry Bird. Larry spoke, too, although he didn't have to say anything. It wasn't the words that mattered. It was his presence, the fact that he was there, even with that injury. I didn't know until the last minute whether he'd make it, and when he did I appreciated it so much.

It was an honor to have the guy there who'd brought out the best in me, who'd really made me the player I became. We would battle each other to be the best, and we'd each try to top the other guy. I used to lie in bed at three in the morning, my eyes open, just thinking about him. The highest respect you can pay any player is to fear that he can beat you. And Larry Bird is the one guy I feared.

It was so strange for these two old warriors to be standing together on the court, all dressed up in suits and ties instead of our uniforms. Usually at least one of us was playing in the game. I don't think the Celtics and the Lakers had ever played before with both of us just watching.

When the halftime ceremony was over, we all went back

into the tunnel area to have our pictures taken. As we were standing there, I turned to Larry and said, "This game is a little slow. Why don't you and I go out there for the last five minutes and liven the place up?" He grinned. He knew I was only partly joking. If we'd both been healthy enough to do it, it would have been incredible.

Seeing my old teammates brought back so many precious memories. Like Jamaal Wilkes, whose nickname was Silk. I could throw him the ball as hard as I wanted. Nobody in the league could catch the passes I threw to Jamaal. And then he'd make that nice, soft shot. He had the smoothest, most delicate motion I have ever seen. Coach Westhead once compared Silk's gentle shot to snow falling off a bamboo leaf. And Norm Nixon, who would drift to his left for the fall-away jumper. And Coop, with all the alley-oops that we'd put together, and the way he and Larry would jaw at each other all day long. And Kurt Rambis, who insisted on being there even though the rest of his team was in Seattle. And of course Kareem.

The ceremony was special, all of it. My parents were there, and they're not used to being on TV. Mom just goes with the flow. She was crying like I was. Dad stayed strong and stern, but I knew what he was feeling inside.

They'd brought Dad into the locker room just before half-time, and the biggest smile came over his face when he was introduced to Wilt Chamberlain. Wilt was his hero, but Dad had never met him before. I'd never seen my father so excited. He was giggling and laughing. "I watched you," he said. "Junior and I used to watch you, and Hal Greer, and Wali Jones, and all those great Philadelphia players." Dad went down the whole roster with Wilt. Man, I wish I'd had a movie camera to record that moment.

Dad and I had spent a lot of time together that weekend. After my workout on Saturday morning, I took him to a little waffle place in Hollywood called Roscoe's. It was so nice, just the two of us talking things over. Then we went home and watched drag racing on TV. The only thing Dad likes better than drag racing is Wilt Chamberlain, so he definitely enjoyed the weekend.

When it was my turn to speak, I got to thank everybody— my teammates, the Laker legends, Larry Bird, David Stern, Jerry West, Jerry Buss, Chick Hearn, Lon, the press, the fans, Andre, my brothers and sisters—"and Mr. and Mrs. Earvin Johnson. Without you, sitting there, every day, every Sunday, right here beside me, pointing out different things about basketball, making me go to work with you, I wouldn't really have learned what hard work was all about. I love you so much. Mom, I stole everything you have. The thing I tried to take the most was your heart. It's so beautiful.''

Then I turned to Cookie: "I thought I was the strongest man who ever lived. But I found out that my wife was a hundred times stronger as a woman than I am as a man. Thank you, Cookie, for being strong, and for being here with me.''

That night, a group of my friends gave a party for me. Four guys spoke, and all of them said pretty much the same thing— that I should come back to the game. And every time somebody said that, all the guests cheered.

Then Arsenio stood up. "Now I know a lot of you are saying that Earvin should come back," he said. "But for selfish reasons, I don't agree. I want him hanging around with me forever. Think about it, Earvin. You've already accomplished everything that's possible to accomplish. You won it all in high school. You won it all in college. You've won five NBA championships, including back-to-back titles. You've been the MVP three times. The only thing you haven't done yet is the Olympics, and that's coming. What else is there?

"It's not about basketball anymore. It's about Cookie, and Andre, and your baby who's coming along. You should concentrate on them. You've already done everything you've set out to do on the court. You've done things that most other players have never done. There's nothing more for you to prove.''

People were stunned when he said that. And I was, too. I didn't know he felt that way. And I didn't imagine that he would talk like that in front of everybody. He was willing to say the unpopular thing, and I admire that.

Later that evening, he took me aside and said it again. "Man, don't come back. You've already done it all. If stress is your worst enemy, you don't need it. You know how you play. When you get out there, it's more than just a game. Let's just sit back and enjoy life a little. Let's eat swordfish, go to Hawaii, and have fun."

I was touched. I knew it came from his heart. I also knew that Arsenio had thought about it. He's a guy who does his homework before he comes at you. He had spoken to a couple of doctors, and to Elizabeth Glaser. She told him that if I took good care of myself, I had a chance to live for a long time.

Arsenio's words had a deep effect on me. Most people, when they saw me on the street or in an airport, would say, "I can't wait to see you back." Nobody other than Lon had said, "Stay home." It took a lot of courage for Arsenio to tell me that. When I got home that night, I woke up Cookie to tell her about it.

I went back and forth a few times on this question, and so did the people close to me. At the beginning, everybody was unanimous that I should retire—Cookie, my parents, Lon, and even me. But as we all learned more about HIV, all of us began to see things a little differently. And after the All-Star Game, when we saw the old Magic Johnson, most of the people around me started to swing over. So did I. I could still play, and the joy of playing is so much in my blood. I started asking myself: Why am I not playing?

Finally, with the new season only a few weeks away, I called a press conference to announce that I was coming back. God put me here to play basketball and to do my thing on the court. There are risks, but I think the positives outweigh them. Speaking for the doctors, Mickey Mellman said something I liked, that nobody knows what's going to happen with this experiment called Magic Johnson.

Now that I'm married, I can't make this kind of decision on my own. Here's Cookie's view on this whole question:

When the two doctors came over to our house and recommended that Earvin retire, he turned to me and said, "What do you think?" I said, "There's no question about it. You're going to retire. I want you around so we can grow old together. I want you to be here for the baby. If you go back, you're shortening your life. It's not worth it." That's what we both thought at the time.

I always used to wonder: What will Earvin be like when he retires? What will he do all day? How will he adjust? It didn't happen the way we planned, but it was fine. Because of how this happened, and because he had something so big to fight for, he was in good spirits. He didn't mope around, and he wasn't moody, which he sometimes was in the past. He was incredibly busy, speaking to different groups, going to meetings, and working out every day. He's had lots of projects, so it wasn't like he was sitting around the house. And he had his businesses, which he loves so much.

Sometimes I looked at his face when he watched games on TV, and I could see it got to him, that he wanted to be out there. And people would say, "I just know he's having a hard time because he's not playing." There was some truth to that. But one night, after we went to a game against the Clippers and the Lakers got blown out, he said, "You know, being retired isn't so bad. I don't have the pressure that I know those guys are feeling. If I was still playing, I'd be storming around the house. Now I can just come home and be fine."

People still come up to us with long faces and say, "We're so sorry." But it wasn't like that. Even if this hadn't happened, he would have retired in a couple of years anyway. The way he plays is not like some players, who can play at different levels. With Earvin, it's always full-steam ahead. And if he continued like that, it might have worn him down. In 1990, when the Lakers lost to

Phoenix in the second round of the playoffs, he played so hard that I thought he was going to collapse. After a while, your body just doesn't hold up any longer.

That Phoenix series was a big disappointment. The Lakers had finished the season with 63 wins. They had the best record in the West. Kareem had left, and Earvin was carrying the team all year. He's so used to winning, and to playing in the Finals. When Phoenix beat them he was crushed. I've never seen him more hurt than that. The Lakers aren't supposed to lose in the second round. Losing to Chicago in 1991 wasn't as bad, because nobody had expected the Lakers to get that far.

It sounds funny, but in most respects he's healthier now than he was before. During the season, or the playoffs, his body was always run-down. He was drained. Sometimes his face was pale. There were times when he couldn't eat. There were times when he could barely crawl into bed.

The All-Star Game was amazing. He was so happy, he was glowing. Even preparing was a joy for him. He was so dedicated, so serious. It was: "Don't mess with me. I have to practice." That was something I'll never forget.

Usually it's just his family that comes to the All-Star Game. But this time my parents were both there, and my stepmother, and my sister. I could tell how proud they were to see him out there. It was like he hadn't missed a beat.

But it never crossed my mind that he would be the MVP. I was just so happy that he was out there playing. I was really surprised when he won it, although Lon predicted it right before halftime. When Earvin took that final three-point shot in the end, even I didn't think it was going in. When it did, I jumped to my feet.

The retirement ceremony was very emotional. It would have been more dramatic, but there was still the thought in his mind, and I guess in everybody's mind, that he might be coming back. When Kareem spoke, Earvin started crying, and I did, too.

I always said I was behind him 100 percent no matter

what he decided. It was such a tough decision, a real tug of war. On the medical side, the doctors were not advising it. But they were not ruling it out, either. And basketball had been his life for so long.

But he also realized that there's another world, and other kinds of joy. And he saw that retirement wasn't all that bad: spending time with me, and the baby. In the end, he went back because he loves the game. But I also think he wanted to retire on his own terms and not because of HIV. This is about Earvin Johnson still being in charge of who he is and what he does. Maybe Earvin doesn't realize it, but I do.

One thing that really makes me mad is when people say that I'm in denial about having HIV. Maybe they think that way because I continue to be upbeat and optimistic. But I'm not going to crawl into a hole. The truth is, I don't have bad days. I don't wake up in the morning and think I'm going to get AIDS. I don't have bad dreams about it. When I dream, it's usually about playing basketball. And when I wake up from that dream, I'm ready for the game.

There have been moments of sadness about the virus, but not many. I've always been that way, thinking positive, with a bright outlook on life. And since this thing has happened to me, I've met dozens of other people who are living with HIV, just like me.

The doctors told me to stay away from people who are sick, and to make sure that I keep healthy and work out. I changed my diet, too. Good-bye to fried food and red meat. I started loading up on fruit, vegetables, juice, grilled chicken, and fish. All that—plus a positive attitude. To which I say, if those things help, I've got a good chance.

To me, HIV is just another challenge. I have the same attitude I always had on the court. I'm going all out to fight it. I haven't lost too many battles in my life, and Larry Bird has been involved in most of the ones I have lost.

But I can't escape the fact that this has happened—even if I wanted to, which I don't. There are so many reminders. I take my medicine every day. And wherever I go, people say things like "We're praying for you." I watch TV and read the papers. I speak to groups and go to meetings.

But last year there was an even bigger reminder for me that things were not the same. For the first time in my life, *I was not playing basketball.* At least not competitively. Until November 1991, that's all I'd ever done.

And that was the hardest part of all. I certainly didn't miss the traveling. But I missed the big games, especially against Michael and Larry. And I missed being one of the boys. I missed chumming around. I missed getting the paper on the road and checking the movie page to see what movie Coop and Byron and I would be seeing.

The Lakers were more than a team. We were a family. When a baby was born or somebody's parent died, we'd all be there. The fans don't hear much about that side of basketball, but we definitely had it. I missed that, too.

But a year away from basketball wasn't all bad, either. One night, just after my retirement ceremony in February, Cookie and I went to see the Lakers play the Clippers. We were spectators, and we sat right behind the Laker bench. The press was all over me, but I explained to everybody that I was there as a fan, and eventually they left us alone.

This was the first time that Cookie and I had ever sat together at a Laker game, and it was a strange feeling. But it was fun, too. It was like going on a date all over again. We ate popcorn, held hands, and talked and laughed all night. We enjoyed each other. Down on the court, the Clippers were definitely enjoying the Lakers. We had always dominated them, but that night the Lakers got creamed as badly as I have ever seen in my whole career. If I had been sitting on the bench, it would have torn me up. Even as a spectator, I felt bad for my teammates because they got embarrassed. But it didn't hit me nearly as hard as I would have expected. After the game, the players had to take those feelings of humiliation on to Seattle. I just went home and forgot about it.

I knew that my absence from the team made a big difference. But that wasn't the only change. In the last couple of years, Kareem had left, and Kurt, and Coop, and Riley, too. Before we knew it, the whole glue of the team was gone. Now only James and Byron were left from our great years. It was tough for the fans, because they'd been spoiled by success and by Showtime. They were used to being excited every night. But things change.

Several times after that Clipper game, I sat in the stands with Cooper and watched games. That was tough. It was the Lakers, but it wasn't the Lakers—not the Lakers we knew. And we didn't like being out of the action. Instead of being in the locker room during halftime, we would sit in Coop's office and discuss the game like a couple of old men.

But when I left the Forum and drove up the ramp on my way out, the security men would say, "When are you guys gonna win?" "You guys"—like I was still on the team. I was glad they still included me, but I also know that if I was playing, the team would be doing better. It was hard for the fans to see the Lakers without me, but it was hard for me, too.

I couldn't stay away, either. Sometimes I still shot with the guys before the game. One night, near the end of the season, they gathered everybody together for the team photograph. I was just a few feet away, practicing my shots. It hurt not to be included. I'd always been a team player, and I definitely wanted to be in that picture. They all asked me to be in it, but it didn't seem right. While they were taking it, I couldn't concentrate on my shots. I even missed a couple of lay-ups.

But there were new challenges, too. Earlier in the month, when Chicago came to the Forum, I made my debut with NBC as color commentator, broadcasting the game with Mike Fratello and Dick Enberg. The trick was to work together and make sure we weren't tripping over one another. Dick was the play-by-play announcer, so Mike and I had to get in and out real quick. I had to learn how to follow their hand signals, but soon I got the hang of it. I was amazed by how quickly they can set up those replays and diagrams while the director is talking into your ear on the headphones.

The hardest part about announcing was trying to be objective. I had to be careful not to say "we" when I was talking about the Lakers, even when I was thinking in these terms. It was difficult to criticize my teammates, but sometimes I had to. If I didn't, I wasn't doing my job. My job was to educate the fans, so I couldn't keep quiet if one of the players screwed up.

At least I didn't have to worry about making a living.

I had Kareem to thank for that. After he almost went broke, I quickly wised up and got my financial affairs in order. When you're playing, it's so easy to get caught up in the glamour. Everybody tells you how great you are, and you start to believe you can walk on water. You think the future will take care of itself. But unless you make real plans, you're going to end up in trouble. The applause dies away before you know it. The glamour fades quickly.

Pretty soon there's another young guy that everybody's crazy about. And then, when it's too late, you realize that you didn't use the power you had when you were hot. When you're on top, everybody spoils you. You think it's going to continue, but it never does.

Right after I switched over to Lon as my business manager, things picked up. I started doing commercials, endorsements, and speaking engagements to pay off my debts. Then, when everything was finally straightened out, we started planning for my future.

Lon helped me put together a business team that could take me where I wanted to go. At that point, I had been in the NBA only for about six years, but when it came to money, I'd always been careful. I lived well, but I'd never gone out and bought crazy things. I always had my eye on tomorrow. Long after I turned pro, I continued working in the summer, and I used that money to live on. I took my regular paychecks and put them away for the future.

I guess it's my dad's influence, but I always thought ahead

to what I would do when I retired from basketball. And one thing I knew for sure was that I wanted to be in business.

One of my advisers was Joe Smith, president of Capitol Records. "I want to start preparing now for life after basketball," I told him. "I'd like to become a businessman. What do you recommend? Who should I be speaking to?"

Joe told me that the man to see was Michael Ovitz. Ovitz had started out in the mail room at the William Morris Agency, but was quickly promoted. In 1985, he and four of his colleagues left to form their own company, Creative Artists Agency. Ovitz didn't represent any athletes, and he didn't really want to. But he was a huge Laker fan. He also admired the kind of team player I was, because he ran his business with a real team approach. He was willing to meet with me to discuss a few possibilities for my future.

One thing I liked about Ovitz was that he didn't flatter me; he didn't tell me what he thought I wanted to hear. He humbled me. He let me know about some of his other clients, people like Stallone and Streisand, Michael Jackson and Robert Redford, who were involved in mega-deals. For all my success in basketball, I knew that I was still an amateur when it came to business. Ovitz didn't say so directly, but I got the impression that I would probably be the smallest client on his list. That humbled me, too.

He gave me some homework, recommending that I start watching tapes of my own interviews so that I could improve my speaking ability and diction. Lon had already been helping me with this—pointing out that I used my hands too much, or that I sometimes fell into using slang. Like many athletes, I used to say things like "you know" and "no question" again and again without even realizing it.

I didn't *have* to improve my speech. I could have gotten away with speaking poorly. But if I had any hope of speaking on behalf of black ballplayers, and if I ever wanted to be successful beyond basketball, I had to communicate more effectively. Over the years, I think I've made a big improvement. I'm no Dr. J., by any means. But Julius Erving has always been a model for me—a man with real class who knew how to express himself.

Another thing Ovitz got me to do was start educating myself about the world of business. I used to devour the sports pages of the newspaper, and not much else. Ovitz explained that I should be reading *The Wall Street Journal* every day— not necessarily in detail, but at least to get a general sense of what was going on out there. He also recommended three business magazines: *Forbes, Fortune,* and *Business Week.*

We both agreed that I was looking for something more substantial than a string of commercial endorsements. Endorsements are fine, but they usually don't last too long. A few years down the road, I didn't want to be just another black athlete who was done with his playing career at the age of thirty-six and had nowhere to go except supermarket openings. Ovitz understood that. He also understood the mentality of most athletes: that there's only a finite amount of time for us, so we want to do everything right away. As a result, we often make hasty decisions without giving much thought to the bigger picture.

Instead of my getting many small endorsements, we wanted to create a serious association between me and a large corporation. Ovitz was interested in developing a real business partnership, which would include some equity on my part. He and his team started going through a list of major American corporations, looking for the right fit. Eventually, they settled on Pepsi, with the idea that I might be able to buy into one of their regional bottling plants or distributorships.

Ovitz then set up a meeting in his office with about a dozen Pepsi executives. I was a little nervous about sitting with these heavy-hitting businessmen in dark suits, so the day before the meeting, I had a kind of rehearsal with the Ovitz team. They briefed me on some of the issues that might come up, and they fired sample questions at me that the guys from Pepsi might want to ask. The meeting went well, and eventually I became a part-owner of a Pepsi distributorship in Washington, D.C.

After all that preparation, I had no intention of being a silent partner. Since becoming involved with Pepsi, I've made several trips to Washington to take care of business and meet with customers, plant workers, and the sales force. One meeting that sticks in my mind was out at Andrews Air Force Base. The woman I met with was a little wary of me. She said, "I don't care about basketball, or who you are."

"That's okay," I told her. "I'm not here as a basketball player. I'm here on business. I'm here to sell you some Pepsi, and to find out why Coke has more shelf space than we do."

When she heard that, this hardnosed, tough military woman broke into a smile. "You're talking my language," she said. In the end, she gave us more shelf space and display.

I always come prepared to these meetings. I know who I'll be speaking to and what their situation is. And I've found that people take you seriously when you know what you're talking about. I'm not Magic Johnson at these meetings, or even Earvin Johnson. I'm *Mr.* Johnson. It's been important to me to try to change the image of the dumb athlete, and I'm glad to see that I'm not alone in this. More and more NBA players are owning their own businesses, and Michael Jordan has been a great leader in that regard.

Bob McAdoo used to talk to me about how important it was that blacks get more involved in business, and I feel the same way. My sports-apparel store is located in the heart of the black community, and we employ young people from the neighborhood. I get my hair cut in Inglewood. I go to restaurants in black neighborhoods. And every year we give out scholarships to my basketball camp at California Lutheran College in Thousand Oaks, so that inner-city kids can come and experience a very different environment.

Power comes from ownership, and until blacks start owning more businesses and *supporting* those businesses, things aren't going to change. But the road to that goal runs through college. In my first years in the league, I didn't understand much about the power a professional athlete has to set an example for kids and to raise money for charity. Then I became involved with the United Negro College Fund. Every summer, I've put together an exhibition game with some of the biggest stars in the NBA. And every time we do it, we raise a lot of money for a great cause. So far, we're up to around $6 million.

Frankly, I can't understand why some players don't get involved in charities or in their communities. There are guys who won't speak, or won't appear, or who seem to care only about how much they'll get paid. Don't they remember that somebody helped *them* out? Lots of people helped me, and I won't forget them: my dad, Jim Dart, my coaches, and businessmen like Joel Ferguson and Gregory Eaton back in Lansing, who taught me that I could have dreams and ambitions.

All kids need is a little help, a little hope, and somebody who believes in them.

CHAPTER 21

A NEW LIFE

The year that followed my announcement had more than its share of drama. But the greatest moment of all was the birth of our son, Earvin Johnson III. He came along on June 4, during the 1992 championship series between Chicago and Portland. I was doing the color commentary for NBC, and I was traveling so much during that period that Cookie and I decided to have the labor induced. I was Cookie's labor coach, and there was no way I was going to miss the birth of our baby.

We knew we were having a boy, but we didn't tell a soul. Although the due date was June 15, the doctors examined Cookie and assured us that an earlier induction would be fine. So right after the Chicago-Portland game on the night of June 3, I flew back from Chicago on a private plane provided by NBC. I arrived home around 3:00 A.M. A few hours later, Cookie and I went to the hospital.

By eleven that morning, she was experiencing real labor. We had taken a couple of Lamaze classes, and I helped her with the breathing, counting to ten so she could get through the early contractions. Later on, when they became too painful, Cookie asked for an epidural. I left the room at that point, because I hate needles. When I returned, my wife was a new woman.

When it was time to start pushing, I turned from a coach into a cheerleader. "Come on, honey, it's the fourth quarter.

Push! We're down by two, and we need a three-pointer. Push! We're down by one, and we just got fouled. Push!''

The doctors and nurses were laughing, but Cookie kept on pushing. When we saw the baby's head, I said, ''Hold it! We've got to start the music.'' Cookie's sister put in a Luther Vandross tape. Now we were ready. ''Okay, honey, push him out!''

Our son arrived at 7:52 P.M., weighing in at seven pounds, fifteen ounces. I cut the cord, and then, with some help from the nurse, I gave little Earvin his first bath. All my feelings were inside, but you should have seen my face. Cookie was in tears. She had been terrified that something would go wrong, but everything turned out fine. We had the baby tested for HIV, just in case. Negative.

Two security guards were just outside the door to protect us from the media. But reporters and photographers from the tabloids were all over the hospital. One paper had supposedly offered $50,000 for the first picture of our baby, but nobody was able to get one. Later that night, Lon met with the press and showed them a Polaroid picture of Cookie and little Earvin.

So Cookie and I have a little son, and Andre, who was eleven when Earvin was born, finally has a brother. Shortly before the birth, Andre had called me from Michigan and said, ''Dad, if this baby is a boy, what are you going to call him?''

''Earvin,'' I replied. ''Earvin Johnson the Third.''

''You know, Dad,'' Andre said quietly. ''That should have been *my* name.''

Wham! As soon as I hung up, I broke down. What Andre had said just tore me up. Cookie and I discussed it, and I decided to ask Andre if he wanted to take on my last name. His mother thought it was a fine idea, and Andre was thrilled. So he's now Andre Johnson.

The older Andre gets, the closer we've become. That's been even more true since my announcement, although we've been tight for years. I'm so proud of him. Andre's a pretty good athlete, but he's even better as a student. And every time he comes out to see us, I make sure he reads a book on the plane.

Although people in Lansing knew he was my son, I kept Andre out of the public eye for a long time. People in Los Angeles started to be aware of him when I brought him to a Lakers game. He sat behind the bench, hanging out with Michael Cooper's son. But it wasn't until my retirement ceremony in 1992 that millions of people became aware of him.

Shortly before Earvin was born, Andre and I got together to shoot a TV commercial for SkyBox basketball cards. Instead of working from a script, we improvised the whole thing. I'd had a lot of experience in front of the camera, but I was blown away by Andre's confidence and poise. Sometimes it's scary to look at him, especially when he smiles, because when I see Andre I see myself.

When Andre got back to Michigan after shooting the commercial, he called Lon. "I had a fun time with my dad," he said, "but hey—where's my check?"

"Your dad has set up a trust account," Lon explained. "And when you're old enough, you'll get all the money."

Long pause. "Oh," he said. "I was planning to take that money and open up a video arcade here in Lansing."

The kid has a head for business, no question about it.

Soon after the baby was born, I was off to La Jolla for the Olympic basketball team training camp. I was a little anxious about joining the Olympic team after not playing all year, but not as nervous as I had been before the All-Star Game back in February. It didn't take more than a few minutes for my teammates to see that I still had my stuff. When you're running up and down the court for half an hour, and you're not breathing hard, and your passes and your shooting are still on the mark, you know you're okay. When we arrived in Portland for the pre-Olympic Tournament of the Americas, it took the fans and the media a little longer to catch on. But they came to the same conclusion: I was still Magic Johnson.

That didn't happen by accident. When you sit out for a

long time, as I had, the most important thing you lose is your discipline. Discipline and hard work have always been the keys to my success, and I started getting them back in March, a few weeks after the All-Star Game.

Although I wasn't playing in the NBA, I had a vigorous routine to help me get in shape for the Olympics. I began each day with two hours of weight lifting. Next came an hour and a half of shooting. Then I'd go home until the afternoon, when there'd be a full-court game at UCLA with a bunch of college and NBA players, including Reggie Miller, Shaquille O'Neal, Pooh Richardson, and others. After the NBA season ended, and word got around that these games were going on, players from around the country called up to ask if they could join us. I appreciated that, because everybody understood that the real purpose of these games was to get me ready for the Olympics.

The best part of Olympic training camp was that once again I became one of the boys. And I got to know the greatest players in the country because we were all on the same team. I never realized that Patrick Ewing was funny and outgoing. He and Larry Bird became good friends, and it was great to see that. I always knew that Charles Barkley was a funny man, but he kept us laughing the whole time. Michael Jordan and I were already friendly, but I got to know him a lot better. Although I'm not a golfer, I spent a morning on the golf course with Michael. At night, most of us played cards together. The All-Star Game is a one-day event, but here we had the chance to create a real team.

People have said that the "Dream Team" was the greatest sports team ever assembled, and they're probably right. I think Michael Jordan enjoyed the fact that not all of the pressure and attention was on his shoulders. And what a thrill it was for me to start games with Michael as the other guard.

Larry Bird and I were named co-captains, and I was impressed that our teammates, who are all leaders on their own teams, were able to defer to us. They gave us their respect, and whenever possible, we gave them the ball.

I've always been proud to play for the Lakers, but putting on the Team USA uniform was something else. Everywhere we went, people called out, "Bring back the gold!" And "Good luck in Barcelona!" Some of our guys had played on other Olympic teams, but this was my first time, and it was incredibly exciting.

What I'll always remember about the Tournament of the Americas was how enthusiastic our opponents were about playing us. In the game against Argentina, the guy covering me was talking the whole time. He didn't speak much English, but he kept asking me to give him my jersey, with an autograph, after the game. (I couldn't give him the one I was wearing, so I sent him a replica.) When one of his teammates got lucky on a free throw that hit the rim and then fell through on a lucky bounce, he came right over to me and said, "That's magic, yes?"

In Portland, our opponents asked us to pose for pictures before each game. What was even more amazing is that this also happened *during* the games. A guy would be dribbling the ball, and suddenly he'd hold it in front of his own bench so one of his teammates could snap a picture of him playing against us. The whole thing was an enormous tribute to NBA basketball, and fun for everybody.

For me, one big thrill was finally getting to play on the same team as Larry Bird. Both of us had always dreamed of doing that. In the very first game, against Cuba, I kept passing him the ball and he kept hitting his shots. But then Larry's back started hurting, and he had to miss a few games. During every one, the crowd yelled, *"La-ree! La-ree! La-ree!"* But Larry didn't want to risk a serious injury that might prevent him from playing a few weeks later in Barcelona.

Then, during the final game of the tournament, against Venezuela, the crowd just wouldn't stop calling for Bird. There wasn't a mouth in that whole arena that wasn't yelling *"La-ree!"* With two minutes left, I said to myself, This is ridiculous. He's got to get in there and play. So I snuck up behind him and tore off his warm-ups. The crowd went crazy, and Larry went in near the end and scored a basket. The whole place went wild.

Then it was on to Monte Carlo, for our final week of training before Barcelona. Some of our practices during that week were amazing—easily the best basketball I've ever seen or been part of. I've never played with, or against, guys who had so much talent. Chuck Daly, our coach, always put Michael Jordan and me on different teams, and the two of us really went at it, competing hard and talking trash. In one of these practice games, my team was up by about 10 points, and I was really letting Michael have it. "Hey, M.J.," I called, using the nickname we have for each other. "I *told* you we could bust you. You guys are *nothing*."

What happened next was an exhibition of basketball that I will never forget. I knew that Michael was the best in the game, but that morning he gave us the real Air Jordan show, complete with inside moves, outside shots, dunks, and soaring leaps to the hoop that were simply magnificent. Until the Olympics, I honestly believed that I could keep up with Michael Jordan in a one-on-one competition. But I was kidding myself. There's no way—he's just too good.

During the Olympics, Michael and I also spent a lot of time together off the court. One night he and I and Larry Bird stayed up practically until sunrise, talking about basketball, our careers, and the NBA. Later in the week, when Cookie arrived with little Earvin for the last few games, she and I hung out with Michael and Juanita.

There were many good friendships on the Dream Team, and when we all flew back together after winning the gold medal, there was a real sadness as we said good-bye. We had all known that the level of basketball would be great, but the personal chemistry was better than anyone expected. We had some big egos on our team, but there was no jealousy or bad feelings. We were all pulling in the same direction and enjoying each other's company.

While we were in Barcelona, Charles Barkley received a lot of attention back home for some of his statements. What can I say about Charles? He thrives on controversy, and I think he enjoys being the bad guy. His remarks didn't bother me, except when Charles said something outrageous and people assumed he was speaking for the whole team. We did ask him to tone it down a couple of times, but Charles pretty much does what he wants—especially on the court. He played brilliantly in Barcelona. When Charles Barkley gets his hands on the ball anywhere near the basket, nobody in the world can stop him.

There was a little grumbling in the media about the fact that the Dream Team didn't stay with all the other athletes in the Olympic Village. But anyone who was with us in Barcelona will understand why that would have been impossible. Every time Team USA left the hotel to play a game, three or four thousand people were lined up outside *just to see us get on the bus.* Whenever we appeared in public, whether it was at one of the other Olympic events or a restaurant or even just out for a walk, we were mobbed. It was like the pope had arrived, and it surprised me every time it happened. Chuck Daly wasn't kidding when he said it was like traveling with twelve rock stars. If we had stayed in the Olympic Village, we would have had no rest at all.

Marching in the opening ceremonies was one of the wildest and most amazing things I've ever experienced. Athletes from other countries started breaking out of line and running over to ask me for autographs, take my picture, or just shake my hand. I'm used to attention, but I couldn't believe that so many athletes from so many different places wanted to meet me.

I wasn't prepared for it, especially with Michael Jordan on our team. But a lot of the Europeans hadn't expected me to make the trip, and they were genuinely excited for me. And while my other teammates had been playing basketball all year, I was being welcomed back to the game. Everywhere I went, people called my name and asked me to smile. "Ma-jeek! Ma-jeek! Please smile for me. Smile for the camera." I still hear those lines in my sleep.

The basketball games were a little less challenging than

we had expected. The teams from Croatia and Lithuania had been built up in the media, and we were sky-high for those games. But the level of competition just wasn't what we anticipated. In part, this was because our defense was overwhelming. There were times when we were able to shut down our opponents for five or even ten minutes at a stretch.

Sometimes it got pretty weird. During our first game against Croatia, I was sitting on the bench with John Stockton and assistant coach Lenny Wilkens. We were talking about how our teammates on the floor had become a little sloppy when I glanced up at the scoreboard and noticed that we were ahead by 34 points.

The truth is that we could have won some of our games by 70 or 80 points if that's what we had wanted. But the Olympics weren't about that. After a certain point, we tried to be entertaining. Our goal was to defeat our opponents, not to embarrass them.

But for those American fans who thought that sending NBA players to Barcelona was a mistake, I wish they could have seen how our opponents welcomed us, and how happy they were to play against us. In that respect, the atmosphere at the Olympics wasn't much different from what it had been a month earlier during the Tournament of the Americas. As Bob Ryan, one of the great basketball writers, put it in *The Boston Globe*, the theme during the Olympics was more or less: Beat me, whip me, take my picture.

The Olympics are a showcase for the best athletes in the world. An American collegiate team would have done well enough, but they wouldn't have won a gold medal, or even a silver. (Croatia and Lithuania would have beaten them.) Every other country sent its best players, and so did we. And a lot of the guys who played against us were professionals, too, either in the NBA or in Europe.

Although everybody knew we would win the gold medal, it was still a magnificent moment when it finally happened. I almost broke down during the playing of "The Star-Spangled Banner," but I had promised my teammates that I wouldn't cry. Still, it wasn't easy to hold back, and my skin was covered with goose bumps. Standing on that platform, I said a silent prayer. I thanked God for giving me the strength and the opportunity to come back, to play basketball again, and to be part of that whole magnificent Olympic experience. It's a memory I will always cherish.

EPILOGUE

A MESSAGE FOR BLACK TEENAGERS

As part of my new job as an educator, I've been visiting inner-city high schools across the country. My main message is that I want these kids to learn from my mistake, so that what happened to me doesn't happen to them. But I've already covered that subject in these pages, and in my book What You Can Do to Avoid AIDS.

There's a second message I give to kids, which has nothing to do with AIDS. It's about making a success of yourself. I never speak from a text, because that's boring. I always speak from my heart. But what I tell them goes something like this:

Basketball was my ticket to success. But if I hadn't been good enough, I would have been successful in something else. I would have gone to college, and worked hard, and made something of myself. You can do that, too.

Basketball is not the best way to get ahead. It's probably the most difficult path you could take. There are 27 teams in the NBA, and each team has 12 players. That makes 324 players who are in the league at any one time. In a country as big as ours, that's not a big number. There are about 1,800 college seniors who play ball, and only a few of them are good enough to be drafted. So even if you're good enough and fortunate enough to play in college, what makes you think you're going to play in the NBA? You have to understand that your chances of playing basketball for a living are minuscule.

The black community already has enough basketball players. And enough baseball players, and football players. But there are a lot of other people we could really use. We need more teachers. We need more lawyers. We need more doctors. We need more accountants. We need more nurses. We need more pilots. And more scientists. And more carpenters. And more professors. And more police officers. And more bankers. And more computer programmers. And more mechanics. And more social workers. And more car dealers. And more politicians.

And every single one of these professions—including doctor and lawyer—is easier to get into than the NBA.

There was a time when blacks couldn't do some of these things, and when sports and entertainment were the best ways to get ahead. That's not true anymore. Today, you have an opportunity to get ahead in many different areas.

You see what I'm saying? Later on, when you become that doctor, or that lawyer, or you have your own plumbing business, I want you to knock on my door and say, "Magic, I've got my own business. I'd like to do your plumbing." Or "I became that lawyer you talked about. Will you be one of my clients?"

If you can possibly go to college, go! I know it's hard. I know that some kids you know will discourage you. If you're ambitious, if you study hard, if your goals are high, some people may tell you you're "acting white." Stay away from those people! They are not your friends. If the people around you aren't going anywhere, if their dreams are no bigger than hanging out on the corner, or if they're dragging you down, get rid of them. Negative people can sap your energy so fast, and they can take your dreams from you, too.

You say, "I'm going to college. I'm going to become a doctor."

"Come on," they'll tell you. "You won't be no doctor."

It's easy to start listening to them. Before you know it, you're having those same doubts.

Don't let anyone tell you what you *can't* do. If you don't succeed, let it be because of you. Don't blame it on other people.

A lot of people doubted me, too. Some people don't want you to make it because *they're* not going to make it. They've given up, so they want you to give up, too. As the saying goes, misery loves company.

Don't give up! Surround yourself with people who are energetic and disciplined. Surround yourselves with ambitious, positive people. If there are adults you admire, don't be afraid to ask them for help and advice.

I know that college is not for everybody. And if it's not for you, find another way to move up. If your skills lie in another direction, maybe you should consider trade school. Maybe you can become a plumber, the best plumber you can be. Maybe you can become a welder, and someday you'll own your own garage. Jimmy Daniels, my neighbor back in Lansing, started cleaning carpets in office buildings. He started small, but he kept growing. Today he owns a whole company, and he's making good money.

I don't mean to tell you it's easy. It's *not* easy. Growing up today is hard. I know that. It's much harder than when I was your age. When I was a kid, there weren't many gangs. Or many guns. There was nothing like crack. Maybe you smoked a little pot, but that was it. Today there's cocaine, heroin, AIDS, and all kinds of things we didn't ever worry about. You might be an excellent student, but you're still living in fear because a stray bullet could hit you.

All of that is real. So is racism. Racism exists, but too often we use it as an excuse. I'm not saying it isn't there, because it definitely is. But if you get your education, you can look beyond that. I don't care what somebody calls you. You can still walk proud because of who you are.

If we keep using that same old excuse, that every time we fail it's because of racism, we'll never get ahead. We'll stay on the bottom. We've got to quit making excuses. Quit feeling sorry for ourselves. We have to go to college. Think about business. Work hard. Support one another, like other groups do.

The government will not save you.

The black leadership will not save you.

You're the only one who can make the difference.

Whatever your dream is, go for it.

POSTSCRIPT

On November 2, 1992, I retired from the NBA. This time for good.

I had come back to the league only five weeks earlier. The Showtime era had ended, but I was looking forward to another winning season with the Lakers. Despite the virus, I was in terrific shape following a year of rigorously working out. And I couldn't wait for our opening game against the Clippers on November 6.

After the Dream Team's great triumph in Barcelona, I had been riding high. But when the summer ended, everything changed. Once again there were doubts and rumors about my sexual past. That sort of thing has come up before, and I could have lived with it. But then, during our final exhibition game, I developed a tiny cut on my arm.

It was a Friday night, and the Lakers were playing against Cleveland in Chapel Hill, North Carolina. The cut was so small that I didn't even notice it. But one of my teammates pointed it out to Gary Vitti, our trainer. I came out of the game, and Gary covered the scratch with a small bandage. But because of the sweat on my arm, the bandage wouldn't stick. Gary covered it with a sweatband, but he couldn't cover up the feeling in the arena. Guys were scared. You could see the fear in their eyes and hear their unspoken questions: Is he all bandaged up? That cut's not leaking, is it?

Normally, I love to inspire fear in my opponents. But this was different. It wasn't my talent that scared them. It was my virus.

On Saturday, when I got home, I told Cookie that something had changed, and that I could see that playing this season wasn't going to be much fun. And I had always promised myself that if that ever happened, I would leave the game. I called Lon that night and told him I was gone.

The next day, a couple of players and one of the owners spoke out publicly against my being in the league. When I read their comments in *The New York Times*, it only confirmed my decision. "You see," I told Lon, "that's all the more reason why it's time for me to go."

I could see what lay ahead. Every time I came into another city, the controversy and the fear would start all over again. And that would be bad for two reasons. It would hurt basketball by taking people's attention away from the game. Everybody would be too busy putting in their two cents about whether I should be playing, and I love the game too much to want that to happen. The other reason is that continuing to play would have led to a lot more pressure on me. And if I'm going to beat this virus, I've got to avoid pressure and stress. That's the last thing I need in my life.

I'm not mad at anybody, but I'm certainly disappointed. If there's one thing I learned during this period, it's how much work remains to be done to help educate people about this virus. It looks like I'll have plenty of time to do my share.

I leave with real sadness. The National Basketball Association has been awfully good to me, and I know that I've played a real part in its tremendous success. If I had to leave, I wanted to do so in a positive atmosphere. I didn't want to stay around one more year if it meant I would be saying good-bye under a cloud of controversy and fear.

I'm also sad because what happened to me may discourage other athletes from getting tested. And if any of them already know they have the virus, my experience certainly won't encourage them to go public, as I did. And what about those guys who think that maybe they can catch the virus from playing against me, but who still don't believe they can get it from a woman? There's still a lot of work to be done.

I don't hold grudges. I never have, and I'm not going to start now. That's wasted energy. This happened, and I'll deal with it and keep going.

Regrets? Sure. These days, when I go to the gym I'm working out by myself instead of with my teammates. When I'm running on the treadmill, I'm thinking about the guys, and wondering how they're doing.

And I wish Karl Malone hadn't gone to the press with his doubts before he came to me. We aren't close, but we did play together on the Dream Team, and he could have pulled me aside to talk about this instead of my reading about it in the paper. But when Karl said he was only speaking out loud what other players were whispering, I'm sure he was right. He's not the only one.

And I do wonder: If all this had happened to somebody else, what would I have done? Sure, I would have had questions. But I'd like to think I would have looked for the answers and not acted on my fears. I hope so, anyway.

As I write these words, there have been something like 250,000 recorded cases of AIDS in the United States. In all that time, there has never been a single documented case of somebody picking up the virus through sports. Does that mean it couldn't happen? Nobody can say that. But how many things in life carry absolutely no risk?

I love the NBA, but I'll survive without it. I'm planning a world tour that would take me to Australia and Japan and several countries in Europe. I hope to put together a team of former NBA players, and we'll take our show on the road. We'll enjoy ourselves for sure, and we'll entertain the fans. But make no mistake—I'll be playing to win.

I always do.